Teaching Information Literacy for Inquiry-based Learning

CHANDOS
INFORMATION PROFESSIONAL SERIES

Series Editor: Ruth Rikowski
(email: Rikowskigr@aol.com)

Chandos' new series of books are aimed at the busy information professional. They have been specially commissioned to provide the reader with an authoritative view of current thinking. They are designed to provide easy-to-read and (most importantly) practical coverage of topics that are of interest to librarians and other information professionals. If you would like a full listing of current and forthcoming titles, please visit our website www.chandospublishing.com or email info@chandospublishing.com or telephone +44 (0) 1223 891358.

New authors: we are always pleased to receive ideas for new titles; if you would like to write a book for Chandos, please contact Dr Glyn Jones on email gjones@chandospublishing.com or telephone number +44 (0) 1993 848726.

Bulk orders: some organisations buy a number of copies of our books. If you are interested in doing this, we would be pleased to discuss a discount. Please email info@chandospublishing.com or telephone +44 (0) 1223 891358.

Teaching Information Literacy for Inquiry-based Learning

MARK HEPWORTH AND GEOFF WALTON

Chandos Publishing

Oxford • Cambridge • New Delhi

Chandos Publishing
TBAC Business Centre
Avenue 4
Station Lane
Witney
Oxford OX28 4BN
UK
Tel: +44 (0) 1993 848726
Email: info@chandospublishing.com
www.chandospublishing.com

Chandos Publishing is an imprint of Woodhead Publishing Limited

Woodhead Publishing Limited
Abington Hall
Granta Park
Great Abington
Cambridge CB21 6AH
UK
www.woodheadpublishing.com

First published in 2009

ISBN:
978 1 84334 441 4

British Library Cataloguing-in-Publication Data.
A catalogue record for this book is available from the British Library.

Typeset by Domex e-Data Pvt. Ltd.
Printed in the UK and USA.

Printed in the UK by 4edge Limited - www.4edge.co.uk

Contents

List of figures and tables

Figures

Tables

Preface

Mark Hepworth and Geoff Walton have had different reasons for writing this book. For Mark the book stems from his long term interest in how people interact with information. This interest developed initially from an academic perspective: what factors influence people's need for information; and from a practical perspective: how do we develop information services that are user-centred and relate to users' needs? Part of this journey included a study of students in higher education. It became apparent that they had significant difficulties using the information around them and needed to be more conscious of how they become informed. This led Mark to develop interventions to help learners learn from their information environment and he became embroiled with 'information literacy'. For Geoff it was the result of working in information services at Staffordshire University, completing a PhD in information literacy and delivering information literacy training. Geoff researched and devised an information skills credit-bearing module in 1996 and since then has become increasingly interested in how students learn and how the virtual domain, especially virtual learning environments (VLEs), facilitates this. In researching for his PhD thesis Geoff became aware of the field of information behaviour and realised that this area of research, largely overlooked in the information profession, is essential to the understanding of how students engage with information and in informing the structure of what we call information literacy, and indeed other literacies such as e-literacy.

The book itself was driven by a feeling that although there are many good information literacy interventions, the underlying reasons why they work, in terms of pedagogy and the characteristics of people's information behaviour, seemed less well understood. There was a lack of appreciation of the complexity of information literacy and hence little time was given to facilitating information literacy. Often information literacy has been interpreted in a very rudimentary and mechanistic way, such as knowing how to search a database or a library. Plus there was a notion that one size fits all, which showed a lack of appreciation of how the context, including the physical and social environment, has an impact on a person's information literacy.

We believe that people who facilitate information literacy or who develop inquiry-based or problem-based learning interventions (which depend on the learner being information literate) would benefit from this text, in which we would unpick teaching and learning theories, and the knowledge derived from studies concerning information literacy and people's information behaviour, and relate these to successful information literacy interventions.

To some extent the book was a journey of discovery because of the breadth of the topic. In addition to the familiar research and practice from information science (on information literacy and people's information behaviour) relevant work can be found in education, media studies, cognitive science and neuroscience. It is also a complex field because of the factional differences between disciplines and different epistemological camps (behaviourist, cognitive, constructivist, social realist and so on) and the relative novelty of the topic.

As a result, people use different labels to talk about the same things and the same labels to talk about different things. The word cognitive, for example, can mean many things depending on the disciplinary orientation of the speaker. Distinctions between conceptual areas are often blurred or contentious. A fundamental question 'How do people learn?' gets a myriad of responses. Different authors advocate a host of explanations (chemical, neurological, behavioural, psychological and social) that play a role in learning.

It was a challenge to know where to stop when writing this book. For example, if we take the broadest definition of information literacy, which could mean the ability for an individual to learn, we should, perhaps, include a discussion of research methods that could be used to generate new knowledge. Finding out, learning, making use of knowledge is a complex process. We go about it using every aspect of our being. We learn in many different ways. The most common and probably most effective way of learning is through experience, trial and error, and talking to other people. Learning can take place without any published information. Participative methods applied in developing countries show how knowledge, data and information can be generated using only the people in the community and systematic reflection on the world around them, and can lead to new, sustainable, strategies.

We have chosen to focus, primarily, on the ability to 'find out' using published (formal and informal) sources (electronic and paper based). We also include the role of other people and how to access the knowledge that other people have. We note that placing oneself in a specific context may be a way of becoming informed. However, this is not the focus of the book and we will not discuss experimentation or other ways of creating primary data and information. Numerous books have been published on how to conduct primary research and how to use the plethora of available methodologies and techniques. For example, if you were buying a washing machine we would focus on the processes associated with defining exactly what you required, identifying and making use of the information available such as consumer reports or people who can provide good advice. What we would not do is to describe how to test five machines and derive data that enables comparisons. We therefore concentrate on exploiting existing knowledge, data and information. This can enable people to address a problem quickly, avoiding reinventing the wheel or repeating the same mistakes as others.

We would argue that a fully developed learner should have an appreciation and consciousness of how to find things out using existing knowledge resources. Even within this remit, there is a complex interplay of factors that have a bearing on this kind of learning, which need exploring. This book attempts to tease out these factors and the impact they have on someone learning to be information literate. It is hoped that this book will contribute to the ongoing dialogue about information literacy and independent learning, and how to develop people's capacity in this area.

Acknowledgements

Mark Hepworth

My interest in this topic has evolved over many years. As a result many people have influenced my thinking. The teachers at the School of Oriental and African Studies nurtured my interest in studying other people, understanding their perspectives and how they make sense of their reality. This interest was directed towards how people interact with information by Tom Wilson while doing a Master's in Information Studies, and later by Nigel Ford, my PhD supervisor at Sheffield University. Exposure to many authors, from different parts of the world, who have tried to unpick people's information behaviour, learning and information literacy, has, of course, been fundamental. The latter include Christine Bruce, Suzie Andretta and Bonnie Cheuk. Bonnie kindly agreed to let us include a workplace information literacy intervention in this publication. I am also grateful to members of the IDEAS team, who have provided a breath of academic fresh air. Recently work with Julie Brittain at the Institute of Development Studies in Brighton has enabled me to make the connection between capacity development and information literacy, and highlighted the link between good pedagogy and participative approaches that value the learner and their knowledge. Reading people such as Robert Chambers has brought this to life. My students have played a crucial role, including those in Singapore at Nanyang Technological University, where I taught information retrieval and the design of user services, and at Loughborough University, where I taught information retrieval and user-centred design. At Loughborough University I developed information literacy programmes for undergraduates and postgraduates, including one for library and information management students on how to teach information literacy. In particular I would like to thank my PhD students who have helped me to explore information literacy, especially Marian Smith, Geoff Walton and Evans Wema.

I would also (one doesn't often get the opportunity to thank people who have enriched life, so forgive the indulgence) like to thank all the creative people (the artists, musicians, writers and performers) who have enabled me to experience and enjoy different worlds: the teachers at Waterford/Kamhlaba, in Swaziland, and Bembridge, on the Isle of Wight, who cared; current and previous colleagues who put up with me and helped me play a role in the 'information business'; old friends who I am lucky to know; friends at the Swan for their conversation and fun; other people I have met in my travels who have reaffirmed my faith in humanity; my family, especially Sian and Joe who have given me intense pleasure and pride, and Joan, my partner, for her help; and, of course, Heather and John Hepworth who bear the ultimate responsibility!

Geoff Walton

My initial interest in this topic stems from my experiences as a library assistant at Staffordshire County Council (under the leadership of David Prescott and Andrew Green) where I became aware of the very diverse information needs of our customers. However, it was only when I took up a subject librarian role at Staffordshire University that I began to appreciate the need for a teaching and learning programme, first influenced by the writings of Eisenberg and Berkowitz (the inventors of the Big6). Also at this time I had the great good fortune to attend the Edulib programme and be taught by Chris Powis, who greatly influenced my outlook on information skills teaching and learning. Probably the greatest set of influences on my thinking came when I began my PhD at Loughborough University, where I benefited from the inspirational guidance of Mark Hepworth, who has, through his leadership, introduced me to the field of information behaviour and its great body of empirical research and its highly influential writers such as Carol Kuhlthau. Now that I have finished my PhD and passed my viva I will miss our regular meetings, the subject matter of which extended far beyond information literacy and information behaviour. My information literacy horizons were also widened at this time and I became aware of Susie Andretta and Christine Bruce, to name but two. In addition I am lucky to work alongside Alison Pope who has also become known in the wider information literacy community; together with Julie Adams we run the Staffordshire University Information Literacy Community of Practice (SUILCoP), which is itself becoming a feature in the UK information literacy landscape.

Like Mark there are a number of other individuals I'd like to thank, first and foremost my wife Caroline, who has put up with my various projects and often proofread articles, book chapters and bits of my thesis, and has shown me that primary school teachers know more about pedagogy than anyone else in education! Also, thanks to Caroline for the primary school example in Part 2. In my other life I am a guitarist, bouzouki and bodhran player and so I'd also like to thank fellow musicians who I've played alongside over many years dispensing our individual (and I have to say very popular) version of celtic folk music: Terry Fox, Adam Fenn, Phil Johnson and in more recent times Scott and Cath Ralph, Deborah MacAndrew and Caroline (again). My two children Katherine and Hannah are a great joy and keep me right. Hannah, who is in year 5 of primary school, very patiently explained to me the other day what imperative verbs are – they are 'bossy' verbs apparently. Of course I would not have been possible without Lily and Wilfred Walton.

We would like to thank Wordle (*http://www.wordle.net/*) for the creation of tag clouds at the start of the chapters and the staff at Chandos for their invaluable suggestions.

Part 1:
Four faces of learning and their implications for teaching information literacy

Introduction

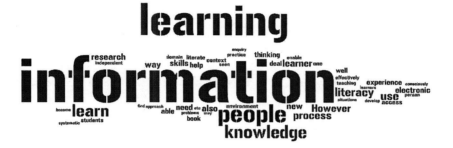

Empowerment is underpinned by information literacy. Being able to learn effectively and independently and use the knowledge, data and information (from now on these three entities are referred to collectively as 'information') around them is likely to result in people having more choice. When people have choice, they are usually better informed about their situation and can see alternatives in a critical light, and then may be able to choose from or create a range of solutions or strategies. This can lead to people having more options when deciding how to participate and interact socially, and how to use and contribute to the resources and services available.

Whether or not this leads to empowerment in a political sense will depend on a person's ability and their social context. Many people find it difficult to access and use the information around them, because of their political, social and physical environment. Recently there have been positive signs that if people have access to information and resources in a highly participative context they can engage politically, which empowers them (Cornwall, 2008). Methodologies have developed that support these changes, for example, participative approaches that promote the importance of people being able to conduct their own research (Reason, 1994) as a way to empower themselves and find solutions to problems in a certain context. This book is likely to help people deal with more common personal or professional situations, however. Nevertheless, the material can be applied to any situation where people need to broaden their horizons and develop new ways of seeing the world.

In the educational context, inquiry-based learning (or enquiry-based learning) has been recognised as a powerful tool for learning about a subject domain, and more importantly for learning how to learn, as it helps people to develop their independent learning skills. Hutchings (2007: 13) asserted that in inquiry-based learning:

> the learning is self-directed because it is driven by students' own decisions about appropriate ways in which an issue or scenario might be approached. They bring to bear on the topic any existing knowledge or experience relevant to the issues. No person comes to the table with no knowledge, and the examination and pooling of what is already known allow students to gain confidence, as well as to practice the habit of reflection. They carry out research and investigations into areas that they decide are essential for a proper response to the issue. Thus they discover *how* to research by engaging in practical examples. In this way, it may be said that the process of enquiry is in the ownership of the students, so that enquiry-based learning is fundamentally concerned with establishing the context, the space, the environment within which enquiry may best be stimulated and students can take charge of their learning. The process is student-centred, with the onus always on the students to take initiatives, propose routes of enquiry and follow them thoughtfully. By these means, students also acquire experience in a range of intellectual and social capabilities. These include critical thinking, reflection and self-criticism, team-work, independence, autonomous thinking and information literacy.

Another way of thinking about inquiry-based learning focuses on the student as a researcher. According to Griffiths (2004) teaching can be:

- research-led, where students learn about research findings, the curriculum content is dominated by faculty research interests, and information transmission is the main teaching mode
- research-oriented, where students learn about research processes, the curriculum emphasises as much the processes by which knowledge is produced as learning knowledge that has been achieved, and faculty try to engender a research ethos through their teaching

- research-based, where students learn as researchers, the curriculum is largely designed around inquiry-based activities, and the division of roles between teacher and student is minimised.

Healey (2005: 70) included another dimension; teaching can also be:

- research-tutored, where students learn about research findings in small group discussions with a teacher (see Figure 1.1).

This approach has become significant in relation to the debate surrounding research-informed teaching. Figure 1.1 highlights the student researcher dimension.

A variant on this matrix has been proposed by Levy and Petrulis (2007: 3), illustrated in Figure 1.2. This matrix also has a staff-led and student-led axis, but it also includes another axis distinguishing between information-led and discovery-led inquiry, in which the former is based on existing knowledge and the latter on new knowledge.

The inquiry-based approach began to be popular in schools in the 1960s but was not fully implemented; more emphasis was placed on learning content than on the process of finding out. However, over the last ten years in higher education, particularly in the health sciences (medicine, nursing and so on) but also in business studies and other subjects, we have seen greater emphasis being placed on inquiry-based learning, as has been the case in primary and secondary education under the Qualifications and Curriculum Authority (QCA) and the Office for

Figure 1.1 Student research–teaching nexus (based on Healey, 2005: 70)

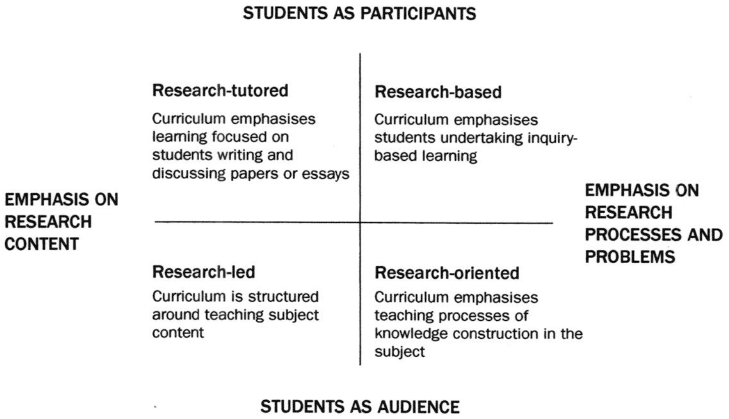

STUDENTS AS PARTICIPANTS

Research-tutored
Curriculum emphasises learning focused on students writing and discussing papers or essays

Research-based
Curriculum emphasises students undertaking inquiry-based learning

EMPHASIS ON RESEARCH CONTENT

EMPHASIS ON RESEARCH PROCESSES AND PROBLEMS

Research-led
Curriculum is structured around teaching subject content

Research-oriented
Curriculum emphasises teaching processes of knowledge construction in the subject

STUDENTS AS AUDIENCE

Figure 1.2   Conceptions and modes of student inquiry (based on Levy and Petrulis, 2007: 3)

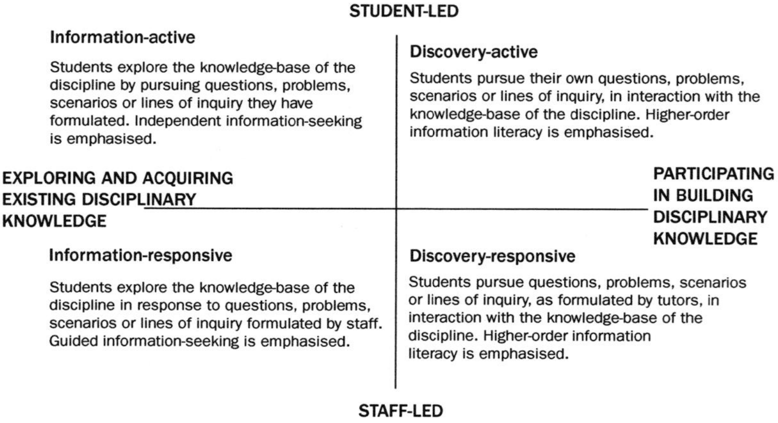

STUDENT-LED

Information-active

Students explore the knowledge-base of the discipline by pursuing questions, problems, scenarios or lines of inquiry they have formulated. Independent information-seeking is emphasised.

Discovery-active

Students pursue their own questions, problems, scenarios or lines of inquiry, in interaction with the knowledge-base of the discipline. Higher-order information literacy is emphasised.

EXPLORING AND ACQUIRING
EXISTING DISCIPLINARY
KNOWLEDGE

PARTICIPATING
IN BUILDING
DISCIPLINARY
KNOWLEDGE

Information-responsive

Students explore the knowledge-base of the discipline in response to questions, problems, scenarios or lines of inquiry formulated by staff. Guided information-seeking is emphasised.

Discovery-responsive

Students pursue questions, problems, scenarios or lines of inquiry, as formulated by tutors, in interaction with the knowledge-base of the discipline. Higher-order information literacy is emphasised.

STAFF-LED

Standards in Education (Ofsted; the official body for inspecting schools) in the UK. This has partly been because of the relevance of the skills that are being developed (the ability to learn independently within a rapidly changing world or knowledge base is seen as valuable asset) but it also has proven to be an effective method to engage and motivate learners. In other countries educators have started to embrace this approach to learning (not of course to the exclusion of other approaches) partly for the reasons given above, but also because they have a belief in the underlying pedagogic strengths of this approach. It is after all not a new idea and stems back to previous thinkers such as Dewey and even further to the Socratic schools of learning.

Although the overall approach to delivering inquiry-based learning is well understood, the knowledge, skills, attitudes and underlying cognitive and behavioural processes that enable learners to be successful in an inquiry-based learning environment are less well comprehended. This book will help to identify these factors and suggests strategies to foster this type of independent learning. Furthermore, the book provides an insight into learners and how they learn and aspects of learners that need to be taken into account when planning an intervention. These insights are relevant to teaching and learning in general, but the intention is to highlight the pedagogy that is particularly relevant to fostering independent learning and hence inquiry-based learning. In addition it is the intention of this book to address the skills and knowledge associated with independent learning in the broader context and not just in schools or higher education institutions. The knowledge and skills are equally applicable to managing in the workplace or the home.

Vannevar Bush's dream was 'to link all types of textual knowledge' (Turow and Tsui, 2008) but in 1945 there was a relatively small number of electronic documents that were in a format that could be easily connected. We now have an incredibly complex web of information sources, some of which are linked, and an ever-growing number are accessible from an internet-connected computer. This increase in connectivity – the availability of information that can be searched and displayed in a common format as well as connections to electronic indexes and more recently access to less formal personal accounts and thoughts, and diverse often freely available multimedia – means that there is a huge opportunity to learn from other people and their experiences. One can come closer to realising Bush's understanding of learning where the human mind 'operates by association' (Turow and Tsui, 2008). Having access to descriptions, stories, explanations and so on enables us to empathise with other people's experiences without having to experience them directly. To do this, it helps to be familiar with this learning environment and how to capitalise on existing knowledge effectively and consciously.

The purpose of this book is therefore to help instructors (teachers, trainers, facilitators and managers) enable people to be efficient and effective in the way they use information to achieve their objectives for personal or work-related reasons. It is for people who encourage others to make critical and systematic use of information, helping them to deal with new and complex situations. Throughout life most if not all people need or would find it useful to be able to learn about new things. For example, a group of people who have lived in state housing and are in danger of being dispossessed, but are not familiar with the mechanics of private ownership and the market economy, need information to be able to make effective decisions about taking out loans to buy their properties. They need to know the relationship between investment, property and value; who can help; what needs to be done; and so on. People's information needs may concern topics such as knowing about how to deal with a particular medical condition, child development, finding a job or effectively marketing a product. In the academic setting a student or researcher needs to be able to tap into existing information and knowledge effectively to develop balanced answers to questions and new insights. In short, what we want to achieve when we enable people to become information literate is to help the learner:

- understand subject matter
- learn when, where and why to use information
- recognise meaningful patterns of information
- develop adaptive expertise
- become metacognitive about their learning so that they can assess their own progress and continually identify and pursue new learning goals
- develop the ability to teach themselves (Bransford, Brown and Cocking, 2000: 50).

Information in these situations can confer power or at least greater control over what is happening. However, what exactly is meant by information and the value placed on different sources of knowledge tends to be governed by the community of practice and may reflect power relationships. There is therefore often a tension between helping people learn for themselves, creating their own meaning (in the most liberal sense) and scaffolding learning so that they learn what is perceived to be 'good' by the trainer. (Scaffolding learning is a pedagogical technique where learners are given an overview of the steps they will go through and the teacher's expectations of them, including learning outcomes and the time expected for certain tasks. Over time the tutor's role diminishes as the learner becomes more independent). Nevertheless, not all people see problems or issues, as information problems and know about the ways, methods and techniques for interacting with information systematically. In fact, people can generally manage without having systematic access to external information. Often the people they know are the best source of information. Nevertheless, we would argue, it is better to be consciously information literate. The lack of consciousness is perhaps surprising since we commonly refer to the relationship between knowledge and power and the fact that new information and knowledge will 'broaden our horizons' or 'expand our boundaries' – in other words give us new choices that can open up new opportunities and make us better able to deal with situations by being 'filled in', 'genned up', that is, informed.

A fundamental challenge to the systematic use of information is the polarisation between practice and research, scholarship and activism – the polarisation between learning by doing and learning from pre-existing knowledge and then doing. By nature people seem to have a preference for doing, getting on with the job, rather than spending time orienting themselves to the problem, seeing what is already known or has been done and then choosing an appropriate strategy. A great deal of learning and new knowledge is of course gained through doing, but the divide is artificial and both domains are interlinked. Investigation can take place through active, experiential research, leading to the generation of ideas, theories and models, which can inform practice. Practice can lead to the generation of theory and best practice. However, the drive to be 'doing' can lead to wasted effort because previous 'research' or knowledge has not been followed up and built upon. One large scale and expensive disaster such as the bouncing Millennium Bridge, for example, apparently could have been avoided if the designers had accessed published information concerning human-structure dynamic interaction.

In the academic setting, where research skills are assumed to be fundamental, remedial interventions have been taking place throughout the world under the banner of 'information literacy', demonstrating that even people who have gone through an 'advanced' educational system are not necessarily information literate. One reason for this is that, although they have achieved high marks in their subjects, these students have achieved them in an environment where there has not been a great deal of emphasis on independent learning skills. Learning for assessment has tended not to encourage or necessitate the independent seeking of information but instead to lead to a pragmatic approach to learning. Also, in extreme cases, learners who have come from learning cultures that are very hierarchical and disciplined, and where the teacher is seen as the person who 'fills empty pots', find the onus placed on them in UK higher education to explore, find, compare, synthesise, criticise and apply information in an innovative way daunting and difficult. Learners who have experienced this kind of education initially tend to dislike the uncertainty and effort associated with seeking information independently; they are relatively uncritical of sources of information and tend to regurgitate it without processing it in any fundamental way. They tend to be highly pragmatic or strategic learners, partly because of the pressure of covering and learning content and preparing for assessment; they derive little joy and few marks from the process of finding out. However, given the opportunity and if supported in an appropriate way, most learners enjoy this kind of learning. This has been demonstrated where problem-based and inquiry-based learning pedagogies have been deployed, for example, with medical students and nurses, where people become familiar with the resources and the process of resolving questions independently.

This is not to suggest that younger people are inherently information illiterate. In a recent phenomenographical study (Smith, 2009) where young people (aged between 12 and 17 years old) were asked questions that elicited their perceptions of information, they spoke about their awareness of the information landscape, the acquisition of information, the processing of information, and the application (use) of information. They were also able to discuss information in a sophisticated way judging its value, relevance, what to keep, what to process and so on. However, these thoughts were not specifically or consciously related to the formal process of learning, nor was there any evidence that educational interventions developed or built on such thinking.

Another challenge to being information literate has been the mistaken assumption that digital literacy and having IT skills are synonymous with information literacy. The phenomenon of the World Wide Web has been a double-edged sword with regard to information use. On the one hand, it has raised awareness of the topic 'information' as a resource, and related issues such as information overload and an awareness of tools and techniques to help create, store and find information. On the other hand, it has led to the belief that people's information problems are easily resolved, implying that one does not need to think about the skills and knowledge associated with being informed and using information in a systematic fashion. Furthermore, discussions of search engines and the web tend to focus only on information access – finding information – and ignore the thinking needed before and after, as well as during, the process of finding information.

However, people have begun to realise that although technological literacy is increasingly a necessity it is not the same as information literacy, which we define as:

> A complex set of abilities, which enable individuals to engage critically with and make sense of the world and its knowledge, to participate effectively in learning and to make use of and contribute to the information landscape.

We are also seeing a link being made between information literacy and capacity development, in general, in developing countries. Capacity development has been defined as 'enhancing grounding/enabling knowledge and skills through systematic learning processes' (Taylor and Clarke, 2008: 4). The ability or capacity to be information literate and increasingly e-literate therefore needs to be fostered.

This book will help instructors foster independent learning, learning that requires the learner to become independently informed rather than being given or directed to the information they need. The learner is therefore seen as an active player in the learning process rather than a passive recipient of learning. This is similar to the ethos of action research, where the researched–researcher divide is replaced by a collaborative research model. In fact, we would argue that without the learner being seen as an equal participant in this process, with genuine discussion and debate about what and how one has learnt, it is unlikely that a person will fully benefit from the intervention. People who are information literate consciously think about and question the way they learn. This can be taught in an abstract way where the learner is told how to go about learning and given strategies and techniques. However, we have found that this approach is unlikely to be successful and learners fail to apply this knowledge. Attempts to teach 'learning to learn' in isolation tend to be met with a lack of engagement and a sense of futility. Learners have to believe that information literacy is relevant to them and will help them solve their problems if they are to engage with it fully. When this is done in a way that systematically integrates information and the task is accompanied by reflection this develops conscious, metacognitive thinking about information use and then it is successful.

This does not mean that schools do not help learners learn about different subjects effectively. This is of course their primary objective and they achieve it to a lesser or greater extent. Ideally, however, if information literacy is taught and embedded in a specific subject or problem domain then it becomes intertwined with the process of solving problems in that domain and ceases to be abstract. The learner then sees how information literacy is linked to being a successful, active, participant in that domain. Particularly if active reflection takes place so that it can be appreciated and absorbed in a fundamental 'deep learning' way, knowledge becomes a part of the individual and influences their actions in the future, and can be applied to different situations. To become information literate people need to explore, debate, reflect and relate the process of learning to their experience, to the goals they wish to achieve. Information literacy is not only the recall of learnt techniques and processes (although there are techniques associated with the effective use of information artefacts) but it also involves new ways of thinking about and attitudes towards how we learn. As with all shifts in thinking this requires genuine engagement with the process – one where the learner sees its purpose and relevance for immediate gain, but also as a form of long-term personal empowerment, otherwise the learning will either be rejected or learnt in a shallow way that the learner will not apply outside the immediate learning context.

The material and ideas in this book relate to the use of information, in general, which may be held in paper or electronic form, or in people's heads. In fact it is hard to separate learning by media since learning is a multimedia experience. Nevertheless, we have chosen to emphasise the electronic environment, as artefacts that contain data, information and knowledge accumulated by people over time, enabling us to learn, tend to be found using information and communication technology (ICT) and held online in forms such as e-pedia, e-books, e-journals or other material accessible via the internet and stored electronically in what has been termed the World Wide Web. Furthermore, in the workplace material is often stored in electronic repositories such as databases or document management systems. The creation of material also takes place primarily in the electronic environment using software, such as word processing software, and there is a host of electronic tools that are used to support the process of content creation, organisation and dissemination that people need to be familiar with. Ironically the electronic domain, initially seen as a panacea for learning, has produced a glut of information of variable quality, which has increased the need to be able to access, use and manage information systematically in a critical fashion.

Much thought has been given to learning and how people learn. There are also many books about study skills, which cover aspects of information access and use, particularly in relation to conducting projects. However, we have not found a text that provides a detailed guide to how people interact with information, and how people learn and integrate teaching and learning theory to suggest practical interventions that will enable them to become information literate.

We therefore intend to provide a guide for instructors or facilitators to understand why they are doing what they are doing and to be able to adapt this knowledge to developing information literacy in different contexts. Our emphasis is on enabling learning in the electronic context, but where appropriate we will draw attention to situations where the non-electronic domain should not be overlooked.

We also, consciously, take note of the current thinking about how to encourage learning (pedagogy) effectively. A great deal has been written about how people learn by populist authors, cognitive psychologists, educators and philosophers. Unfortunately the circulation of literature tends to be confined to the domain of the author. There has been little cross-fertilisation and few works consciously talk about how people learn and relate this to learning how to be information literate. We address this issue by discussing learning and ideas about how people learn, as well as how to help the learner to learn. We then integrate and apply these ideas to the teaching and learning of information.

This book draws on:

- our experience of teaching information retrieval in electronic environments
- our experience teaching information literacy
- our experience teaching postgraduate students in library and information management how to teach information literacy
- research we have conducted over the years on how people use and interact with information
- research we have conducted into different methods for teaching information literacy
- other people's experience in these areas
- current thinking and wisdom about how people learn and effective methods to facilitate the learning process
- current thinking from the information behaviour school of information science, which specialises in studying and modelling people's interaction with information.

This book is particularly timely due to the importance being placed on human capital and people's capacity to learn and apply new knowledge, and the ever-expanding access we have to information and the tools to deal with it creatively, whether as text, graphics, speech, video or animation, either individually or in collaboration with others around the globe.

2

Learning and information literacy

What is learning?

Learning is interpreted here as taking on board new ideas that change the way people see a situation or the world around them, resulting in a transformation in their thinking and/or behaviour akin to the view of learning espoused by MacKeracher (2004). Phrases such as 'broadening one's horizons', 'seeing the world afresh' and 'shifting boundaries' encapsulate the impact of learning. We do not mean the learning of discrete, isolated items and being able to recall them at some future date. Learning implies a complete shift in how we see and interpret the world around us; it is connected with language that helps to conceptualise these new thoughts; it is associated with the ability to do new things. If a person is without information, other than that in their immediate vicinity, it is unlikely that they will have thought of alternative ways of being. That being may be concerned with what one can do with a particular subset of knowledge, such as scientific or agricultural practice and whether to believe, disbelieve or disagree with the opinions of others.

What is literacy?

The most basic definition of literacy is to 'be able to read and write' (OED, 1998). However, people have argued that 'to be literate is more than being able to read and write. It is about access to ideas that challenge our thinking and promote new ways of looking at the world' (Gamble and Easingwood, 2000: 4). 'It also involves speaking and listening' (2000: 12). To be literate is a major factor in information literacy since without literacy learners are limited to oral sources of information, which may limit them due to the need to store knowledge and information in one's memory or to access it via personal contacts. Having said that, the oral transmission of information and knowledge via story telling, for example, has been recognised in recent years as a powerful mechanism for learning.

A plethora of literacies: transliteracy and information literacy

E-literacy encompasses the ability to access, use, manage and create information in an electronic environment and is therefore a subset of information literacy. It includes the capacity to use electronic networks to access resources, create resources and communicate with others. It is related to the 'process of extracting meaning from, and recording and presenting your own meaning through, the full range of [electronic] media' (McFarlane, 2000: 20). Unsurprisingly it is one literacy in a veritable panoply of literacies which we see as related to the emerging concept of transliteracy. Transliteracy is defined as 'the ability to read, write and interact across a range of platforms, tools and media from signing and orality through handwriting, print, TV, radio and film, to digital social networks' (Thomas, 2008). Figure 2.1 illustrates the other terms relating to transliteracy in circulation; the terms people use tend to reflect their background. All would either form a part of information literacy (above the dashed line) or be a product of it (below the line).

Oral literacy concerns the ability to use and create information in an oral form. ICT or digital literacy concerns basic IT skills, including the ability to use software to create, organise, use and communicate information, data and knowledge. These may vary depending on the role of the learner. Media literacy is a term stemming from communications and media study and tends to be used to refer to the critical use of information and communication. The term numeric literacy is used to describe the capacity to manipulate and express numerical relationships. Text literacy implies knowledge of how texts are structured and of methods to extract, manipulate, critique and produce text. Visual literacy is used to describe a similar set of skills but in relation to the

Figure 2.1   Transliteracies

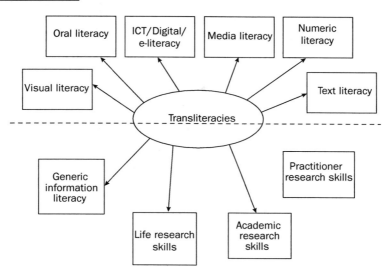

image. The skills are encompassed under broader headings associated with 'doing'. The term 'life skills' (or 'life research skills') tends to be used to describe a host of skills associated with managing in various contexts, such as dealing with money or communicating with others, which information literacy can facilitate. Academic research skills and practitioner research skills, commonly used terms, relate to 'research skills' and 'work skills'. 'Research skills' tends to be used to describe the skills of the professional researcher in the academic, commercial or industrial context. The term may be seen as a subset of 'academic literacy' and includes a number of techniques to gather evidence that may generate, confirm or refute ideas.

Numerous books provide descriptions of research techniques, which perhaps should be treated as a part of information literacy in the sense that they are ways of learning about the environment. However, information literacy currently (as in this book) focuses on access to and use of the processed intellectual response to primary data. Research skills are embedded in ideas about epistemology and ontology (what we can know, how we can find out and what it is called) and are associated with a host of qualitative and quantitative techniques. 'Work skills', as implied, relate to the workplace and include the ability to manage information and time, to plan and to collaborate. 'Study skills' are the skills associated with study in school, further and higher education. The latter tend to be associated with independent projects but encompass other techniques to aid learning. Study skills are pragmatic and do not take into account any philosophical notions of knowledge. They tend to be driven by the tasks students perform in formal education. Study skills writers discuss specific tasks that can be learnt, such as note taking or essay writing. They help people to conform to the learning culture and expectations associated with the educational environment. They also provide skills that can be applied to learning in general and help the learner to be more effective. 'Independent study skills' are those skills associated with independent study outside the classroom.

There are turf wars around such terms. These are probably redundant. However, such debates do at least force us to reflect on what exactly people need to know and how they can be helped. In fact all these skills or categories of learning are intertwined. Information literacy in this book is seen as a thread that runs through all these areas. The common thread is the ability to apply conscious thought systematically to defining information needs, identifying, accessing and using information that may involve any of these literacies and it is a key building block for various contexts, whether or not it leads to 'answers'. In practice, because of the need to situate independent learning in a particular context, information literacy may then be set within a specific domain such as health, economics or science.

What is information?

Understanding what is meant by information helps to frame teaching and learning interventions. It gives an appreciation of the impact or significance this phenomenon has on a person and processes we are trying to facilitate. It gives us a goal.

A great deal of debate has gone on to try to reach a satisfactory definition of information. Case provides a broad definition of information and terms associated with people's interaction with information:

- 'Information can be any difference you perceive, in your environment or within yourself. It is any aspect that you notice in the pattern of reality.

- Any information need is a recognition that your knowledge is inadequate to satisfy a goal that you have.

- Information seeking is a conscious effort to acquire information in response to a need or gap in your knowledge.

- Information behaviour encompasses information seeking as well as the totality of other unintentional or passive behaviours (such as glimpsing or encountering information). As well as purposive behaviours that do not involve seeking, such as avoiding information' (2007: 5).

It can be seen that information is not necessarily provided in a formal codified form, such as a book. It may be an experience; it may feed tacit knowledge that helps to make sense of experience. The fact that information may be 'any difference you perceive, in your environment or within yourself' implies that information can take many forms of complexity and form. Bystrom and Jarvelin (1995) distinguished between different situations that may lead to information needs: 'genuine decision tasks', where information demand and need may be high; 'known genuine decision tasks', where tacit knowledge may be sufficient; 'normal information processing', which may be so formalised that little critical thought is required; and 'automatic information processing', where people may unconsciously absorb content, ideas and so on.

Other authors describe the information we need as the filling of a gap (Dervin, 1983). This is similar, intellectually, to a traveller coming to the edge of a canyon with no idea of how to cross. Information enables one to make sense of a situation, which is comparable to providing a bridge over the canyon to enable the traveller to continue on his way. Dervin sees information as a sense-making process of becoming informed rather than a thing in its own right. A lack of knowledge has also been described as an anomalous state of knowledge (ASK) (Belkin, 2005), like a gap in knowledge that one needs to 'fill'. Others associate information need with uncertainty (Spink et al., 2002). It becomes clear that information and information literacy are not just associated with the use of published sources found in physical collections in libraries, bookshops, homes or offices, or electronically in personal or organisational websites, e-books and e-serials via search engines, portals and databases. These terms recognise the broader context of making sense and the need to understand one's information need. Information resources may include video, personal accounts, pictorial information, cartoons and stories. Information could be gained through an informative experience mediated through one's senses. This broadens the scope of information literacy and enables teachers to think more realistically about people's information literacy. They are, therefore, more likely to develop more appropriate interventions. 'Texts' are important, however. They are after all 'signs purposefully structured by a sender with the intention of changing the image structure of a recipient' (Belkin and Robertson, 1976) and hence the main focus of information literacy. This quotation brings to mind the word 'imagination' (Ledochowski, personal communication): accessing information and learning is in a sense a way to stimulate the imagination.

Over the last 500 years in many parts of the world there has been heavy emphasis on text. It was and still is a powerful tool for communicating secular and non-secular ideas. Now as a result of the range of multimedia in the electronic domain this emphasis is starting to change and an even richer communication is possible. Increased public access to the range of information tools and information resources draws attention to one particular aspect of information literacy, empowerment. Freire describes how 'in the process of learning to read, men and women discover that they are creators of culture' (Freire, 2007) rather than the passive objects responding to change. Similarly the ability to seek one's own answers has connotations of critical reflection and empowerment. The new tools may also facilitate the social nature of the 'process of knowing' (2007: 17), which is fundamental to the process of reflection and theorising – it tends to be more productive as a collaborative exercise. Furthermore, those who have a liberal approach to where they obtain evidence, and question the voice they are listening to, may be led to new sources of information and knowledge. This is instead of listening to the voice of the powerful or the media or 'experts', such as academics or consultants, who are traditionally thought to be the fount of knowledge and wisdom, although they may not have had direct experience of the problem. In other words people in the community or practitioners may have more pertinent insights and could be of more value than external experts. However, in order to manage their environment better, people in the community would probably benefit from using information from outside the community as well as their own knowledge.

Case's (2007) definition of information behaviour (as an area of research in information science) highlights the fact that information behaviour may not be highly directed. Information and knowledge can be gained through many channels, often in an unconscious way. In practice the immediate environment is where information seeking generally starts. This could include family, friends, people in the community or colleagues. This process of horizontal learning has not been given the recognition it deserves until recently. In the corporate and civil area innovative methods, including the use of cartoons, have been used to capture ideas, norms and practice as part of organisational learning (Snowden, 2001). In the corporate domain this has fallen under the heading 'knowledge management'. People have noticed how informal gatherings, for example, around the water cooler, where people chat about what they have been doing, or situations they have been in or dealt with, are important for learning contexts. Xerox found it useful for technical staff to share their experiences with each other and the developers (Choo, 2007). Therefore, from an information literacy perspective it would be important to facilitate people's ability to engage with and learn from these kinds of situations, perhaps by improving their capacity to network or enabling them to develop mechanisms to 'capture' aspects of such knowledge. People who place themselves in certain contexts may learn from others.

Many communities, particularly in remote or deprived areas, have little access to information resources other than the people around them. Again, from a Freirian perspective an appreciation of the knowledge that exists at a grass-roots level is in itself empowering, but knowledge, data and information may not necessarily lead to empowerment. However, one positive example is the Arid Lands Information Network (ALIN), which set up knowledge centres in Kenya where farmers go to share and exchange knowledge. These centres also organise and produce other information resources and conduct sessions in school and with farmers. Interpersonal communication, knowledge management, horizontal learning and placing oneself in a social context are important aspects of information literacy.

Case (2007) also provides a healthy reminder that people do not always seek information even when, from an outsider's perspective, it would be useful. This may be because people are unconscious of their information behaviour or may not have developed their information literacy. Previous negative learning experiences – fears of what they may find, feelings of isolation, fears of appearing stupid, fear that information will complicate things, a lack of knowledge of what is known, an unreasonable confidence in their own knowledge, a predisposition to just having a go and learning 'on the job' – may all inhibit information literacy.

Being aware of the multiple perceptions of information and different dispositions to learning in terms of how people prefer to learn, attitudes to learning, motivational characteristics such as confidence or a sense of self-efficacy and their use of information is important for teaching information literacy to be successful and to build on or change information behaviour.

It is fundamental for information literacy to build on the previous experience and knowledge of the learner and to provide information literacy training that is based on strong pedagogic practice and an understanding of the various contexts within which the learner wishes or needs to learn.

Why are we seeing such an emphasis on how we learn and independent learning?

Historically changes have taken place in how people see the world politically. Over the 20th century roles and relationships have been defined and redefined. Quite recently knowledge was perceived to be the remit of the few, the elite. It is only in the last 30 years that more than 15 per cent of the population has gone into higher education in the UK. Before that the majority of people were expected to earn their living in jobs that were not perceived to be information intensive. The 'educated elite' tended to be teachers, priests, professionals, government employees and industrialists. They were generally more economically powerful and tended to be in the upper echelons of hierarchical organisational structures, and in the UK this was associated with the class system. Newer societies that started from a more egalitarian ethos tend to have a more inclusive view of learning, which has led to more thought about how to make learning easier and how to give more people greater opportunities. It has been assumed that it is the right of any individual to have an even chance of success whatever their background. This is evident in countries such as the USA, Australia and New Zealand, which have an explicitly egalitarian ethos and where class structures are less evident than in the UK. However, a liberal ethos is reflected in the UK in organisations such as the Open University, which values inclusion. Other countries motivated at a governmental level to improve the capacity of the nation to enable them to develop economically, such as Scandinavia, Singapore and Bahrain, have increased access to information and more creative learning environments – although this has occurred only recently in Bahrain.

All in all from the individual, organisational, community, national and international perspective we can see that a higher proportion of people are expected to use information and knowledge and to learn continuously. Phrases such as 'human capital', 'capabilities', 'the capacity to learn', 'knowledge-based economies' and 'information society' indicate that information and knowledge has been recognised as a valued resource for society in general through which activities can be managed, and in the commercial sector profits made and goals achieved. Hence our capacity as human beings to use data, information and accumulated knowledge effectively has been given an economic premium and seen as a part of 'human capital' and social or organisational capital, which can be transformed into economic capital. Companies are increasingly willing to allocate resources that help individuals to make efficient use of their information and knowledge. The ability to create and manage intellectual capital such as patents (a record of knowledge) is increasingly used to assess an organisation's worth. In the academic and commercial domain the combined force of people to use their intellect is also at a premium and collaborative research networks, for example, are encouraged by research councils. Global virtual communities are increasingly seen as a way to leverage knowledge and are commonly promoted by large corporations, such as IBM, as well as other organisations, such as the World Bank. In government and non-governmental organisations information management is increasingly seen as fundamental. Despite these changes and the steady stream of poor information management stories there are surprisingly few initiatives to train staff in information literacy and information management.

Nevertheless, emphasis on information and valuing information and knowledge has led to greater dependence on the ability of individuals to make use of information – their information literacy and their ability to communicate and exchange information and share knowledge with other people. In the developing country context the importance of information literacy has begun to be made explicit as an important contribution to capacity building. This link with 'development' helps us to put information literacy in a wider context and is a further indication of its significance. A recent publication by the Institute of Development Studies (Taylor and Clarke, 2008) highlights the importance of learning and how capacity development involves enhancing knowledge and skills through systematic learning processes. The authors say that '[an] individual's capabilities of many different kinds are limited by their capacity to construct useful knowledge, to share that knowledge with others, and to apply that knowledge in practice and in ways that may lead to further construction of knowledge through critical reflection on their practice' (2008: 7). Later they make the important point that 'education is about conceptual change, not just the acquisition of information' (2008: 11). This echoes the notion that being information literate is not just having the ability to define needs, to access information and to use that information, but is a way of thinking about problems from an information perspective – it involves a change in outlook.

Information literacy is increasingly valued as a significant portion of the transferable skills that society 'wants'. From an individual's perspective these skills (skills is used here as a shorthand for attitudes, knowledge and skills) are seen to be important since they imply the ability to solve one's own problems or the problems of the community that one is a part of; to be in more control of one's current situation and future; and to be able to create new knowledge. Having transferable skills can therefore help people to make better decisions and to create new knowledge contributing to social and organisational goals, as well as to manage more effectively in their personal life.

Another factor lending weight to the value of information literacy is the explosive increase in the amount of information that is being created around the world. This trend – the massive increase in the generation and communication of information – preceded the digital revolution. The digital revolution has been both a response to managing information effectively and, ironically, has been one of the factors leading to the increase in the quantity of information generated. This increase in available information has also led to an awareness of the research and knowledge that is not being used. In the development sector the focus of some funders, at present, is to help ensure that policy makers as well as intermediaries and people at a grass-roots level get access to (previously funded and other) evidence-based research. This is similar to the relatively newly established practice of evidence-based medicine that has been emphasised in the health services around the world over the last 15 years.

In the past information and knowledge was primarily communicated face to face using oral communication. Rich, multimedia techniques were used to access and communicate knowledge about the world, including dance, song, poetry and story telling; the use of voice, facial expression, narrative, engaging characters (heroes, animals and so on); and artefacts that held meaning, including art and other man-made objects. Thus knowledge was assembled, communicated and transferred. In some societies, such as the Egyptian, texts and written images were deployed primarily to record data but also to explain roles, relationships and world views. These tools were primarily in the hands of the few, often political and religious leaders. This continued into medieval times. Oral communication was the primary public medium. With the advent of the printing press text moved into ascendancy and was interwoven with the explosion of scientific knowledge, the growth in population and the need and desire to share information and knowledge.

Text has been the primary tool for information exchange and learning since this time. Computerised ICT has largely followed and spread the dependence on text. Other media have not been explicitly valued for their educational role although television, theatre and cinema (a visual and audial form), radio (an audial form) and literature (text) do play a significant information and educational role. They all provide a means to access different 'worlds' and make sense of the world around us. This may be achieved through story telling, which creates 'rich pictures' in our minds that help understand and share the processes and conditions that people experience. However, in the formal educational system we still see an emphasis on the skills of reading and writing (as well as numeracy) in the curriculum although we are seeing a shift in emphasis as teachers become more proficient with new technology, understand its role and begin to place more emphasis on other media. In addition there is greater appreciation of the needs of different learners and a willingness to cater to these learning needs, but the recognised need to share and build on pre-existing information and knowledge is paramount. The drive to do this has led to a rekindling of interest in older methods of knowledge transfer, including story telling and the use of narrative to capture and communicate knowledge, particularly in the corporate context (Snowden, 1999). This dovetails with the expanded definition of information described above and the need to draw on a broad range of knowledge, including ICT, to ensure people are effective members of the information society.

The increase in the usability and accessibility of computerised applications – in particular information retrieval tools such as those offered by Google and the Web 2.0 technologies, which enable the creation, use and distribution of a wide range of content (pictures, film, animation, voice as well as text) – has implications for information literacy training. On the one hand, they are the tools that can be used to access, use, manipulate and communicate information that the information literate person needs to know. But they are also the tools that the 'teachers' can use to foster information literacy. Indeed Walton et al. (2007a; 2007b), Pope and Walton (2009) and Walton (in press) have demonstrated that information literacy can be fostered via online discourse. In completing a set of online collaborative learning (OCL) activities via an online discussion board they found that students became highly focused on an information literacy task, engaged in high level cognitive processes (analysis, synthesis and evaluation) as defined by Bloom et al. (1956) and demonstrated information literacy skills associated with the ability to evaluate web-based information in a highly sophisticated fashion. By scaffolding online learning interventions with set questions to be answered, rather than information to be absorbed, information literacy was fostered. E-learning not only enabled students to read information about evaluating websites but also, via online discourse, to engage in analysis, to devise their own evaluation criteria and in turn begin to create a shared meaning regarding a topic.

Using such applications in combination with ideas of social, situated, personalised and continual learning we are seeing a change in the learning context, and the tools that enable the application of different pedagogical views of the learner can be used to help people learn. However, the learner also needs to have access to and be familiar with this myriad of tools and content. It is possible that via the application of these tools the richness associated with the face-to-face oral transmission of information and knowledge can now be better emulated in the electronic medium and can be achieved from a distance using the telecommunications infrastructure.

A combination of the issues described has therefore led to an appreciation of the importance of information literacy. But exactly what skills and knowledge does this emphasise? Should it include the confidence and motivation to form and ask questions and independently seek answers or the ability to deal with multiple sources and types of information with variable quality and functionality? Is it knowing about multiple sources, including people? Is it being able to extract and process information effectively and efficiently? Is it to do with using information tools and technologies, or is it familiarity with the norms of information use and production? These questions give an indication of the breadth and complexity of information literacy and the degree of thought needed to develop such skills, attitudes and knowledge.

Information literacy

The capacity of individuals, organisations and communities to have an element of control over their lives is constrained by their knowledge. Knowledge, as we have so often been told, is linked to power. Access to knowledge can be constrained socially by norms and social structures. If people do not have access to information it is difficult for them to make well-informed decisions. They would have no knowledge of different viewpoints that may contradict commonly accepted and perhaps unfounded beliefs, beliefs that perhaps support the continuation of social structures and practices that do not benefit sections of society. A lack of knowledge makes it difficult for people to participate in a dialogue or debate with others who have more knowledge and access to information and data that supports their views. A lack of knowledge means that it is hard for people to reflect critically on their situation, to take new directions or to develop new ideas. Within specific domains, those without knowledge of the area, current ideas, theories and practices find it is impossible to engage with other practitioners or even to be listened to.

Ignorance leads to a lack of choice or poor choices whether at an individual, organisational or community level. It imposes boundaries that constrain. The ability to learn, so that it is possible to achieve one's own short or long term objectives or the objectives of people one is working or playing with, is therefore fundamental and leads one to have some control over and to shape conceptual boundaries. Information literacy is one building block in the construction of knowledge.

The concept information literacy is concerned with learning, in its broadest sense. Learning maybe 'directed learning', where people actively seek answers to problems, or 'passive learning', whereby people absorb information and knowledge from their contact and interact with the information landscape around them in an 'accidental', unplanned way. The latter is often called serendipity. Learning takes place in an information landscape that includes people who can inform; published or communicated sources such as leaflets or stories; and natural events that tell a story (the natural events are given meaning through prior knowledge, such as knowing that when a particular cloud forms there is a likelihood of rain).

Being information literate therefore means having the ability to access representations of meaning, generally as language in the form of texts, but also voice, images, performance and meaningful objects that encapsulate ideas which communicate information, reflections of knowledge. These ideas have meaning to the person and provide a mental framework that facilitates understanding and enables action and purposeful, successful, interaction by the individual or group with the world around them. People are information literate when they are able to use information and knowledge to be informed so that they can solve problems, make decisions and have some control of their world, and be active participants in a social context that shares a common reality, common objectives and a common learning culture. The common learning culture includes both what is deemed knowledge as well as the accepted methods to generate new knowledge. The individual is of course a member of many groups, plays many roles and participates in a host of activities, whether in the workplace, the home or on the street; each one requires different types of knowledge, different ways of learning and access to multiple types of content.

Beyond their immediate situation, individuals may be a part of a particular learning community, a community of practice. This is a group of people who share similar goals, have common beliefs and work together to achieve those goals. The concept 'community of practice' (Lave and Wenger, 1991) tends to be associated with the workplace.

However, this concept could be extended to encompass any interdependent interaction with other people, such as a group of friends, the family, workmates or people involved in a political organisation. A community of practice could be tomato growers who want to grow and sell their produce. It could be mothers who need to take care of the health of their children. Community is therefore used here to refer to people who share a common information need as a result of their common goals, and who share a common information and knowledge environment. To be a part of a community of practice one needs to know the language of that practice. The language represents and enables communication of shared ideas and meanings. The artefacts associated with that community, the 'tools of the trade' that help people achieve outcomes, such as the telescope for the astronomer, extend their physical capability, in this case sight, enabling them to see far-off and 'invisible' objects. Tools may also be repositories of ideas, information that is, in a sense, a frozen conversation that informs and enables them to learn new mental constructs and become a part of the community. The individual or for that matter the organisation or society may become so well informed or steeped in a particular dialogue that they eventually contribute to the wider discourse. Then they are seen as experts who can benefit (or manage or control) others, developing and communicating new information and knowledge that 'helps' that community 'perform' – interact with the environment in a way that achieves common goals and enables sustained survival. These are the 'experts', the knowledgeable.

A number of factors may affect the information literacy of an individual or a group of individuals. The current information and knowledge landscape that the individual or community of practice inhabits will be one significant factor that will govern the information literacy of the individual and the information literacy they need. The efficacy of the information literate individual, group or organisation will be influenced by their knowledge of the information resources that they have access to and their ability to use information in an effective way. This will include their cognitive ability, their familiarity with and ability to use the thought processes associated with interacting with and making use of information and knowledge – the products of other people's thought processes. It will also include their physical ability and familiarity with accessing information resources, making use of information and possibly communicating their newfound insights. The use of a book, for example, implies both cognitive and behavioural skills and knowledge. The cognitive skills associated with processing information such as analysis, comparison or categorisation, and the behavioural skills such as physically using certain sections or features of the book to help access information, or tasks such as scanning or note taking. Similarly the ability to store knowledge as stories and to be able to recall them is a cognitive skill and the ability to use effective modes of delivering and telling is a behavioural skill. The information literacy of an individual and the wider group may also be influenced by an individual's motivation and how they perceive themselves and their self-efficacy. In the same way the perception of a group as a collection of people with shared interests and their combined efficacy may influence their use of information and whether they proactively seek it to achieve their common needs.

Norms associated with how we learn will also be influential. These norms tend to stem from the community of practice, for example, who we learn from or actively seek information from, what information and knowledge we value, who provides information, the evolved form that that information takes, and the values attached to these. The values and norms can vary from individual to individual, group to group, and culture to culture. There may also be power structures, economic forces and divisions of labour that affect the creation, storage and communication of information and knowledge, which again may have bearing on the information literacy of people and groups. These may have a positive or negative impact and create an opportunity or a barrier to being information literate. They may drive the need to become more information literate. They may determine who is information literate. In developing counties, having access to the radio may influence a person's opportunity to be informed and act. For example, women may have less access than men (Beardon, 2004). The lack of access to ICT due to a lack of funds or infrastructure, the digital divide, may limit the opportunity to become information literate. The power and ability to control access to and charge for scholarly academic journals can inhibit access to information. Historical initiatives such as the setting up of public libraries and current initiatives such as the Creative Commons and the Open Source Initiative are attempts to address these issues.

Information literacy is therefore a multidimensional phenomenon that can be thought about from different perspectives, including individual, social, cultural and global. At a societal and group level, it can seen as human capital or social capital as Bordieu (1986) saw it. Social capital can be converted into economic capital, as with intellectual capital such as a patent. This is associated with the ability and opportunity for people to access shared explanations and interpretations of their world and the ability to mould and react to that perceived reality. At an individual level we see information literacy as part of those human capacities and behaviours (human capital) that enable people to satisfy physical, social and emotional personal goals, including being a part of and taking part in the wider human endeavours that contribute to our sustainability. Through this participation they are seen as and feel that they are valued members. This may be converted into economic capital, as a wage.

Understanding this broad and rich context within which the phrase information literacy sits has direct implications for what is taught and how it should be taught. For example, bearing in mind the exploratory and sense making aspect of learning tends to foster a constructivist approach to designing appropriate teaching interventions. Furthermore, the realisation that one function of information literacy is to enable participation in a community of practice implies that communication and discourse are likely to form a fundamental part of the learning process. One challenge of teaching information literacy is that it is abstract. People are not generally conscious of how they use information, nor are they prepared to conduct independent research in schools effectively. Young people in schools tend to see information as something given rather than something they seek, because their experience of school is a place where they are generally given the information they need to complete tasks or are directed to it (Smith and Hepworth, 2007). There are situations where school children do independent research, but they tend to do it in an unsupervised way, often at home, with little guidance. Assessment tends to be of the finished product rather than the process of gathering and processing information. Hence, information literacy is not greatly developed among school children and they do not become conscious of it. There are exceptions. In some subjects such as English or history there is a more conscious approach to information, particularly the critical evaluation of information (where it has come from, its validity). However, these attitudes and this knowledge tend not to be transferred to other subject domains. The social engagement aspect of information literacy – as well as enabling independent decisions and learning that in turn help people to fulfil their study, work or non-work objectives – needs to be emphasised, as does the power it gives to people to question and challenge the powerful and how it can lead to greater control by people over their lives. This latter aspect of information literacy has been recognised as an essential component of democratic participation (Catts and Lau, 2008).

The following is an adaptation of a definition of an information literate person published by Unesco (Catts and Lau, 2008; Horton, 2007). The information literate person:

- realises that information or knowledge is required to solve a problems in the workplace, to understand civic needs and to provide for the health and wellbeing of the individual, the family and community
- is aware of the information landscapes (information artefacts – books, manuals, indexes and so on) people and information rich environments relevant to their situation and can locate and access that information
- knows how to evaluate, interpret, manipulate, capture, organise and store information in a way that is appropriate to their situation and applying accepted norms
- knows how to communicate and present information effectively to others
- knows how to dispose of information no longer needed and safeguard information that should be protected.

Information literacy therefore encompasses cognitive and behavioural skills and knowledge, and an awareness of social and cultural norms that relate to the use of information and generation of knowledge. With e-literacy these skills and knowledge are applied in an electronic environment, and assume familiarity with the related technologies, but they can equally be applied in the paper-based or oral domains.

As indicated by Friere (2007), this may not only serve a utilitarian purpose. Whitworth (2006) argues that by becoming information literate people can move far beyond this into the realms of becoming actively engaged as critical citizens in an overtly political fashion. What is missing from the Unesco definition is the word 'critical'. It is recognised that this notion is used in other definitions of information literacy, for example, by the ACRL (2000, 3):

- 'Determine the extent of information needed
- Access the needed information effectively and efficiently
- Evaluate information and its sources critically
- Incorporate selected information into one's knowledge base
- Use information effectively to accomplish a specific purpose
- Understand the economic, legal, and social issues surrounding the use of information, and access and use information ethically and legally.'

However, Whitworth (2006) argues that in this definition of information literacy (as well as others) the word 'critical' is used to mean a way of categorising information via criteria of reliability, accuracy, relevance, authority and so on, and tends to insulate expert discourse from public scrutiny, rather than to enable learners to scrutinise the validity claims of all texts and utterances, and act within principles of justice and having respect for others.

What do we need to know about the learner and learning to help foster information literacy?

There are different vantage points from which to view learners. These vantage points, views, lenses or explanatory frameworks have their origin in different epistemologies and ontologies. Some emphasise the socially embedded nature of learning, others the physically embedded nature of learning and our interaction with the world. The former tend to emphasise the situated nature of learning – the impact of norms and accepted ideas, and the importance of language, discourse, and political and social structures. The latter tend to draw attention to the material world and people's physical interaction with it. Some try to bridge the two. Figure 2.2 illustrates the relationship between learners and their social, psychological and behavioural context in relation to the information landscape.

Figure 2.3 illustrates the context within which the independent learner and maker of meaning can be placed. It highlights the interactions with the social and material world, and the impact of the individual's physicality and their cultural and physical context, and how this may influence their experience.

At the top level of Figure 2.3 we have the products or repositories of social interaction with the environment. These legacies of thought, records of experience, traces of information, data and knowledge are current and living as well as rooted in the past. Below are the individual interactions – where using and creating information, data and knowledge within social and material contexts leads to the production of new information products and requires the use of existing intellectual resources. The individual's interactions over time lead to learning and capacity development within specific contexts.

The individual's capacity is influenced by their physical (biochemical and physiological being), cultural, social and physical context (technology, materials and so on); through experience they can become an independent learner and communicator, a person who understands, constructs and conveys meanings in a systematic way.

Figure 2.2 The Hepworth and Walton model of information literacy behaviour

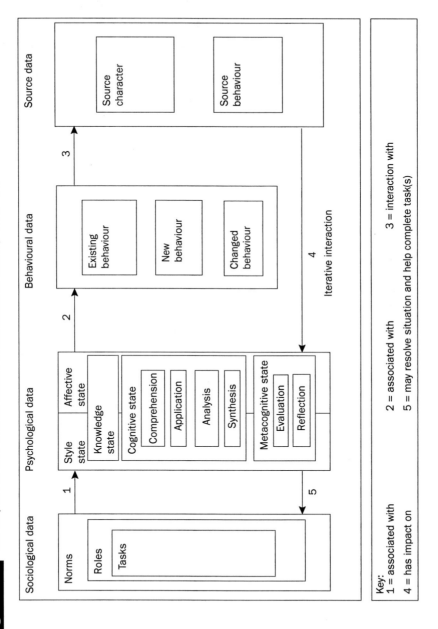

Key:
1 = associated with
4 = has impact on
2 = associated with
5 = may resolve situation and help complete task(s)
3 = interaction with

Figure 2.3 The social and physical world of information

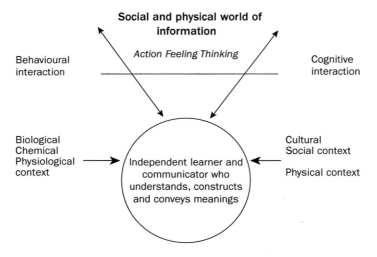

Working backwards the person is involved in a task where they need to be informed and to understand their world (and we inhabit many worlds – domestic, consumer, work, study). Depending on their role and situation they may contribute to that world by constructing meanings via social interaction and the production of narrative (oral, textual, visual and auditory) while they conduct tasks, deal with situations, and achieve goals and objectives. To do this they need to be active learners and motivated to learn independently. Learners are a 'product' of their being (biochemical and physiological), their socio-cultural and physical experience and context. They interact with and are constrained by their socio-cultural and physical context. The form of this interaction depends on their biochemical and physiological make-up. This is reflected in the individual's interaction (cognitive and behavioural) with their material and social world, for example, with information artefacts or information organisations. The latter have changed and developed over time due to a variety of social, economic and technological drivers. People are actively involved in creating and adapting to this environment. Explanations for what motivates this activity range from the organic (an evolving organism doing what it can to survive in the world), to the materialistic (the securing of resources); some explanations emphasise the social nature of being and becoming part of and belonging to a wider social group. In addition there are the individualistic affective explanations, such as satisfying emotional needs, and psychological explanations, such as resolving uncertainty. These 'frames' help us to think and identify meaningful facets of our information experience.

Those following the 'scientific paradigm', who tend to empiricist and positivist assumptions, imply that there is a direct relationship between ideas and reality. Knowledge is based on empirical evidence, which enables people to achieve certain tasks or predict outcomes. Interpretivists believe that we have no direct access to knowledge about a concrete 'reality' and that our conceptions of reality are mediated through our perceptions; these conceptions are mental constructs that help us to mediate our environment. Empiricists are associated with behaviourist ideas about the learner and tend to see quantitative tests of learning as a direct reflection of learning. They tend to see cognition as building blocks of knowledge, one building on another, tested through the ability to achieve certain tasks or to predict outcomes. Cognitive characteristics of thought tend to be viewed here as 'hard wired' or embedded. From an interpretivist viewpoint, cognitive constructivists tend to emphasise the notion of people making sense of their reality through the construction of mental maps and schema, whereas social constructivists emphasise the socially situated and constructed nature of 'reality' and the role of language that defines 'reality'. In fact the lines between these points of view are blurred and less distinct than is often argued. Different authors focus on different aspects of the learner and the learning process. Empiricists and behaviourists focus primarily on the individual and the biological and physical (in the neurological and sensory sense), whereas interpretivists draw attention to the social nature of the learner and the context within which the learner learns. By context we mean the cultural and socio-economic environment that has developed over time. This in turn, as a result of people's participation, creativity and ideological standpoints, has led to and been influenced by a technological environment that enables the individual and society to interact with and manage their world. An appreciation of these aspects may seem unnecessarily philosophical and yet an understanding of these broad perspectives has implications for us as teachers since they throw a spotlight on the different factors that affect the learner and learning.

Each view serves its purpose in understanding the nature of the learner and has implications for understanding how people learn and the nature of teaching and learning interventions that the educator should foster. The following explanations regarding the different 'faces' of learning, or ways of viewing the learner and learning, start at what could be conceived as the inner core – the person as an organic form, and moves to the outer core to thinking of the person as part of social and cultural space. The proverbial onion would be another way of thinking about this with its inner and outer layers. The inner layer, the heart of the onion, represents people as physical beings. The outer layers are the social and cultural perspectives.

3

The learner as a physical being – a sensory approach

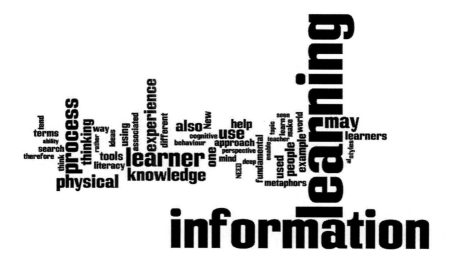

This chapter focuses on the physicality of the learner. Our physical 'construction' has an impact on how we learn. From birth we try to make sense of our physical interaction with the world around us. These interactions are governed by our physicality, form and internal structure, including the neurological pathways that are laid down and associated with behaviour and thought that stems from our experience. Our physical senses, sight, hearing and so on are intertwined with how we learn. Preferences for using different senses can develop. Appreciating the embodied nature of the learner is important in the design of effective learning interventions.

In 1999 Lakoff put forward the view that a learner is a product of themselves as a physical being in a physical environment. As a physical being we are a biochemical phenomenon made up of structures that have evolved in a specialised way, which is affected by and affects our interaction with the world with the underlying 'purpose' of being and sustaining itself as a living organism. This has evolved through chance and adaptation, quite simply because it can. Lakoff bridges the gap between positivism and interpretivism. From this perspective reason could be seen as evolutionary and reflects our evolution as a species. At a neurological level, 'the nervous system sets up a large number of connections; experience then plays on this network, selecting the appropriate connections and removing the inappropriate'. Then throughout life additional synapses are added based on experience (Bransford, Brown and Cocking, 2000: 116). Our experiences and exposure to information is part of this developmental process. New structures develop in the brain as a result of learning. Lakoff argues that our conceptions are not a direct reflection of an objective, mind-free reality because the sensor–motor system plays a crucial role in shaping them. Reason is therefore not disembodied. From this perspective what we do and how we work is an embodiment of our being – our physical being, our neurones, sensory organs, physical experience of the world (for example, our sight, hearing, sense of touch and physical form, such as our verticality and the fact that we have a front and back), our awareness of movement, our experience of physical force and our awareness of temporality. All of these become highly developed at an early age. Young children have a bias for 'biological concepts, early number sense and early understanding of basic physics' and 'co-ordinated schemes of looking, listening, and touching' (Bransford et al., 2000: 80). An infant, for example, as young as three months old, 'expects' a box placed on another to be stable but not when there is no supporting platform (2000: 84). A 12-month old child uses a schema such as a push–pull plan and applies it to a range of objects and situations (2000: 87). At the age of 24 months a child can choose the right tool. Three to four year olds have some understanding of the different properties of inanimate and animate objects, and can give sensible answers to questions about inside and outside. These indicate the kind of fundamental conceptions, as a result of physical predispositions, the child forms that become the basis for thinking thoughts about the world.

Lakoff (1999) has argued that this physicality has led to fundamental conceptual structures that we use to think about things and to express our thoughts. These enable us to make sense of the world and to communicate through shared concepts and hence interact with others to help manage that world. These conceptual structures, Lakoff argues, are embedded at a neurological level. Neurones 'fire' when physical things are to be done but also when thoughts are to be had. Combinations of neurones 'fire' in conjunction with specific thoughts. Notions of up, back, front, movement, inside and outside are shaped by our physicality and are used to help conceptualise our interaction with the physical world around us. These physical experiences are associated with and get translated into verbal structures and language, which enables us to develop knowledge and communicate our experience. These experiences can be seen in fundamental metaphors we use to explain, conceptualise and communicate with others about the world around us. Many cultures, Lakoff argues, use these structures to compare, contrast and categorise – to process data, information and knowledge. He identifies fundamental metaphors that he states are grounded at a neurological level and stem from our physicality, as described above, which we use to interpret and think about our experience of the world around and to communicate with others. From a teaching perspective they help us think about becoming informed by identifying specific metaphors that are related to how we think about the mind, thinking and learning, which helps us to concretise concepts associated with information literacy. They provide a frame within which the learner can predict future situations and place new knowledge. For example, considering a line of thought as a path immediately gives the learner a structure and a set of expectations – it has a beginning and an end; there is a likelihood of having to choose between different paths and the expectation of dead ends, short cuts and so on.

Physical metaphors as a means of shaping thinking

Such metaphors are therefore useful because they have a fundamental resonance and help to concretise abstract mental processes. This is one of the major challenges when talking about and teaching thinking associated with information. We would argue that awareness of the individual at this neurological level is important in helping to communicate and share concepts with the learner. Metaphors provide a 'rehearsal'; they help to orientate the learner to what may be in store. Practically we can consciously incorporate this language, which reflects fundamental cognitive structures, in our teaching. This will become evident in the teaching interventions discussed later in the book. Table 3.1 provides a list of examples of fundamental metaphors that are used

Table 3.1	How metaphors used when people talk about the mind are incorporated in information literacy instruction
Metaphor	**Use in information literacy instruction**
The mind is a body	Build an understanding. Develop a state of mind (as in 'body building'). Conversely the implied physicality of the mind signifies that a representation of the product of the mind – intellectual output – could be described as a physical object. For example, an essay or report could be described as building a house with a foundation drawn from the literature and previous knowledge using the tools (search engines, catalogues, databases etc.) and raw materials available (articles, e-books, web pages etc.).
Thinking is moving	Thinking about a topic one may wander, stray, arrive, race, lose track, go off course.
Ideas as locations	Information can be placed in an information landscape. An answer can be a destination. Information can be stored in a location, a pile, a nugget, closer to home, a database (a base of data), a glut, overload (buried) or something that contains information, where data, information and knowledge may be outside or not central to the 'container' – the topic or domain. We can also talk about a cultural or, closer to home, information landscape.
Reason is force	Reason is used to narrow a topic down, to whittle away at a subject, to broaden a search; an idea may give leverage, to condense a topic. Each metaphor implies bringing to bear a physical force on the 'object' – the idea or concept. Knowledge is power has similar connotations. A key (the power to turn) can be associated with information.
Rational thought is	It is a direct, step-by-step process. Frameworks, models, ordered instructions (first, then…) are used to describe and help understand information literacy and information behaviour processes and procedures. They resonate with their implied 'rationality', reason. They purport to be a rational description of factors, and to follow them implies systematic and 'deliberate' reasoning. Models for learning information literacy could be seen as deliberation.
Being unable to think is being unable to move	Terms like being blocked, feeling overloaded or stymied, coming to a dead end, and not being sure which way to go are used to describe obstacles experienced in the learning process and when undertaking research.

Table 3.1 How metaphors used when people talk about the mind are incorporated in information literacy instruction (*Cont'd*)

Metaphor	Use in information literacy instruction
A line of thought is a path	Learning, thinking about or finding out can be described as a journey of discovery. Finding out involves charting or navigating the information landscape, exploring the topic. We refer to the path to reason and/or understanding. A (cognitive) process that takes place over time is also conceptualised as a journey. Paths can split, peter out or join larger paths.
Rethinking is going over the path again	Terms like back tracking, going over the arguments again, reflecting on what one has done or found on the way, retracing our steps can all be used to describe the process of reflection (something that comes back in reverse!), which is fundamental to become conscious of metacognition associated with information literacy.
Communication is guiding	Informing others of how, what, when and where is a fundamental concept. This seems to be also related to the power of story telling and its function to guide and help explain to others the nature of things.
Searching, seeing, noticing	Searching, seeing, noticing, hearing (I hear what you say), looking at (paying attention) and demonstrating preference (taste) can all be part of interacting with information.
Thinking is object manipulation	Turning over in one's mind, playing, grasping, recalling, retrieving an idea.
Acquiring ideas is eating	Having an appetite for a subject, swallowing, digesting; indigestible ideas.

when people talk about the mind. The column on the right-hand side indicates how they can be incorporated and applied in information literacy discourse.

Whether or not one believes, as Lakoff does, that these metaphors are fundamental and 'hard wired' at a neurological level as a result of our evolution and interaction with the world as beings, they can be seen to have a distinct, intuitive, resonance. They are commonly used in European and other cultures around the world. As teachers we can see that choosing such metaphors carefully when teaching information literacy can make the processes and experiences associated with this subject more intuitive and concrete. The nature of these metaphors helps learners to relate to and understand the situation they are experiencing. They would also help learners to extrapolate and infer what may follow in terms of what actions or thinking to take.

Fundamental metaphors for thinking

Fundamental metaphors can therefore be used to enable people to absorb, understand and draw inferences. They can provide a guide as to how to think. For example, topics can be represented or perceived as *containers* – physical entities of the sort that we have experienced from birth. Databases are already visually represented as *tubes*. Ideas can be conceptualised as things we grasp as a child *grasps* an object. Our experience of movement and the temporal nature of experience lends power to the description of a project as a *journey* the learner can take. They can then make assumptions about the nature of the new experience. That it takes place over time. It may have *dead ends*. It may go in different *directions*. There may be tools that enable them to undertake and complete this journey. We can talk about the information *landscape*, our term for the data, and the information and knowledge environment around us that they are likely to experience. Knowledge *spaces* can be used to represent communities of practice, which share a certain language and norms that need to be understood and learnt if we want to engage with them, learn from them, and be seen as a proactive participant and a valued contributor to them. Information can *overload*, be a *morass*. We can find *smaller* or *finer elements* among a *larger mass* – information as *nuggets* of gold among *piles* of information; the *needle in the haystack* (Hughes, Bruce and Edwards, 2007: 64). Hughes et al. use a number of metaphors that help to conceptualise the progression and develop expertise of the learner through the information-seeking process. These include seeing information seeking as *finding a way through a maze*, then *using tools as a filter* and then *panning for gold*.

Thinking about appropriate metaphors that can help the learner conceptualise what they are expected to learn and the way they should go about the learning can therefore be a powerful tool. The power of metaphor can also be seen in oral cultures, where physical representations in textual form are absent as a means to capture information and knowledge. Metaphors are used to allow people to conceptualise and place their learning in a context that is already 'understood', to learn new things and enable them to be held in the mind as memories. As a teacher of information literacy, partly because of its abstract nature, it is therefore important to choose appropriate metaphors that help the learning process through their power to concretise the abstract and provide a frame that in itself allows the learner to make predictions and choices.

At the sensory level of analysis we can also think of artefacts and tools we create as extensions of our bodily ability. A magnifying lens increases our power of sight. Information tools enable us to view large numbers of representations of thought, such as documents, at one time. The tools, such as databases or filing systems, enable us to sort, categorise, store and find information. They also provide an extension to our individual and collective memory. Tools embody our ideas about what we do and want to achieve, and information forms part of the landscape that the learner needs to become familiar with. This is important since the tools enable learning and are a part of the information, knowledge creation and dissemination process. Part of becoming information literate is to be knowledgeable about the tools that are available, their strengths and weaknesses, and how to use them effectively to support the learning and communicative process. Tools include portals and organisations' websites, which help us to identify useful information; applications such as mind mapping and visualisation software help us access and represent our thinking processes; other methods, such as social computing applications and Web 2.0 technologies, enable us to communicate our ideas with other people.

A great deal of information literacy training in the past has focused on the ability of people to use tools. This is obviously necessary and a certain amount of behavioural training is required where people learn about the range of sources and specific functions (such as commands) that are required. However, although necessary, we have found that if behavioural training takes place in isolation from its role in supporting learning and the goals associated with the wider social context within which they have a purpose, such as achieving work, pleasure or study goals, it has little impact. Without embedding these goals in the wider context as well as known similar contexts (represented perhaps through metaphor), learning tends to be shallow and learners find it difficult to transfer the training to other situations. This has an implication: that ICT training, which enables mastery of one set of tools, does not lead to information literacy. Unfortunately this has been a mistaken assumption, which has led to an emphasis on how to use technology rather than how to manipulate information using technology. This may be partly for pragmatic reasons, such as the time and effort needed to integrate these tools into the learning process, and an emphasis on content rather than process, with less emphasis placed on the manipulation of content.

Developmental aspects of learning

The learner as a physical being also has developmental aspects. Within broad boundaries it has been shown that certain types of thinking are developmental. Young children seem to find it more difficult to think in the abstract, as a result of either their neurological development or their sociological experience. This may be because between the ages of approximately 30 months and five years children's language (sentence structure, syntax and vocabulary) is relatively underdeveloped (Gross, 2005). The length of their utterances lengthens and the extent of their vocabulary increases through childhood and into adolescence. Given that some argue that language is dependent on thought it is essential to be aware of such developmental stages and how these might affect the structuring of learning interventions. For example, young children are likely to find the relatively abstract process of 'defining an information need' difficult because they have not fully developed their language ability; additionally, they do not use their memory as efficiently as older children when solving a problem (Gross, 2005). Borgman et al. (1995) found that young children found it difficult to think of a range of terms that could be used to describe a topic. They found it much easier to go through a list and identify single words instead.

In addition, a young person is likely to be unfamiliar with a subject and hence will have a limited range of vocabulary relating to it. This is exacerbated by the fact that most English-speaking children at the age of 13 have a vocabulary of 20,000 words, which is less than half of the 50,000 words that a young adult of 20 years will be familiar with (Gross, 2005). Knowing a range of vocabulary that describes a topic is of course particularly important when searching for material in the electronic domain and where the computer, generally, depends on the user to think of terms to search for. Clearly the fact that children have a smaller vocabulary than adults has implications for teaching searching skills to children of secondary age (12 to 16 years). It should also be noted that this difficulty will be further compounded when people have to search in a language that is not their first language.

Approaches to learning

These developmental considerations discussed above are not as critical in young adults and it therefore seems more useful at this stage to consider approaches to learning. Young adults and older people have an approach to learning which is relatively fixed and can fall into three broad categories: 'deep', 'surface' or 'strategic'. Marton and Saljo (1997) investigated the interaction between students and set learning tasks where students' written answers to a question were scrutinised using the technique of content analysis to measure their levels of understanding of a particular topic. They concluded that a student's approach to a task (their intention) determined the extent to which they engaged with the subject and thus affected the quality of their learning. From this they identified two types of learning: 'deep' learning and 'surface' learning (Biggs and Moore (1993) and Race (2001a) identify a third; see below). As trainers or teachers it is useful to be aware of these degrees of intention, to identify which approach to learning their students have, and then find ways to help learners become 'deep' learners.

'Deep' learning involves an intention to understand and seek meaning, leading to an attempt to relate concepts to existing experiences. In addition, deep learners distinguish between new ideas and existing knowledge and critically evaluate and determine key theories and concepts. This approach results from the student's intention to gain maximum meaning from their studies. This is achieved through high levels of cognitive (and metacognitive) processing when learning. In essence, facts are learnt within the context of meaning and in the ownership of the process. Ramsden (1992) argued that deep learning is the only way that students will understand learning materials effectively. Moseley et al. (2004) argued that critical thinking facilitates this approach and Ford (2004) regards these approaches to learning and thinking levels as essential factors affecting information behaviour.

'Surface' learning involves the intention to complete the task at hand and memorise its components; there is no distinction made between new ideas and existing knowledge. Students treat the task as extrinsic (externally imposed), for example, in the case of learning by rote. Students may offer the impression that maximum learning has taken place, which is achieved through superficial cognitive processing. Here facts may be learned, but this learning takes place outside a meaningful framework. This may underlie a misconception among students that a subject consists of a large number of facts to be learned, which one needs to absorb. Students may feel that it is sufficient to learn a large number of historical dates rather than to understand why the events occurred. Ramsden (1992) maintains that this view must be challenged directly by designing curriculum and assessment that maximises the opportunity for deep learning.

Race (2001a) has identified 'strategic' learning as another form of learning. This parallels the notion of 'achieving learning' espoused by Biggs and Moore (1993). Strategic learning, underpinned by a motivation to achieve, is characterised by being focused on the product; this is akin to surface learning, where the student maximises the chances of obtaining high marks while maintaining only a pragmatic engagement with the task. Such engagement in strategic learning is the means not the end, unlike deep learning.

Biggs and Moore (1993) argue that these approaches should not be seen as fixed but as modifiable within the teaching and learning context and are themselves learned. Some writers have argued that learning approaches change over time and that adult learners learn differently and have differing motivations. This theoretical perspective is known as 'andragogy'. These approaches may be habituated and are not easy to change, as with the drilled, pragmatic, learner (Fry, Ketteridge and Marshall, 1999). Ramsden (1992) warns that at times, particularly during examinations, students can imitate a deep approach when in fact they have adopted a surface approach. He has named this phenomenon 'imitation learning'. It could also be argued that this is in fact a student operating in strategic learning mode in that the student is focused on the product rather than on new knowledge (Newstead and Hoskins, 1999).

In addition, from the individual and physical perspective, the individual learner may have a propensity or a bias for using specific visual, auditory or kinaesthetic senses (Gardner, 1993). Furthermore, people may prefer to have an overview, a holistic view, of a subject domain or task rather than receive information in a bit by bit, sequential, stream. These are examples of learning styles.

Although students' approach to learning may be changed or people may apply different learning styles in different situations, their learning styles are important (Fry, Ketteridge and Marshall, 1999). There are many theories surrounding learning styles. Kolb, Rubin and Osland (1991) have suggested a number of learning styles based on their learning cycle. Kolb's learning cycle (Kolb, Rubin and Osland, 1991) is conceived as a four-stage process: experience, reflection, abstract thinking and active experimentation (this learning cycle is explained more fully in Chapter 5). Pask (1976) identified two types of learners: serialists (who prefer a step-by-step, narrow focus) and holists (who prefer the 'big picture' and work with illustrations and analogies). Studies have found that holists tend to use broader searching strategies and engage in a larger number of searches; they are more aware of broader and narrower terms, and more likely to use serendipity than serialists when using information sources (Ford, 2004).

Honey and Mumford (1982) put forward a four-fold classification of learning styles:

- 'Activists' respond best to new experiences and problems.

- 'Reflectors' best engage when learning activities are well structured and where they have time to observe, reflect and think.

- 'Theorists' respond well to logical structure where they have time to explore methodically and question.

- 'Pragmatists' work best with practically based immediately relevant learning activities.

Ford (2004) draws attention to the 'field-dependent' – 'field-independent' cognitive styles continuum (of which Honey and Mumford's categories may be a part) in that:

- 'Field-independent' individuals tend to experience the components of a structured field analytically, as discrete from their background, and to impose structure on unstructured fields. They tend to work best where they are required to mediate their own learning.

- 'Field-dependent' individuals tend to be less good at such structuring and analytical activity and to perceive a complex stimulus as a whole. They tend to favour a 'spectator' approach where learning is structured for them.

Ford (2004) reports that 'field-independent' individuals make more use of truncation, use more keyword terms, are less confused when using the web, are more focused in their thinking and tend to be quicker than 'field-dependent' individuals. Recognising these differences can help to explain why learners behave differently and the kind of support they may need.

'Kinaesthetic' (also 'kinesthetic'), 'auditory' and 'visual' learning styles are derived from the theory of 'multiple intelligences' or ways of thinking developed by Gardner (1993). 'Kinaesthetic' (more correctly 'bodily-kinesthetic') learners learn by manipulating and doing tasks rather than reading about them. They use their sense of touch more than other senses, respond to physical rewards, are physically orientated and move a great deal, memorise by walking and seeing, use action words, cannot sit still for long periods, like to act things out and like being involved in games.

'Aural' (more correctly 'auditory-musical-rhythmic') learners use sound, rhyme and music, and aural content in visualisation, for example, sound effects. According to Gardner, these learners enjoy reading out loud, find writing difficult but are better at telling, speak in rhythmic patterns, learn by listening, enjoy discussion, remember discussions better than written text and are not good at doing projects that involve a large amount of visualisation.

'Visual' (more correctly 'visual-spatial') learners prefer using images, maps and pictures to organise and communicate information, and they enjoy drawing. These learners memorise by visual association, have trouble remembering verbal instructions and are good readers.

These last two categories have strong parallels with the verbaliser–imager cognitive style continuum mentioned by Ford (2004). On this continuum individuals are regarded as being located towards one or other of these poles and will tend to perform better in tasks that require the associated form of information representation in memory that is visual or verbal. Unsurprisingly, imagers tend to prefer visually orientated information sources; interestingly, although their retrieval effectiveness in web-searching is low they tend to feel less disorientated when using it than verbalisers.

Finally, the last dimension to include is that of 'divergent' and 'convergent' thinkers. Divergent thinking is used almost synonymously with creative thinking, where individuals tend to generate links between wide-ranging, disparate items of information. In contrast, convergent thinkers tend to have a narrow, logical approach.

All of these differing theories indicate that any learner will deploy one or more of these styles in a particular learning situation. An awareness of these learning approaches and styles helps to structure activities to include all learning styles. Therefore, activities should be contextualised and take place within a motivational context that engages learners as much as possible to encourage deep learning. Ford argues that these notions must be embraced in order to understand the information behaviour exhibited by students as they progress through higher education.

Current thinkers doubt that any one person necessarily prefers one learning mode more than any other; instead they argue that people may tend to favour one mode or another in specific types of situation, and recognise that people can develop their ability to use different senses. However, it is currently still thought that to create a richer learning environment, teachers should provide learning in a way that relates to these different sensory needs. In other words, presenting learning in only a textual or auditory way is likely to be less successful than also providing it in a visual form or one that incorporates activity. It might also be preferable for people to seek information in a form that relates to their learning style.

In extreme cases, if someone has some form of physical disability, it will have an impact on their ability to process information in different forms. People who have difficulty hearing will not be able to use auditory information and this may affect their textual literacy, but they are likely to have a heightened ability to process information visually. The teacher should therefore spend time considering how to communicate information to these learners visually, using pictures, diagrams and colour. Other physical conditions may also affect information processing. People who experience severe fatigue, for example, prefer information to be presented in a brief form and through video and moving image rather than text.

Generally younger people expect information and learning to be provided in an engaging way, because of their experience of a rich multimedia world and innovative teaching methods, which are far more diverse than those experienced by people now in their middle age or older. Hence there is a need to provide information literacy learning in a way that engages all senses and dispositions. This is challenging because of its abstract nature and a greater need to make the learning concrete.

From a different perspective and still viewing the learner as a physical entity, as beings we interact with our environment; we act, we receive sensory feedback, and from a positivist view we 'learn' what is there and the characteristics and properties of the experienced phenomenon and how we can manipulate it. Language represents ideas of the world and enables social interaction with other people through negotiated shared meanings. From the teacher's perspective this implies we need to create learning environments that emulate the kind of learning outcome where the learner can physically engage with a phenomenon. In terms of information literacy this means interact with knowledge, data and information, being aware of and using various artefacts (blogs, books, e-search tools, social bookmarking and so on) and where people can experiment. The Pavlovian notion of learning through stimulus and response sees a learner as an organism who through experience and usually through repetition and reward learns new behaviours, ideas and norms. These explanations stem from a neurological and physical conception of the learner. In the same way athletes talk about muscle memory where repetitions of a particular activity become embedded in the physique of the sportsperson, and musicians repeat, over years, combinations of co-ordinated activities until they become 'natural'. The physical process of interacting with information artefacts and tools can also become embedded. Similarly, types of thinking and knowledge can become a part of the cognitive structures in the brain. An example of information literacy learning that takes the stimulus, response, and positive and negative feedback mode was an online tutorial called Liberation, developed by the University of Northampton. Using a trial and error approach, learners identified key elements of a reference and assembled the reference in an appropriate order, thus learning how to write references that conform to a recognised referencing style. Featured in the tutorial was an animation of a cat. If the student entered correct answers the cat gained rewards and did well. If incorrect answers were given the cat might have lost one of his 'lives'. The learners therefore received immediate feedback on their actions; those who did not get answers right at first were able to modify their work and learn so they eventually entered the correct answers.

Tied up with this conception of learning is the idea that learning is an incremental process. One block is built on another. Complexity is built on simpler understandings. New knowledge needs to build gradually on pre-existing knowledge. This has parallels with the cognitive constructivist ideas of learning discussed later. This incremental approach to learning has obvious implications for teachers. It is important that teachers have a clear understanding of what learners already know, for example, their experience of search engines or their lack of experience of online databases. In addition, teachers need to understand the type of learning environment that learners have experienced in the past, as this will affect their learning strategies. For example, a student who had been punished for introducing knowledge that had not been taught in a school (the experience of a Tanzanian student) is unlikely to seek information independently. In fact trainers need some understanding of learners' previous experience and perception of information and learning, which may have been unpleasant or unfruitful.

The need to build on previous experience, the incremental approach to learning whereby learners incorporate new learning with existing knowledge, is generally accepted (although in practice seldom explicitly addressed). In addition, recognising previous knowledge shows that the learners' previous knowledge is valued. It makes new learning less intimidating as learners are not immediately cast adrift in completely uncharted waters. An example of introducing new concepts incrementally is to ask learners to reflect on the use of a simple internet search engine that they are familiar with. They could be asked to consider its functionality and the fact that generally most simple search interfaces default to ANDing (in the Boolean sense) terms and then rank output on the frequency and position of these terms in an e-document or record. Learners are also likely to have developed their own strategies, which can be shared and built on.

Metaphorical analogies can also be used to align new knowledge with previous experience, such as the similarity between choosing apples OR pears or apples AND pears! This creates an opportunity to introduce the concept of Boolean logic and other Boolean commands, and be able to move on to other functions such as proximity operators and being able to specify where search terms should appear in a document such as the title. This behavioural approach to learning and training emphasises the need for repetition as a way to embed learning, and the value of reflection on the effect of different operators. Reflection helps to embed learning; it helps learners to appreciate the difference various strategies make and to develop abstract principles from that experience, which they should be able to apply to other situations. This type of learning can easily be tested using summative tests, which in turn provide feedback to learners and help the teacher determine whether the learning intervention has been successful. Reward in the form of marks, praise or recognition will reinforce this kind of learning.

An explanation of motor schema by Narayanan (1997), also taking this kind of behaviourist and biophysical viewpoint of the learner, has echoes of models of information-seeking behaviour. This implies that there may be a more fundamental explanation or underpinning to information-seeking behaviour, which could be useful when designing an intervention. Narayanan argued that there are fundamental states associated with motor action. These echo with our knowledge of information seeking, information literacy and information behaviour. He identifies the following states:

- getting into a state of readiness (preparing oneself emotionally, intellectually and physically to engage)
- the initial state
- the starting process
- the main process
- the option to stop
- the option to resume
- the option to iterate or continue the main process
- checking to see if the goal has been met
- the finishing process
- the final state.

Implications for information behaviour

Kuhlthau (1991) identified various cognitive states or stages associated with the undergraduate independent study project, including initiation, selection, exploration, formulation, collection and presentation, and linked these phases to uncertainty, optimism, confusion, clarity, sense of direction and relief. Ellis (1989) among engineers identified starting; chaining, browsing and monitoring; differentiating; verifying; and ending. Marchionini (1995: 50) also identified a similar process: recognise and accept; define problem; select source; form query; execute query; examine results; extract information; and reflect and stop. He pointed out that at each stage the search would possibly stop and retrace any part of the process. Hepworth (2002) also found a similar situation where student searchers exhibited a highly iterative process when using e-sources. They tended to stop when they encountered a search problem, then resumed (generally in a different source), trying new terms, eventually reaching a final state and generally feeling insecure and worried that they had not been completely successful.

It is important for teachers of information literacy to be aware of these broad stages and associated cognitive processes and emotions. They can then scaffold and provide an overview of the learning process so that learners are aware of what is to come; this helps to foster consciousness of these generally unconscious states. This enables learners to plan and reflect critically on different stages and processes, helping them to determine whether they have been effective or not, and why not. Learners are therefore encouraged to think strategically about the process and how they can make effective use of the tools, and to react rationally, rather than randomly choosing another source when confronted with an obstacle. One challenge is that the search can be viewed on two levels. The first sees the search as a linear process with a beginning and an end: select terms – choose source – search – find – finish. But on another level within this overall process it is highly iterative, 'messy' and depends on accident and serendipity. Terms may change or be added to; sources may be rejected or returned to. Although the overall process may be linear, it is important not to give the impression that the process is necessarily sequential. This is particularly the case when the topic or information landscape is unfamiliar, because then it is likely to be highly exploratory, and full of dead ends and backtracks. Unfortunately this is often not recognised by teachers of information literacy, which leads to a high degree of frustration as learners are given unrealistic expectations. Unrealistic expectations have also been fostered by the hype around Google, which has given the impression that information retrieval is always simple.

Narayanan's work is another example of the embodiment of the mind where in contrast to the mind being considered situated independent of the body, it is seen as linked to sensory-motor characteristics of the body. Whether this is the case or not, this theory does provide an organic image or metaphor of information seeking and problem solving that people can relate to. This process of finding out, sometimes linear at other times iterative, sometimes through intention at other times through the luck of finding useful material, reminds one of another activity, foraging, which term has been used to describe information seeking. We have probably all seen films of ants moving across the forest floor in a trial and error fashion, fanning out, encountering opportunities, obstacles and rewards; gradually 'learning'; and sharing a chemical memory that enables them to use their environment successfully as individuals and members of a community.

Implications for information literacy

From an information literacy perspective the positivist philosophy and behaviourist approach has led to a behaviourist conception of information literacy. This has led to the identification of a discrete set of concrete behavioural skills that can be learnt and whose performance can be measured. The information literacy outcomes noted by the Association of College and Research Libraries (ACRL), in the US, to some extent reflect this view. Practical wisdom, based on experience, is perceived as a higher order of thinking, which enhances skills to the level of expertise (Simister, 2007). This metacognition is the process of becoming conscious of and making explicit the actions required for gathering, analysing and using information. In other words, in the information literacy context metacognition means knowing about one's learning and acting on this knowledge. Metacognition about our learning process enables us to manage our learning, to plan, monitor and correct.

Other developmental processes can have a bearing on learning. One that relates to information literacy is the development of strategies and knowledge of when tools can be used – this is in addition to the ability to remember how to use them. For example, to cluster ideas under a common theme can enable recall and the act in itself is an ability. With information literacy training we hope to see evidence of metacognition that reflects knowledge of the efficacy of behavioural strategies in addition to the thinking processes and procedures associated with becoming informed that are discussed below. This 'behaviour' can be reinforced, repeated and refined. The behavioural perspective can be seen to focus on physical action. It is hard to make what is probably an artificial distinction or separation between behaviour and cognition, however. In information behaviour research the same terms are often used to describe both activities; for example, 'browsing' has a cognitive and a behavioural meaning. But bringing either to the foreground is likely to make the tacit more explicit. In fact, it could be argued that the processes embodied in information literacy models offer a framework which can make these processes explicit rather than tacit.

4

The learner as a thinker – a cognitive approach

The cognitive approaches to learning oscillate between positivistic notions and interpretivist or constructivist notions of the learner. This chapter focuses, primarily, on thinking about thinking as a concrete phenomenon, which it is implied is connected with the physical aspect of the learner described in the previous chapter.

The term cognitive implies any kind of mental operation or structure that can be studied in precise terms. Cognition became the focus of attention in information behaviour research in the late 1970s and 1980s. Before that research focused on behaviour – what people did. At that time it was assumed that this provided a direct insight into people's information needs or at least threw a light on needs. This could be true, but what people do may not be an indication of need. For example, people may request an item of information because they think that that is what is available rather than what they actually need. However, in the 1970s and 1980s greater attention was paid to people's thoughts and feelings. The individualistic cognitive approach that implies inherent cognitive structures can be seen in a number of explanations by writers who highlight specific cognitive processes associated with learning. They provide useful tools for thinking about thinking and provide frameworks for constructing learning interventions; they also highlight specific cognitive processes that the teacher should encourage and can identify and measure.

These thinking skills may be 'real' phenomena – cognitive skills apparent in all beings because of their neural make up, which can be developed, measured and learnt in a positivist sense, or as abstractions or representations of constructivist thinking whereby people make sense of their world. The concept of thinking skills has been very influential and Moseley et al. (2004) have analysed and classified the main theories. 'Thinking skills' theories, which include the concepts of critical thinking and problem-solving, reflect such thinking. These are considered here because they relate to the quality of information gathering, building understanding and productive thinking. Problem-solving and critical-thinking skills form an essential part of information literacy models (Bruce, 1995; ACRL, 2000), and information behaviour models; see especially Ford (2004). Moseley et al. (2004) identified over 50 thinking skills frameworks and evaluated in detail 35 of them.

Thinking skills frameworks

Moseley et al. (2004) offer precise definitions for the concept of thinking and the notion of skills:

- *Thinking*: 'A consciously goal directed process, such as remembering, forming concepts, planning what to do and say, imagining situations, reasoning, solving problems, considering opinions, making decisions and judgements and generating new perspectives.'
- *Skill*: 'expertness, practical ability facility in doing something [...] Skill overlaps with ability but more often refers to specific areas of performance – it implies performances are of a high standard and adapted to particular requirements.'

The authors identify three common factors which are central to the notion of thinking skills: 'metacognition', 'self-regulation' and 'critical thinking'.

Metacognition is characterised as the knowledge one has regarding one's own cognitive processes and products and anything that relates to them. For example, when a person engages in metacognitive activity a realisation emerges that they are having more trouble learning fact X than fact Y; a person may doublecheck fact X before accepting it as a fact or the person may feel they have to make a note of fact Y because they may forget it. In essence, metacognition is an active monitoring and consequent regulation and orchestration of these processes – usually to achieve a goal. It is awareness not just of one's own processes but also of the ability to plan, monitor and evaluate that thinking. This appears to detail the iterative process mentioned in many learning theories, and information literacy and information behaviour models.

'Self-regulation' is strongly linked to metacognition and presupposes it (Moseley et al., 2004). It is regarded as a systematic process and involves cognitive, motivational, affective and behavioural components, echoing the style and affective states in information behaviour as identified by Hepworth (2004a), enabling a person to adjust their actions to achieve desired results in changing circumstances. Self-regulation is strongly context-specific and comprises:

- setting goals for learning
- attending to and concentrating on instruction
- using effective strategies to organise, code and rehearse information
- establishing a productive working environment
- using resources effectively
- monitoring performance
- time management
- seeking assistance when needed
- holding positive beliefs about one's capabilities, the value of learning, factors influencing learning and anticipated outcomes of actions
- experiencing pride and satisfaction with one's efforts (Moseley et al. (2004: 9).

This analysis resonates strongly with the concept of 'self-efficacy' as put forward by Wilson (1999) and Ford (2004) in that a learner deploying the characteristics set out above will feel more in control and confident in a learning situation, and therefore may do better in finding information to support an argument. Hepworth (2004a) found that informal carers who had a low sense of self-efficacy tended to have small interpersonal networks and had taken longer to find information and help. Clearly self-regulation, like self-efficacy, is underpinned by affective or emotional factors.

In the US, critical thinking and thinking skills are synonymous (Moseley et al., 2004). This equates with Bloom's higher order thinking skills (Bloom et al., 1956) implying that good critical thinkers are proficient in analysing, inferring and evaluating. These ideas are also found in 'higher-order' information literacy skills in Bruce (1995), SCONUL (1999), ACRL (2000) and Big Blue Project (2002). Philosophical definitions include a normative component, also found in information behaviour models. This component is inextricably linked to values where 'good thinking' depends on two dispositions: caring about making the right decision and caring to present the decision honestly and clearly; these dispositions may vary according to external norms and expectations. These ideas are specifically mentioned in the ANZIIL (Bundy, 2004) and CILIP (Armstrong et al., 2005) information literacy models. The elements of critical thinking (related to these dispositions) are interpretation, analysis, evaluation, inference, explanation and self-regulation.

Moseley et al. (2004) helpfully divide the thinking skills frameworks they have evaluated into four 'families':

- 'All embracing' frameworks, which cover personality, thought, learning and deal with emotional and motivational influences as well as the structure of cognition.

- 'Designer' frameworks, which deal specifically with instructional design and have cognitive rather than a more comprehensive theoretical base. These are more relevant to, and are used within, the educational field.

- 'Higher' order frameworks, which are more philosophical in nature. They include critical and productive thinking and are concerned with higher-order processes leading to a judgement or decision (educational or political) where an individual strives to make the right decision or present a position honestly and clearly.

- 'Explanatory' frameworks, which are strongly grounded in psychological theory, are concerned with cognitive structure and or development either in intellectual aptitudes or stages of progression towards more complex or mature ways of thinking.

What is clear from his evaluation is that Bloom's taxonomy (see Figure 4.1) still underpins many of the theories analysed, which indeed pervade education generally (Moseley et al., 2004). Interestingly, some of the main information literacy models use Bloom et al. (1956) explicitly (ACRL, 2000) or resemble them implicitly (SCONUL, 1999; Big Blue Project, 2002).

Importantly, Moseley et al. (2004) identify the practical applications of the theory families. Hence, Bloom's model is recognised as important in designing thinking skills programmes.

Figure 4.1 Bloom's taxonomy

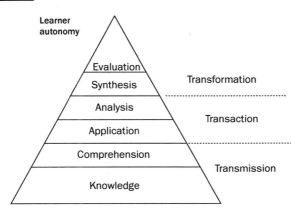

These thinking states can be stimulated and made explicit. *Knowledge* relates to remembering and retaining information and can be brought to the foreground by asking learners to say what they know, remember or have learnt. This could include an awareness of the process they have gone through, for example, determining their information needs, choosing various sources and choosing methods that are effective for narrowing or broadening a search and obtaining more relevant material. In addition, knowledge may be embodied as fact, for example, knowing that *Web of Knowledge* is a secure database containing peer-reviewed references in the sciences and social sciences. The reflective process to elicit this knowledge helps to concretise and make it conscious, enabling the learner to know what they know and make it more likely that they can apply this knowledge to other situations.

Comprehension relates to interpreting and understanding where learners describe information in their own words, tell how they feel about it, say and/or explain what it means, and compare it with and relate it to other information. This could include descriptions of the tools and services that they use to access information.

Application relates to making use of information and can be highlighted by asking learners to state where information leads to and using it to solve a problem or demonstrate its use in some way. Application could also include, for example, the use of a search strategy following comprehension of the alternative approaches.

Analysis relates to taking the information apart, including identifying the constituent parts of the information, its order, its causes, the problems and/or solutions it generates and its consequences. It could include an investigation of the style, appropriateness or authority of different sources.

Synthesis relates to putting the information together; it can be cued into the thinking process by asking learners to identify common ideas, differences between authors, what is missing, how it can be improved or developed, or how the information can be re-formed by the learner in their own way.

Evaluation relates to judging and assessing. This includes the learner stating how they will judge the information, considering the answers to questions – does it succeed in its purpose?, does it satisfy the learner's need for information?, are there omissions or bias? – and justifying their reasons for their judgements. Evaluative techniques can be applied to other aspects of the learning process, for example, the evaluation of various search strategies, choice of sources, communication and presentation methods.

These are fundamental cognitive processes that need to be highlighted and encouraged in the independent learner in all aspects of information literacy.

Assessing thinking skills

The Biggs and Collis (1982) Structure of Observed Learning Outcomes (SOLO) model is useful to assess critical thinking (see Table 4.1). We will consider this model in more detail as it is vital in understanding the outputs within the educational context in general, and may offer a potential way of measuring information behaviour and information literacy in particular.

It is argued that this model provides a systematic way of describing how a learner's performance may grow in complexity when mastering new tasks, particularly those undertaken in education (Biggs, 1999). It is useful for defining curriculum objectives that describe performance targets or goals as well as for evaluating learning outcomes so that the levels at which individual students are performing can be identified.

This can be used to discern levels of information literacy understanding. The following examples of responses to the same question about using evaluation criteria in order to select good quality information illustrate how these may appear.

Table 4.1		The SOLO model of Biggs and Collis (1982)	

Learning outcomes	Capacity	Relating operation	Consistency and closure
Pre-structural	Minimal: cue and response confused	Denial, tautology, transduction Bound to specifics	No need felt for consistency: closure without seeing the problem
Uni-structural	Low: cue and one relevant datum	Can generalise only about one aspect	No need felt for consistency: closed too quickly, jumps to conclusions, so can be very inconsistent
Multi-structural	Medium: cue and isolated relevant data	Can generalise only about a few limited and independent aspects	Feeling for consistency: closure too soon on basis of isolated fixations so can reach different conclusions with same data
Relational	High: cue and relevant data and interrelations	Induction: can generalise within given or experienced context using related aspects	No consistency in given system, but closure is unique to given system
Extended abstract	Maximal: cue and relevant data and interrelations and hypotheses	Deduction and induction: can generalise to situations not experienced	Inconsistencies resolved: no need for closed decisions; conclusions held open or qualified to allow logically possible alternatives

How the SOLO learning outcomes relate to information literacy, in this case, evaluating information

Pre-structural outcomes

> Q. What new knowledge have you learnt regarding evaluating information?

> A. You need to find good quality information in order to write a good essay.

This almost goes without saying and does not show any understanding of the question.

Uni-structural outcomes

> Q. What new knowledge have you learnt regarding evaluating information?

> A. You can get good quality information from reading books and journals.

This response has at least begun to scratch the surface. The learner uses some appropriate terminology, for example 'journals', and is on the right track.

Multi-structural outcomes

> Q. What new knowledge have you learnt regarding evaluating information?

> A. You can get good quality information from reading books and journals. You need to concentrate on using academic text books, peer reviewed journal articles and good quality websites only.

This is much better and shows much more detail but does not address the specific question regarding evaluation criteria.

Relational outcomes

> Q. What new knowledge have you learnt regarding evaluating information?

> A. You can get good quality information... Text books are usually written by academics or experts in the field, they usually contain many references to previous work and the author's own research. Peer reviewed articles have gone through a lengthy process before being published; they have been reviewed by experts in the field. There are many ways to identify good quality websites and it is always a good idea to have some evaluation criteria in mind when deciding whether to use them.

This shows facts and an explanation addressing a point in order to make some sense of the question.

Extended abstract

Extended abstract statements have all of the above but with one essential and important difference: they contain what Biggs refers to as a 'breakthrough statement', which goes beyond what is given and changes the way we think about a concept (Biggs, 1999: 39). In this case the same question might be answered in the following way:

> Q. What new knowledge have you learnt regarding evaluating information?

> A. All information is biased; it's a question of getting to know what to look for to understand which are the most balanced and best researched sources.

It must be noted that this model has some limitations: the taxonomy does not take into account the social nature of interactions or the influence of affective and conative dimensions of thinking because its focus is on student performance. These dimensions are vital to an understanding of information behaviour and information literacy. However, because the overall context is an educational one this model is worthy of consideration.

Thinking skills programmes based on these ideas typically (as argued by Moseley et al., 2004) require students to plan, describe and evaluate their thinking and learning, or more succinctly 'plan–do–review', and imply that these activities can induce processes which produce desired mental products. Furthermore, the outputs from these activities can be assessed in a structured and meaningful way. In summary, thinking skills can be seen as a way of managing attention and working memory to enable conscious and unconscious activity to work together productively. This core idea has much resonance with information literacy models and explicitly forms a part of Ford's information behaviour model (Ford, 2004) particularly regarding levels of critical thinking that students deploy in their information behaviour.

Induction and deduction are other cognitive processes related to the process of discovery and research. They influence the nature of information gathering and analysis and therefore have implications for information seeking. For example, an inductive approach will emphasise the gathering of a range of material and identify questions, patterns or themes in that material (as in inquiry-based learning). A literature review will often take this approach whereby the learner, having read texts, will identify themes shared by different authors and unique ideas requiring analysis, synthesis and abstraction, and will critically reflect on the coverage of previous writers. Most educators have witnessed the difficulty learners have with this process of identifying structures in the document or text (Laurillard, 2002), identifying common themes, synthesising arguments, and critically reflecting on other people's ideas. Poor literature reviews provide descriptive accounts of individual author's viewpoints, little synthesis and minimal critical comment or application of the ideas to their own specific problem or question. Induction and deduction are essential in most workplaces; to be able to understand the business environment, for example, an individual needs to identify patterns, such as 'players' and trends, critically evaluating alternatives that stem from conversations, documentation and so on, identifying possible solutions.

Knowledge and understanding

The expertise of the individual is a factor that will have a bearing on the person's information literacy and learning needs. An expert can monitor their own understanding; they recognise problem types based on schema;

they notice more and they organise, represent and interpret information in a more sophisticated way (Bransford, Brown and Cocking, 2000). Expertise includes declarative knowledge (system settings, how to perform searches) and procedural knowledge (search task execution, problem solving associated with the subject domain) (Ingwersen and Jarvelin, 2005). Teaching and learning needs to be synchronised with level of expertise. Lack of knowledge about how information retrieval systems work has been found to be one of the key experiences of student searchers (Hepworth, 2004b), who are therefore unaware of strategies that could help. This makes it difficult for them to use sources effectively or to adapt their searches strategically. Lack of procedural knowledge about information-seeking processes leads to misconceptions about the nature of searching. For example, searchers may assume that a search is a sequential linear task, moving from term to search, to retrieval, to completion, rather than an iterative one. This may be the case where someone knows the topic, exactly what they were looking for, and the possible answer, or in situations where anything relevant will do. However, in situations where the topic is complex or poorly understood, the search task is likely to be highly iterative. Furthermore, in these cases the process of searching is intrinsically linked with learning about the topic. In this case the learner gradually defines the topic through interaction with retrieved material en route. This will be associated with continually refining the search strategy and only in the latter stages developing strategies that retrieve highly relevant material. If the searcher does not appreciate this then they are likely to get frustrated and may abandon the search (Hepworth, 2004b).

Lack of knowledge of the subject domain poses specific problems for learners, including not knowing the appropriate terminology to use as search keys because the learner is unfamiliar with the language of the domain. They will also be unfamiliar with the standardised terms (controlled vocabulary) people have chosen to index records (documents, images). The process of identifying relevant and reliable retrieved items will be difficult as the learner will not know exactly what is appropriate and what information is deemed authoritative. Furthermore, information retrieved may be at an inappropriate level for the learner. For example, school children have been shown to have difficulty understanding information retrieved from the World Wide Web because it has not been written with them in mind (Smith and Hepworth, 2007). Hence the searcher needs to know how to be able to identify relevant resources of an appropriate kind and where they may be found. They also need to be knowledgeable about the appropriate criteria for judging the value and relevance of the information.

As a result cognitive skills need to be used to identify appropriate information resources. To a great extent these require a knowledge of information representations, the artefacts that hold information (people, organisations, communities, books, articles, web pages or database records). Through their knowledge of the key artefact characteristics can be used to choose appropriate sources. This may be through features such as coverage, an author's name, organisations involved, publication name and reputation, document type (academic, news, personal accounts) and topicality, quality, novelty, availability, authority and format (numeric, textual, pictorial). The searchers need to consider whose voice is being heard. How these are applied will depend on epistemic, functional, conditional, social and emotional values and may lead to acceptance of ideas, possible acceptance or rejection (Ingwersen and Jarvelin, 2005: 201). The pragmatics of 'fit for purpose', available time, as well as motivation will play a part. The learner therefore needs to be aware of the characteristics of information artefacts (form, content, style, currency, authority, credibility and so on) and be able to use them to evaluate and select material that will meet their information needs.

The learner needs to be conscious of how documents are physically structured and be able to use the structure to help find information, process and assess the document, including using titles, abstracts, introductions, headings, indexes and descriptors. For example, a learner might orientate themselves successfully with a topic by browsing a series of titles to get an idea of the extent of the domain and themes within the domain. They would use the features of a text, such as contents pages, headings, diagrams or the index, to provide an overview of issues that are covered. Diagrams often encapsulate what is being said. Summaries and conclusions give further detail; in the text before the last few paragraphs of a conclusion alternative solutions tend to be proffered. This is related to what Ingwersen and Jarvelin (2005) describe as successful mapping between cognitive representations of the searcher and those of the document and/or document collections.

Demonstrating knowledge through language

Expertise also relates to knowledge of the tools that facilitate the retrieval of information, for example, how search engines, databases, portals or libraries work. Without knowledge of classification or how a body of information is structured it may be difficult to use an information resource. People reveal their expertise through the language they use. An information literate person will use a richer set of language to talk about information and information resources and learning (Walton, 2009). Students use their greater confidence in language to demonstrate their new information literacy skills. For example, first-year sport and exercise science undergraduates who had participated in a blended information literacy learning intervention reported that they now knew 'how to' do something:

> I now know how to look for e-journals and e-books on Swetswise and E-brary, something I did not know how to do before.

> I have learnt how to use the online library.

> I understand how to use the library more effectively.

These comments display knowledge and application as well as feelings of confidence. Expertise can also be shown by using some technical language, thus demonstrating new knowledge regarding using and searching e-resources. For example:

> I am now confident in using search connectors like 'and' and 'not'. I also know how to use advanced searches properly.

> [I can] use AND/OR in between search words.

> [I] finally found a number of sources by changing the keyword in the search box.

> By typing in certain words I can find good articles and abstracts that will come in handy.

The last statement indicates that the student has an ability to apply their knowledge and can use technical language to achieve this.

These extracts, taken from students' reflective practice statements, reveal that they are becoming information literate because they clearly feel confident about the resources they should draw on, and they use technical language in an appropriate way. These show us that qualitative data of this sort can open a window to signpost how students feel about the skills they have learnt in participating in an information literacy learning and teaching intervention. This gives valuable feedback to tutors.

5

The learner as a sense maker – a constructivist approach

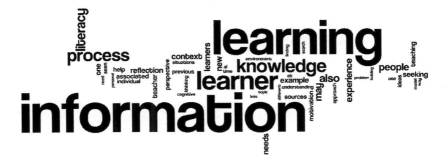

The constructivist approach falls within the cognitive domain, in the sense that it focuses on the mind. However, constructivists place more emphasis than cognitivists on the higher level experience of learning than on the more fundamental thinking skills discussed previously. It is difficult to separate out the cognitive constructivist and social constructivist. Both tend to emphasise that people individually and socially construct 'reality', whereas the purely cognitive approach implies a common set of thinking processes and hence an implied physicality to them, such as Bloom's model (Bloom et al., 1956) of thinking states.

Cognition in terms of information retrieval 'implies a continuous process of interpretation and cognition in context by all participating actors on both the systems side and on the human actor during IS&R [information seeking and retrieval]' (de Mey in Ingwersen and Jarvelin, 2005: 29). Authors tend to veer between cognition of the individual in an isolated sense and in relation to the context within which they find themselves. Stemming from the individualistic view, in information science, information needs have been defined as 'anomalous states of knowledge' (Belkin, 2005) implying a physical gap in understanding.

Satisfying information needs has also been associated with reducing cognitive uncertainty (Spink et al., 2002). Information seeking was seen as mapping the individual's conceptual 'world model' with the 'world model' of the generator of information and the information objects they produce (Ingwersen and Jarvelin, 2005). This implies that mapping will be facilitated if the searcher is conscious of the conceptual world of the author and how it may impact on the structure of the information they provide, knowledge that could be used to find material.

Others such as Dervin and Nilan (1986) argue that information is constructed in the mind of the learner and as a situated sense-making process. As we have already seen, learning is highly situated and contextualised. The focus here is on constructive, active learners; it takes into account events and actions that precede and follow information use. Assumptions include 'moving, process, discontinuity, situationality, gap bridging and information seeking…; information is seen as an 'individual process of construction, not a process of utilising ready made information bricks' (Ingwersen and Jarvelin, 2005: 60). When a person's movement through time and space is halted a gap is envisaged that needs to be bridged and information may help to achieve this. From a teaching perspective this signifies a gap in the learner's knowledge that needs to be highlighted, as well as previous knowledge and experience that may relate to the situation. The gap facilitates access to resources that may help 'bridge that gap' and through reflection on this process develop metacognition, which enables the learner to review the process critically. Developing cognitive processes and meta-cognitive processes that support this is seen as a direct way of enabling better decisions.

The constructivist approach is based on personal construct theory (Kelly, 1955). Some authors describe learning as the continuous building and amending of previous structures as new experiences, such that effective learning involves individual 'transformation' (Squires, 1994; Fry, Ketteridge and Marshall, 1999; Race, 2001a). MacKeracher (2004) in her 'dialectical' learning model argues that this transformation occurs first when individuals add a greater degree of detail to their existing knowledge ('differentiation') and second by combining this new knowledge ('integration') into their personal understanding of reality. In this approach it is believed that people actively construct their own knowledge (Kolb, Rubin and Osland, 1991; Biggs and Moore, 1993; MacKeracher, 2004). Some recent studies in the field of visual perception suggest that there may be physiological evidence to support this theory of an individualised reality (Hollingham, 2004). Experiential learning and the use of reflection are based on this constructivist theory, where higher order learning involving understanding can only take place when the learner's underlying schemata are changed to incorporate new understanding.

Constructivist learning theories (experiential learning in particular) currently underpin most learning theory and practice within higher education (Fry, Ketteridge and Marshall, 1999; Race, 2001a; Race and Brown, 2001; Gibbs and Coffey, 2004) because they are regarded as inherently student centred in approach as opposed to didactic behaviourist models. In addition, these theories have much in common with theories of 'critical thinking' (Moseley et al., 2004).

It is self-evident that the experiences we have, whether in life, at work or in education, play a central role in the process of learning. Kolb, Rubin and Osland (1991) expound the notion that ideas are formed and re-formed continuously through experience and that we bring our own ideas and preconceptions at differing levels of elaboration to the process, which is in essence an iterative process. Kolb's learning cycle is conceived as a four-stage process and viewed as most applicable to work-based learning, teaching laboratory and practical work, action learning, role play and small group teaching (see Figure 5.1). Snowball (1997) has successfully used this model to structure information skills workshops for medical postgraduates. Webb and Powis (2005) also found it a useful model for structuring information literacy teaching.

In this model learners employ these four processes in this order:

- *Concrete experience*, where learners should be fully and freely involved in the new learning experience. This could include working in groups brainstorming terms to describe a domain, topic or question, or working in pairs using a search engine or other information retrieval tool – one person could document the search process.

Figure 5.1 Kolb's learning cycle (adapted from Kolb, Rubin and Osland, 1991)

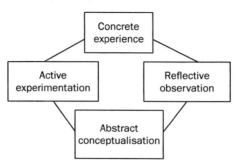

- *Reflective observation*, where learners need time to reflect on new learning experiences from different perspectives and are closely linked to the notion of feedback. In addition to reflecting on the new subject matter and its implications every task or process associated with finding out can be reflected on; this is necessary to help develop metacognition. It helps to concretise the experience, so that ordering, categorising and prioritising events and interactions associated with learning are more likely to be applied in other learning situations.

- *Abstract conceptualisation*, where learners are able to form and re-form, process, take ownership and integrate their ideas into sound logical theories. From a subject perspective new information and knowledge needs to be internalised. From an information literacy perspective this is an extension of reflection and the identification of general and specific strategies stemming from their personal experience and discourse with others.

- *Active experimentation*, where the learner uses theories to make problem-solving decisions and tests implications in new situations. Here the learner uses methods that have proved effective to present and communicate information in the past.

In summary, this cycle involves doing, reflecting, processing, thinking and understanding; these activities are governed by the learner's needs and goals, and all elements are necessary for learning to be achieved. As the learners continue around the cycle they not only become more skilful but also notice more, such as the structure of documents or reflecting on their choice of terms, sources, access, search strategies and so on and make better connections, understand more and make more informed decisions regarding what to do next, such as where to place themselves to become better informed. The cycle concerns learning concepts or symbols, such as Boolean or 'phrase search' as well as skills; in effect it is about learning by doing, not just learning to do (Gibbs, Morgan and Northedge, 1998). In addition, where students are expected to learn practical skills such as how to search a database or use other tools, several cycles may be involved, each of progressively longer duration and greater complexity. The cycle is envisaged by some writers as a learning spiral, each loop more advanced than the previous one (Northedge and Lane, 1997; Gibbs, Morgan and Northedge, 1998). MacKeracher (2004) identifies this advancing or articulation of learning as 'differentiation'. This model offers us a view of learning as a highly personalised iterative activity. It is noteworthy that this view has parallels with Hepworth's (2004b) findings

Figure 5.2   Race's Ripple on a Pond (Race, 2001b: 1)

regarding the iterative nature of information behaviour. In contrast, some (Bloom et al., 1956) regard learning as a hierarchical activity moving from lower to higher order learning (see figure 4.1 for more detail).

Race (2001b) argues that this sequential cyclical model does not sufficiently explain the nature of learning. Other writers (Gibbs, Morgan and Northedge, 1998) agree with Race (2001b) that learning is 'messy'; Race suggests a new model, which he calls the 'Ripple on a Pond' (Figure 5.2).

This model focuses more directly on the motivation of the learner to learn and the notion of continuous feedback. This idea suggests that learning is dynamic (learning achieved by doing, gaining feedback, making sense of what is learned and using reflection), iterative and driven by internal (intrinsic) and external (extrinsic) motivations. Within this model reflection, the metacognitive element of the model becomes the dominant component. Metacognition or reflection is important to learning because it helps learners to monitor, evaluate and change as they progress and gives rise to further learning and understanding (Biggs and Moore, 1993; Metcalfe, 1994).

The role of reflection in learning

Reflection appears to be an essential component and may even characterise deep or strategic learning (Biggs and Moore, 1993; Hepworth and Brittain, in press). Reflection is therefore not only a pedagogical method recommended by Squires (1994), Kolb, Rubin and Osland (1991) and Race (2001b), in the traditional learning setting. It is included in MacKeracher's 'dialectical learning model' (MacKeracher,

2004) and Mayes' dialogical model (JISC, 2004) for e-learning contexts, and is a learning outcome in its own right, in that students are expected to learn to become reflective learners as they progress through an award (Mayes and de Freitas, 2004; QAA, 2006). Reflective practice as a professional issue from which some of these ideas are derived, especially those involved in teaching and learning, can be found in Schon (1987), Bell (2001) and Trigwell (2001).

Race (2002) gives a useful definition of reflection:

> The act of reflecting is one which causes us to make sense of what we've learned, why we learned it, and how that particular increment of learning took place. Moreover, reflection is about linking one increment of learning to the wider perspective of learning – heading towards seeing the bigger picture.

This idea of using reflection to build on previous understanding is also used by Jonassen et al. (1995). Moreover, the idea of reflection can be found as a component closely linked to metacognitive processes in many thinking skills frameworks (Moseley et al., 2004) and as central to the iterative process mentioned specifically by SCONUL (1999) and Big Blue Project (2002), and implied in the ACRL (2000) and ANZIIL models (Bundy, 2004). In addition it is implied in information-seeking behaviour models (Wilson, 1999; Ford, 2004; Hepworth, 2004a) as well as learning theory as mentioned above. Vygotsky in particular posits this relationship (Hung and Chen, 2001) and argues that these processes provide a form of self-regulation which causes the learner to internalise learning from the social to the individual dimension.

Cowan (2002) argues that it is only when learning outcomes provide opportunity for reflection that they engage the learner. Teles (1993) reports that reflection is critical to the notion of 'online apprenticeships' and Walker (2003) states that asynchronous delivery enables reflection because the learner is given more time (than in a face-to-face situation) to do some reflecting on a topic and contribute a considered response. The process of reflection can be further assisted by the provision of formative feedback. For example, an English literature tutor might critically evaluate versions of an English student's poem by giving feedback via comments and suggestions, and providing support for each version of the poem, with a view to fostering reflection in the learner and helping her master the skill of writing poetry (Teles, 1993). Littlejohn and Higgison (2003) regard the provision of continuous feedback as an essential component within the e-learning context.

Cowan (2002) states that it is not enough simply to ask learners to reflect. What tutors need to do is structure learners' reflections in such a way that they are provided with questions they may find useful to answer, such as 'How did I construct that last search strategy and how might I improve on it next time?' In this way the outcome should be an effective process analysis of the approach they have followed. The purpose of the reflective activity will dictate the questions to be posed. Kolb, Rubin and Osland (1991), Teles (1993), Race (2001b) and Cowan (2002) believe that those who become more aware of how they do something on the whole become more effective learners, but this awareness can come some time after the event (Cowan, 2002).

Constructing meaning

The iterative construction of meaning, knowledge and skills described above can be seen as a subset of activities associated with the wider sense-making process. Dervin's (1983) description of learning stems from an interpretivist and constructivist epistemology. This approach also focuses on the thinking of the learner but places greater emphasis on the relativistic and individualistic nature of this experience. The world, in a sense, is inside the head of the learner. The interpretivist would argue that we have no direct knowledge of the world around us and would give less weight to acknowledging specific cognitive structures. Thus we construct mental maps and schema that make sense of the world. We develop language and concepts through our collaborative interaction with the world around us; these are efficacious as long as they provide explanatory frameworks that enable us to share meaning and achieve our objectives. Constructivism can be viewed from both an individual and a social perspective. Each has a bearing on how and why we learn and these perspectives have implications for the learning environment we create. The social element will be the focus of the next chapter.

From an individual perspective learners are seen as involved in a process of making sense of the world around them from birth, perhaps in the structured, cyclical way described above. They create mental constructs that individually and together help them make predictions, explain why things happen, and manipulate objects and materials. This perspective echoes to some extent the sensory conception of learning.

Learners are seen as constructing meaning rather than acquiring knowledge. Intelligence is seen as an incremental process rather than a fixed entity. From a pedagogic perspective this leads to people emphasing the gradual nature of this 'building' process as indicated above, building on previous knowledge. In comparison with the behaviourist orientation, it implies a more dynamic relationship between the learner and their learning. For example, this sort of teaching allows time for students to engage with a topic, building on pre-existing knowledge, identifying gaps in understanding, starting to map the domain by brainstorming the topic to elicit vocabulary, and helping them to start to appreciate what is within or outside the topic. This in fact echoes to some extent the behavioural notion of a building block, in that it implies the assembly of cognitive building blocks, from simple to complex, and that complexity stems out of initial simplicity. This language could imply a set hierarchy of learning and knowledge, which would be mistaken. Part and parcel of being information literate is that all possible ways of becoming informed should be considered, so the traditional source of highly valued 'expertise', for example a consultant, may be considered less valuable than the experience of a less highly valued practitioner.

The experiential approach to learning of Kolb, Rubin and Osland (1991) could also be explained in these terms, where the learner goes through a cycle of theory, experiment (doing), abstraction of the lessons learnt and further application of learning. Kolb depicts this process as cyclical, starting with exploration and experimentation, leading to reflection and abstraction of principles, further application and eventually generating theory. One can view this in behaviourist terms – the physical cognitive conception of doing leading to reflection and learning from experience, and then further application reinforcing the learning – an action–reaction–feedback–action loop or a cognitive thinking process or a constructivist process of building a 'deeper' mental map of a learning context. Whether people take a behavioural, cognitive or constructivist interpretation of this cycle, it has implications for the design of the teaching intervention.

Learning as an active participative process

It is fundamental that learners should be seen as active participants in the formation of ideas rather than passive recipients of information. For example, relatively unstructured browsing for related information would help learners to 'bump into' related material, concepts and terms that gradually enable them to put the new learning in context, define the topic they are learning about and develop a new way of thinking about their world. This line of thinking therefore tends to be associated with notions of the individual creating personal meaning, where learning outcomes are less prescribed than is usually the case, and where the learning is more in the hands of the learner. The way learners interpret the experience may not be the same as the way the teacher interprets it. Learners are thus seen as equal participants. This approach therefore has a political component and has been connected with the notion of empowerment. Here making sense of the world through learning can be linked to the idea of the individual gaining satisfaction and resources; learners may be able to take more control over their lives, be better able to cope and less likely to be exploited. Freire (1974) described this as 'conscientization', whereby people developed a critical understanding of their reality; learners shift their intellectual boundaries and develop new horizons. These ideas have fed into participative approaches to learning, such as participatory action research, where people's knowledge is valued and their capacity to conduct their own research is fundamental, allowing them to explore their problems from their own perspective (Reason, 1994) rather than being 'researched' or having ideas imposed on them by external 'experts' or governing bodies.

The idea that learners are active participants in the learning process can be challenging for the teacher, as it implies that learners have the opportunity to take the learning in a direction not foreseen by the teacher. Some teachers may have difficulty in coping with this if they feel they are losing authority and control. The teacher becomes a facilitator, focusing on process and less on content, and do not see themselves as 'filling empty pots'. This idea also implies that the learning intervention should ideally be personally meaningful to the learner, moving from a teacher-centred to a learner-centred view of teaching and learning. Having a positive view of learners and their capacity to learn, and trusting learners, contrasts with traditional views of learners and an authoritarian approach to teaching and learning. It can pose a challenge when a teacher is dealing with large number of learners at one time, however. If one is presented with large numbers of learners it is easier to take the teacher-centred position where information is provided in an asynchoronous direction with little participation from the relatively passive audience. This also raises challenges when one is planning learning. How do you enable individual experimentation within a formalised, constructed, learning environment (especially e-learning environments)? It means that time is needed to engage learners and to generate motivation. It also implies that there should be opportunities for learners to present their different experiences and get feedback.

Motivation

If one focuses on the individual one is led to think about motivation – the motivation to take on board new information and learn about new things. Motivation is key to any learning. From a behaviourist perspective motivation can be explained from the organic perspective – the need to satisfy physical needs, the gratification of rewards, and the need to avoid negative consequences. The importance of assessment to the learner – the acquisition of positive rewards – has been emphasised by many writers (Laurillard, 2002) and there is an implication that they are a key driver from the learner's perspective. This is why Biggs (1999) states that learning interventions must be made in tandem with the desired learning outcomes; these are often made explicit through some form of assessment.

The individualistic nature of this perspective also tends to draw attention to the personal motivation of the individual and the need to spark that motivation through genuine enthusiasm rather than authoritative assessment 'sticks'. Authors have demonstrated the need to allow choice of topic when teaching and learning information literacy (Barranoik, 2001; Smith and Hepworth, 2007), or where learners develop their own questions within a broader question. Going through the process of identifying questions also helps to define learners' information needs and information-seeking goals, which leads to identifying appropriate sources. The very process of making a choice tends to foster engagement with the process, encourages learners to think more deeply about the problem and gives them a greater sense of ownership of it. It provides an opportunity to identify and incorporate previous relevant knowledge. This is fundamental and serves two purposes. First, it builds learners' confidence as it (probably) demonstrates that they already have some knowledge on the subject, which is comforting; further, it shows that they can make a valuable contribution to the learning process and are not a passive recipient. Second, the knowledge that a learner already has about the subject provides a context on which to 'attach' new knowledge, just as an analogy helps transfer knowledge of one context to another.

Similarly, in interface design representations of familiar objects are used to help the user know what to do. For example, to help a user get the computer to carry out mathematical calculations a picture of a calculator can be placed on the screen. The user can then draw on previous experience to know what to do. Without relevant previous knowledge a person who has no knowledge of computers will tend to desperately jot down instructions to be learnt and follow them in a mechanical fashion, without any real understanding of the wider context. One strategy for developing new knowledge and building on old is to highlight naïve ideas and build on them. For example, one could illustrate that the statement 'Google will retrieve the best articles' is false by accessing a subject-specific search engine where content is filtered or a fee-based database where more relevant authoritative articles may be found. Previous knowledge can therefore provide a bridge to new knowledge.

Sometimes learners lack motivation when they are told to find out about a specific topic, without being given a choice. Unfortunately this is still common practice in many schools (Smith, 2009), leading to a lack of engagement. If the importance of choice is recognised, learning interventions can be made that are inquiry-based, project-based or problem-based, where learners can determine, to a lesser or greater extent, the direction of their research. Problem-based learning assumes that the 'individual's construction of reality is transformed as a result of reflecting upon the experience and plotting new strategies of living as a result' (Savin-Baden, 2007). One strength of inquiry- and problem-based learning or experiential learning, as it tends to be called, is that it encourages the independent inquirer to use a range of sources rather than, for example, depending on set texts. Problem-based learning tends to incorporate the opportunity to reflect on the process of learning and what has been learnt, what helped, what were the problems, how they were resolved, and identifying good strategies. These can be shared via peer-to-peer learning. Time can also be devoted to discussing how the process of learning can be applied to other situations. It also facilitates the gradual building of knowledge and tends to involve activity. Generally it is agreed that active learning leads to deeper learning and the greater chance that the learner will be able to develop learning strategies that can be applied to other problem contexts. This approach was popularised by Barrows and Tamblyn (Savin-Baden, 2007: 8) following their research into the reasoning ability of medical students at the McMaster Medical School in Canada. Problem-based learning is challenging, however, in the sense that the outcomes and the 'journey' may be less well defined than is often the case for learning interventions.

Teachers need to be flexible and able to adapt to unpredicted outcomes – to 'think on their feet'.

In developing countries these kinds of approaches have been taken further in participative learning approaches to dealing with specific local problems. In one such method, participatory action and learning (PAL), the 'teacher' is the facilitator and fellow researcher along with the community. These approaches have led to successful and sustainable change.

Motivation is a recognised 'driver' of engagement with the learning process. An overheard student conversation epitomises a lack of motivation associated with information seeking. One student appeared with a bundle of books. The other, surprised to see the person with so many books, asked if they were 'good ones', implying that looking for books may be a wasted effort, and received a non-committal response. The student then justified the bundle by stating that it required less effort than locating journal articles: 'no way they would look for journal articles. Too much effort.' There was no indication that finding out and learning about the topic was intrinsically interesting. Nor was there any judgement placed on the quality of different sources other than the effort required to find them! The questioner, who had made even less effort to find material, went on to describe how poorly they had fared in their studies. No connection was made between their lack of motivation to seek out material and the use of information and their success or failure. The tone implied that this just happened and that they had little control over these events. Independently seeking information was perceived as a chore. To be fair it could have been the case that the topic did genuinely bore the learner – maybe they were on the wrong course; perhaps the learning interventions were dull!

One lesson from this is that teachers need consciously to foster ways of developing motivation and attitudes that encourage information seeking in learners. Assessment rarely explicitly rewards the information-seeking process and the information literacy of learners. Previous experience can affect learners negatively, for example, if they have had an educational experience or come from a learning culture where seeking information independently is discouraged, or when pragmatic forms of learning are emphasised and all the resources are provided. Revision textbooks that highlight the parts learners have to remember to get good marks foster a highly pragmatic approach to learning and discourage learning for personal knowledge. Zipf (1949) reminds us that with regard to seeking information 'least effort' tends to be the norm. This puts even more onus on the teacher to help foster motivation among learners of information literacy.

A number of strategies have evolved to help foster engagement and motivation. Some overlap will be seen between them and echoes will be found of pedagogy already discussed. Keller (1987) developed the ARCS (Attention–Relevance–Confidence–Satisfaction) model of motivational states that need to be generated. Attention involves capturing the attention of the learner through a novel, fun or strange image at the start of the learning – applying the familiar to a new and unforeseen context. Relevance implies that the learner needs to know how the new learning can be applied and how it will help them. Confidence can be encouraged by making clear the level of performance expected, but also allowing the learner to set goals. Satisfaction can be achieved by providing a situation where the learner can demonstrate their newfound knowledge and initially meet goals relatively easily. This has been shown to be the case in gaming environments where in the early stages of a game levels are clearly defined and relatively easily to achieve. Later levels are further apart and harder to achieve (Gee, 2003).

Gagne (1985) also identified conditions for learning and gaining motivation: gain attention; inform the learner of the learning objectives; stimulate recall of similar previous learning; stimulate the learner, for example by providing vocabulary and examples of application; cue lesson content; provide guidance to the learner; elicit performance; provide feedback; assess performance; enhance retention; and transfer knowledge by showing how learning can be applied to other situations. Reigeluth (1987) identifies slightly different aspects of the learning intervention: elaborate a sequence of learning; highlight prerequisite sequence; summarise and show how sequences (steps) are interrelated; synthesise by asking the learner to elaborate on what they have learnt; develop analogies where the learner draws parallels with previous learning and other learning situations; highlight underlying cognitive strategies; and develop learner control and the ability to review their learning (for example, evaluate their choice of sources, monitor their competence, and evaluate the information they have retrieved and whether it addresses the questions).

Motivation is therefore stimulated through a learning context, part of which is to show the relevance and applicability of the work or thinking. So for information literacy learning to work, relevance and applicability need to be embedded in an information intensive task and be seen to help achieve a real goal. In fact, although learners can be taught the functionality and features of an information retrieval system, unless these are linked to achieving a learner's personal goal, the teaching is unlikely to be successful in providing depth of learning and the ability for the learner to transfer that knowledge to similar circumstances. Situations that foster such motivation (in addition to the more obvious 'study' or 'research' contexts) include people who research their genealogy or a specific goal such as buying a house or investigating a medical condition that affects them personally. The challenge for the trainer is therefore to be sufficiently knowledgeable about this context, by being familiar with the information and information resources needed to complete the task. For example, a trainer developing the information and knowledge needs of agricultural extension workers would need to know about the importance of market prices, how to make compost, pest control and so on, to embed the information literacy learning within this context.

Inquiry-based approach to participation in learning

Inquiry- or problem-based learning requires information literacy and is also a way to increase the learner's motivation. The two terms seem to be used to describe similar learning contexts although advocates of inquiry-based learning tend to place more emphasis on the learner identifying the question to be investigated. Inquiry-based learning motivates and is more likely to engage learners because they are more actively involved and have to take responsibility for the investigation. They can also see the relevance of the learning as it tends to be placed within a real world context and taps into the social dimension of learning, which will be discussed in the next chapter. Inquiry-based learning emphasises reflection, which we have seen is a fundamental feature associated with 'deep learning'.

Inquiry-based learning tends to take the following form:

- 'Establishment of the area of investigation, a stimulus to questioning usually in the form of a scenario, a task or a problem;
- Identification by the student group of key issues and appropriate questions; the absence of a specified reading-list means that resources are discovered by students. Decisions about which resources are appropriate are taken by the students, thus following a full research method;
- Investigation of sources and evidence by individuals or sub-groups;
- Reporting outcomes to the whole group;

- Group reflection on the process so far, identifying remaining gaps and analysing the scenario afresh in the light of new learning;
- A process reiterated, re-circling until a provisional halt is called by the exigencies of assessment deadlines' (Hutchings, 2007: 21).

In the health domain problem-based learning has been more common than inquiry-based learning but as indicated the two types of learning share common characteristics. Problem-based learning has been shown to be effective in promoting self-directed learning in health professional training programmes (such as medical, nursing and occupational therapy). This method, drawing on authentic situations encountered by practitioners, is aimed primarily at facilitating the transfer and application of knowledge and skills to clinical settings. The focus on independent learning has been seen to have additional long-term benefits, particularly in laying the foundations for a lifetime of continued education essential to meet the demands of professional practice (Boud and Feletti, 1997). Both approaches need to be consciously accompanied by information literacy training. Currently this may or may not be the case. By default inquiry- and problem-based approaches to learning will encourage information literacy due to their emphasis on independent learning that requires learners to use the information resources available to them. However, we would argue that this is not enough and even when these approaches are taken information literacy should be fostered systematically so that it becomes conscious rather than implicit.

There are many techniques to help foster engagement and enable participation, such as crosswords and quick quizzes, methods that can also provide quick feedback to the learner (and the teacher) so that they know whether they are on course. The Cephalonian technique is based on asking trainees to ask questions from prepared colour coded cards. This takes the pressure off them having to come up with their own question, and ensures participation. Audience response technology, whereby learners can answer questions electronically via handheld devices, is another method of ensuring participation and enables learners to respond without feeling exposed. Cardiff University's *Handbook for information literacy teaching* (Gaunt et al., 2007) provides a practical guide to many of the techniques and tools as well as tips for training. There are numerous other books that suggest specific, successful, techniques. Robert Chambers (2002) provides a comprehensive guide to techniques that have been used to help ensure participation in a learning intervention. These have been successfully applied in varied contexts, particularly in developing countries where gaining the involvement and participation of learners has been shown to be fundamental to fostering sustainable change and solutions that relate to the needs of the community.

As implied above, scaffolding the learning intervention helps learners to feel at ease since they know what they are going to do and what is expected of them. It also provides the basic knowledge of how to start the learning process. This is related to Biggs' (1999) notion of constructive alignment, which serves the purpose of scaffolding learning and makes sure that the teaching intervention is actually designed to achieve the learning objectives of the teaching intervention.

Implications for information literacy

An information literacy intervention therefore needs to be placed in a familiar context (fostering confidence), allowing learners to build on previous knowledge and experience, for example, their past experience of using a search engine or reference books. This could mean investigating with learners how they learn and find this out in another context, and then unpicking that learning process and applying it to the new learning context. This serves various purposes, including valuing learners and recognising their previous knowledge, and making it easier to integrate new knowledge with existing 'schema'. It has been shown that the following activities help to engage learners: spending time on the initial stages of information-seeking tasks; determining the subject matter or domain; reviewing previous knowledge; breaking down questions into sub-questions; deciding on the outcome; and discussing the information needed to complete the task.

Scaffolding learning instils confidence, direction and hence motivation. In some cases, where there is little choice and the topic is given – perhaps in unspecific terms such as 'find out about the Romans' – little time is spent discussing what the topic is about, allowing the learner to see the various nuances of the subject, or finding a particular angle that interests them. This is demotivating and encourages learners to go online and download apparently relevant material (in some cases without reading it) and presenting that. When this happens learners have gained little knowledge about the topic, and have not developed any information literacy by learning about the processes associated with finding out about the subject they are studying (Smith and Hepworth, 2007). Although this example was drawn from the secondary school environment, the same experience occurs in further and higher education and the workplace. In any information literacy training session where the assessment is given for the finished product, for example, a report, learners are unlikely to value the process of finding out or synthesising information. Therefore summative or formative assessment must include assessment of the process, in order to encourage reflection on it. Techniques such as quizzes, or learning contexts where learners are required to make reflective statements, for example, on discussion lists or through peer-to-peer presentations, can be used to encourage reflection, for assessment and to embed learning.

It has been found in the school environment that learners feel uncertain about how to approach the process of independently seeking information and want more support during the finding out process. Little conscious teaching and learning is directed to the actual process of finding out and the information literacies underpinning the task. As a result learners are uncertain and insecure, which is demotivating (Smith and Hepworth, 2007). For example, providing 'marks' for an initial mind map that identifies key concepts and terms associated with a topic gives value to the process and provides an opportunity for feedback to the learner. An assessed rationale for choice of sources would serve a similar process. Written reflection and reporting back on search strategies used is also a valuable strategy, encouraging reflection and the identification of strategies that can be applied to other situations; this leads to deeper learning. Diaries, whereby learners keep a log of their finding out experience, can be used to foster this kind of personal reflection. Short quizzes provide the opportunity for teachers to give immediate feedback, supporting learners during the learning process; this helps teachers to be aware of problems experienced by learners (Hepworth and Wema, 2006).

Oral reflection on the experience of searching (or in fact any part of the information-seeking process) has many benefits. The reasons for this will be discussed later in more detail when we look at the social aspect of learning. Suffice to say, from a motivational point of view, having to present to peers encourages a good performance. We have probably all experienced that the pressure of presenting to one's peers is greater than presenting to an anonymous marker or panel or even to the 'teacher'. It tends to lead to ownership since the individual or group is identified with their presentation. In addition it leads to peer-to-peer learning, which can be an effective way of learning. This can of course be emulated at a national and global level through tools such as YouTube, a wiki or a blog.

Evaluating impact

Pre- and post-information literacy diagnostic tests can also encourage motivation. The pre-diagnostic test helps learners identify knowledge gaps. However, feedback needs to be provided quickly for learners to really benefit from this exercise. In today's environment where younger people have developed the basic skills to use Google, they tend to assume that this is all they need to know about 'finding out' and do not appreciate the range and complexity of other search tools and techniques that can help them to be effective independent learners. The pre-diagnostic test helps learners to become aware of gaps in their knowledge; it also enables teachers to identify gaps in knowledge and helps them to orientate their teaching to meet the needs of the learners. The post-diagnostic test serves the function of determining whether the teaching intervention was successful, showing learners what they have learnt, and encouraging them to reflect on the learning intervention that they have experienced and to consolidate that knowledge. A number of authors have used diagnostic tests, including Andretta (2005) and Hepworth and Wema (2006).

Other cognitive factors that have an impact on learning and the way people interact with information include the learning style of the learner discussed earlier. People tend to learn in different ways – active, auditory and so on – and to organise information in different ways (holist, serialist) (Ford, 2004). Providing learning material in diverse ways caters to these needs and fosters a positive learning environment. Learners could also be given a choice of how they wish to present the 'product' of their learning, whether as a textual report, a visual poster or a performance.

Other distinctions have been made, for example between operationalist (command–precision focus) and conceptual (subject–recall focus). The point of knowing this from the learner's perspective is that it is useful to be conscious of one's own learning style since it will have its own strengths and weaknesses, and it suggests the possibility of choosing a strategy that may be less intuitive. It also might help the learner to become conscious of possible states of mind that could have a negative impact on their learning, for example the very broad distinction between 'blunters' and 'monitors' (Baker, 1994). 'Monitors' tend to proactively seek out information. 'Blunters' tend to shy away from information, perhaps thinking that it will lead to more 'bad news' or further complications. This was found to be the case among informal carers (Hepworth, 2004a) where their information seeking was mapped. Blunters had small networks of information sources (artefacts or people) and took a long time to find useful information which could have helped them deal with their situation. This could be for a host of factors, such as previous experience, knowledge of the information environment, ability to communicate, wealth, health, their sense of self-efficacy or locus of control and so on. In an informal study of carers a 'monitor' went to extraordinary lengths to get hold of material, including befriending the hospital librarian. A study by Heinstrom (2003), where she surveyed 298 people, showed there was a relationship between information-seeking behaviour and personality type. In particular she investigated the following character traits: 'extrovert/impulsive and hasty' people tended to prefer ease of access and material that confirmed their previous ideas; 'competitive' people were impatient and did not allow sufficient time for searching; 'conscientious and conservative' people were less open to material that challenged their previous views; and 'neurotic' people – who were vulnerable to negative emotions, insecurity and doubt – made less effort to search and had difficulty in dealing with alternative views. Heinstrom points out that these character traits are far from deterministic and individuals are heavily influenced by contextual demands. She argues that these traits are more apparent in routine situations.

From the perspective of a teacher of information it is nevertheless useful to be aware that aspects of a person's character may influence their learning style. This may have an impact on the learner's information needs, for example whether they require pictorial or factual information, and how they may prefer to represent their information needs, for example choosing between mind maps and hierarchical visualisations. It may affect how willing they are to spend time on tasks, particularly those that have an indeterminate outcome. It may affect their approach to creating search strategies and whether they are willing to plan and spend time deliberating on search terms, or the need to act and explore. It is therefore important for learners to be aware of these factors and how their learning style can influence their success as a learner so they can modify their behaviour where appropriate. Appreciating the factors that may influence individual learning and information seeking is also important for the teacher to appreciate, since the factors may influence the material and the training intervention that they design.

Investigating information literacy

Others investigations of people's information behaviour and information literacy such as Smith (2009), Bruce (1997) and Cheuk (1998) focus on the way people experience information literacy. These investigations have posed a challenge for information literacy models that have been developed in library and information science in that the conceptions belong to this community tend to be abstractions of what takes place. People outside the community do not recognise these conceptions or the terminology and this can lead to a lack of engagement. Hence understanding how people actually experience information literacy can help frame teaching. The following paragraphs give an indication of how people experience and think about information and information literacy.

Smith (2009) in her phenomenographical study found that young adults perceived information as having four levels:

- *Level 1*: the information landscape. This is associated with having knowledge of sources of information, the range of sources and their characterisitics.

- *Level 2*: the acquisition of information. This includes receiving information, in an unplanned way, which is used to build a knowledge base, and the process of finding information from a range of sources.

- *Level 3*: the knowledge base of internalised information. Here a distinction is made between information stored in an unprocessed way with the potential for future use, and information that is processed and builds a knowledge base or directly connects with information already internalised.

- *Level 4*: the application of information, where information is used for a range of purposes.

Bruce (1997) investigated faculty perceptions of information literacy and detailed them as the seven faces of information literacy:

- the information technology conception (tools to access, network, stay informed)

- the information sources conception (knowing and finding sources)

- the process conception (executing a process, strategies, dealing with situations)

- the information control conception (managing information, storage, retrieval)

- the knowledge construction conception (building personal perspectives)

- the knowledge extension conception (developing novel insights)

- the wisdom conception (wise use, involving personal values) as perceived by the learner in higher education.

From the perspective of teaching information literacy and e-learning it is important that these perceptions are taken on board; then it is more likely that the learner will relate to what is being taught and therefore be more engaged in the learning. This is less likely if they are confronted with abstractions about information literacy that stem from academics or practitioners who have developed their own schema to describe it.

Cheuk (1998) also elicited the perspective of the individual. Interestingly this study was carried out in the work context rather than higher education and reflects that context, although similarities can be seen with other models of the information-seeking experience and process. These situations were associated with different information sources, relevance judgements and types of information. Studying auditors Cheuk highlighted seven perceptions of information seeking and using situations, including:

- 'task initiating' (learners perceive they have a new task)
- 'focus forming' (learners gain a better understanding of going about a task or solving a problem)
- 'ideas assuming' (learners form ideas about how to conduct the task)
- 'ideas confirming' (learners try to confirm the idea they have assumed)
- 'ideas rejecting' (learners encounter conflicting information or cannot get the answers they need to confirm their assumed ideas)
- 'ideas finalising' (learners seek formal consensus to finalise ideas)
- 'passing on ideas' (learners present ideas to a targeted audience). Here the teacher is alerted to the experience of the learner and might ask themselves how they could facilitate 'focus forming', and whether there are tools or cognitive or behavioural strategies that could help.

Markless and Streatfield (2007, 29) highlighted three fundamental activities associated with information literacy and key thinking processes and behaviours:

- 'connecting with information', including exploring – browsing, networking, picture building; locating – systematic searching; orientation – identifying sources, reviewing, defining problem
- 'interacting with information', including thinking critically – filtering, knowing enough, synthesising and analysing, questioning and challenging; constructing new knowledge, concepts; transforming – refining and interpreting, imposing structure; evaluating and verifying

- 'making use of information', including transforming – restructuring, taking ownership of the learning; citing and referencing; communicating.

At a more micro level, Hepworth (2004b) gathered data about students while they were searching for information and found that they experienced common negative information retrieval situations, including:

- unfamiliarity with sources, where to go and which were the most appropriate
- unfamiliarity with the functionality of information retrieval tools and how to use them effectively
- retrieving either too many or too few items and not knowing how to narrow or broaden the search
- error messages (which implied they had used the system incorrectly).

In these situations students tended to abandon their original approach and try a totally new strategy, often trying another source, rather than thinking about how to rectify their current situation by, for example, modifying their search strategy.

The learning context and its implications

Paying attention to how learners experience and perceive their interaction with information is important. One challenge presented by previous research is that different studies work at different levels of abstraction, for example the overall perception of information (Smith, 2009), being information literate (Bruce, 1997) and interacting with information via information retrieval systems (Hepworth, 2004b). It is therefore important to know where and how to use these frameworks when fostering information literacy. Teasing out these conceptions of learners' information experience can help them think more imaginatively about their information seeking, its usefulness and how information supports their learning and helps them in their daily life. It helps the teacher to identify different aspects of the learning process and communicate information literacy in a way that should be recognisable to learners. It can also help the teacher to create learning situations where one or more of these concepts is explored, stimulating a more conscious approach to using information.

We therefore need to understand information literacy from the perspective of the learners. These are likely to vary to some extent, depending on the context of the learners in terms of the environment they find themselves in, the types of roles and tasks associated with that environment, whether at school, at home or in the workplace. Although the overall processes are to a great extent consistent, the goals, tasks and content will alter; the tools will vary, as will their functionality, which is likely to be content or subject specific. The roles and interrelationship between people and the norms associated with them, such as the collaborative nature of the work, will have an impact. One therefore needs to ensure that information literacy interventions are embedded in the context of the learner, whether, for example, conducting a piece of biology coursework or developing a marketing strategy in a company. Furthermore, the terminology used by the learners to describe their learning process, such as 'ideas confirming' or 'ideas finalising', need to be recognised and used to frame information literacy interventions and to communicate to the learner how it will help them with their tasks.

One of the problems associated with much information literacy literature is that it tends to come from the educational context (school, further and higher education) and refers to student learners; it is very much grounded in that reality, emphasising processes associated with individual, independent study and research. This does not mean that it is irrelevant to learners outside the educational context. Common cognitive and behavioural processes as well as common tasks associated with information seeking can be identified, but there are significant differences between different learning contexts. Therefore to foster information literacy among a group of people it is very important to understand the context within which they learn and their experience, so the training is pertinent and genuinely addresses their needs. A limitless range of contexts can be envisaged: older women exploring their history, choosing and assembling material, editing and organising it, creating some form of presentation based on the material; union workers investigating a health and safety accident; people learning about useful agricultural practice drawing on indigenous knowledge; school children finding out about the environment around the school; researchers investigating pollution and fish farming; or individuals learning about commerce or the market.

The Information Seeking In Context (ISIC) bi-annual conference and the e-journal *Information Research* are good sources of studies of people's information behaviour in different contexts. They provide a useful reference tool for trainers to contextualise training, particularly when they are working with people from a different background. If previous studies of people's information behaviour are not available then it is likely that the trainer will have to conduct a preliminary inquiry into the information needs of the people they wish to train. Trainers need to understand the knowledge generation, storage and use in that domain and the questions that are asked and how they can be answered drawing on the available knowledge, data and information around. This is extremely important in the workplace context; trainers need to understand how people work and like to be helped.

One consequence of information literacy coming out of the educational context and having been the concern of information professionals (librarians, information officers) is that the terminology used is drawn from information professionals (academics, practitioners) who deal in abstractions of the information seeking process and use words such as location and access. These concepts mean little to learners. In the academic environment information literacy tends to be seen as a solitary, individual activity and until recently was associated with a linear activity that reflected the processes undertaken when completing a project. The higher education interventions in Part 2 of this book to some extent also reflect this context, but could, we think, be adapted to other contexts.

Understanding the experience and the difficulties of learners and developing training material grounded in these experiences are more likely to be recognised as relevant and taken on board in the academic environment. A recent study that explored the information literacy experience in the workplace (Hepworth and Smith, 2008), where the information literacy of administrative staff in higher education was explored, found that respondents did not recognise the labels we use. The term information literacy, for example, was associated with having knowledge of ICT. One fundamental difference from the academic study context was the hierarchical and segmented nature of the workplace. People seldom started by identifying a problem and information need, as tasks were generally given to them by their manager, who needed to understand the overall process. In addition the division of labour within the workplace meant that information literacy tasks associated with the work were distributed among a team, for example, one to find information, another to manipulate and organise it and another to communicate the results via a presentation to people outside the team.

One aspect of the workplace that has been underemphasised in traditional models of information literacy is the importance of interpersonal and networking skills as a fundamental part of information gathering, evaluation and management. To be able to identify who to go to for information and experience and be able to interact with them effectively was found in this study to be a fundamental part of a person's information literacy. In addition, the traditional importance given to sources of information that originate outside an organisation was found to be inappropriate in the workplace studied. Here far more emphasis was given to internal information sources such as internal databases. Less emphasis was given to evaluating the quality of the information, particularly where tasks were repetitive and sources were known to be reliable. This is less likely to be the case in exceptional or novel situations, what Engestrom (1999) called 'contradictions'.

The emphasis on the importance of people as a source of information and learning has been underplayed in information literacy teaching. Knowledge management, whereby people hope to gain access to and share what is known by the individuals and community around them, is the most valuable source of information and learning for most people, as they are generally available whereas other information resources may not be. People have knowledge which has developed through experience and hence is grounded in their reality; they can share that knowledge to some extent. It is generally believed that tacit knowledge, held in the mind of the individual, can never be transferred in its entirety, but an oral description by a knowledgeable person tends to be richer than a written text. People also have the ability to understand the needs of listeners and can adapt, condense and filter their knowledge in a way that is appropriate to the listener, something that a static information object such as a book cannot do. The use of hypertext, extended style sheets (XSLT) and extended mark-up language (XML) has enabled people to have an individualised view of an electronic document. But these are still relatively crude. Providing links to frequently asked questions can also at least enable user-specific views of content and relate them to the situation of the learner. However, oral transmission, in the form of narrative, perhaps due to the construction of narrative, seems to have an intrinsically powerful communicative and memorable quality.

Any information literacy intervention should focus on other people and their knowledge as a learning resource – what has been termed 'horizontal learning' (Reeler, 2005). Mapping the information environment should therefore include mapping the people who may be useful, the knowledge they are likely to have, and how one can successfully access and extract information from them. Collections of people, such as organisations, should be seen and included as possible sources of knowledge and information.

For teachers to relate their teaching to the context of learners, they need to have some understanding the learners' learning environment. Therefore, as indicated above, it would be beneficial if not essential if they carried out a preliminary information needs analysis and study of information seeking before the training started. Alternatively teachers need to have experience of working in the learners' learning environment; otherwise their teaching is likely to be seen as irrelevant. Or, a highly participative approach could be taken whereby the teacher facilitates the exploration of the information and knowledge environment with learners.

It is evident that one issue that complicates the teaching and learning of information literacy is that people interpret it in different ways. Bruce, Edwards and Lupton (2006) highlight some of the differences. For example, teachers may see information literacy as 'using IT for retrieval and communication, finding information, executing a process, controlling information, building up a knowledge base in a new area, working with knowledge to gain new insights, using information wisely for the benefit of others'; information professionals may see information literacy as 'acquiring mental models of information systems, a set of skills, a combination of information and IT skills, learning skills, a process, a way of learning, the ability to learn, ways of interacting with the world of information, information behaviour, part of the literacy continuum'; and students may see information literacy as 'fact finding, finding the right answer, finding information to form a personal standpoint, critically analysing information – trying to reveal values, finding information located in information sources, initiating a process, building a personal knowledge base for various purposes'.

Bruce, Edwards and Lupton go on to define different frameworks that help us to think about the various approaches for teaching information literacy. These are useful to help teachers think about what they are doing and how. These six frameworks include:

- the content framework (focusing on what needs to be known) – a behavioural view of learning

- the competency framework (focusing on what the learner should be able to do) – again, a behavioural view of learning

- the learning to learn framework (focusing on what it means to think like an information literate professional in a relevant field) – a more cognitive perspective

- the personal relevance framework (focusing on the usefulness of information literacy from the learners' perspective) – a more individual constructivist view of learning
- the social impact framework (focusing on how information literacy impacts on society) – a social constructivist or social realist view of learning
- the relational framework – again, a social constructivist or social realist view of learning.

Using these frameworks in combination with an understanding of people's conception of knowledge and information and the information-seeking process, as described earlier, can help the teacher to adopt consciously a specific focus for instruction and address the different needs of learners. For example, an information literacy intervention could focus on 'information as a process' in a 'learning to learn' framework, and deal with problems individuals may experience.

6

The learner as a social being – a social constructivist approach

This chapter highlights the social nature of learning. We have therefore moved from the physically embodied nature of learning (Chapter 3) to learning as a socially embodied phenomenon, alluded to in the previous chapter. Learning tends to occur as part of a social activity and can be seen as one part of becoming a participant in a group activity. This has implications for how information literacy is taught, placing emphasis on the social dimension – highlighting the social benefits of being information literate and making explicit how the social norms may affect a person's information literacy. In addition, the social perspective brings to the foreground techniques that stem from our social being, for example the importance of discourse about negotiating, shaping, confirming and sharing our conception of information literacy.

There are many theories that emphasise the social dimension of learning. Over the past 40 years researchers from information science have studied people's information behaviour. More often than not, as indicated in the previous chapter, these studies focused on particular social groups or social contexts. Recently activity theory has been used successfully to model the social aspect of information seeking (Wilson, 2006). This highlights the importance of roles, norms, actions and the use of (information) tools to achieve objectives.

Learning as a community of practice

Wenger (1999) views learning as synonymous with becoming part of a community. This sense of community can stem from shared characteristics of people's experience, for example a person's social context – role in an organisation, a family or a group of practitioners – which tends to imply a common geographical or technological environment, and common or interdependent roles with tasks that people participate in to achieve prescribed or agreed goals. Learning in this sense is socially embedded. The community may be local, national or global and may span common or connected practices. Each community has a host of normative values to do with the articulation of relationships and ways of behaving, beliefs that enable them to function in the world and a language to communicate and share these ways of viewing the world. Practice-based communities or what have been termed communities of practice (Lave and Wenger, 1991) exemplify this. These are communities of people, such as engineers, chemists or postmen, that take part in a common endeavour. This idea is similar to Kuhn's (1970) identification of epistemic communities which share a common belief in what can be known and how we can go about learning about that world and share common paradigms.

From a theoretical standpoint this notion is characterised by focusing on the ways in which knowledge is distributed socially (Mayes and de Freitas, 2004). In this sense knowledge is regarded as 'situated' when learning outcomes enable individuals to participate in the practice of a certain community. This focus moves away from analysis of sub-tasks towards patterns of successful practice. In essence this notion is regarded as a necessary attempt to reconnect behavioural or cognitive levels of analysis that have become disconnected from the social dimension. Within this analysis the assumption is that learning is shaped by social forces and that successful learning must be personally meaningful where a learner's activity, motivation and learning are related to a need for a positive sense of identity (or positive self-esteem).

Two themes or 'flavours' relate to situated learning. These are referred to as 'socio-psychological situativity' and 'community of practice situativity' (Mayes and de Freitas, 2004).

Socio-psychological situativity

This is centred on the importance of context-dependent learning in informal settings where the learning activity, in which the skills or knowledge are normally embedded, is given as authentic a social context as possible. For example, problem-based learning (as discussed in the previous chapter), anchored instruction and cognitive apprenticeships embody this approach. In this instance the design focus is on the relationship between the nature of the learning task in an educational setting and its characteristics when used in a real situation.

Community of practice situativity

The emphasis here is on the individual learner's relationship with a group of people rather than the relationship of an activity to wider practice. In this learning model the learning of a particular practice is characterised by a process where beginners are initially peripheral in the activities of the community but as their learning increases their participation becomes more central. As with constructivist theories, meaning is constructed by individuals. However, the main difference here is that meaning is generated through negotiation, participation and reification through mutual engagement with others in this community (Wenger, 1999). Negotiation of meaning is defined as interaction and gradual achievement within a given context. Participation is defined as the process of taking part and is therefore active. Reification is the process of treating abstractions as real entities. For example, in the legal system the abstract notion of justice is represented as a blindfolded person holding a set of scales. Hence, it is a shortcut to communication where we project our meanings onto the world and then perceive them as existing and having a reality of their own (Wenger, 1999).

This is similar to the idea of 'habitas' (Bordieu, 1986), although Bordieu focuses on a disposition learnt or absorbed through upbringing and the effect, for example, of class rather than socialisation in the workplace. Bordieu also uses the term 'field' to describe the arena in which people struggle in pursuit of resources. The fundamental point is that people take part in activities that form a common reality, sharing and exchanging common ideas, and tasks are undertaken to achieve certain goals. Conceptions associated with this reality are held as explicit and tacit knowledge and communicated via language, symbols and artefacts; they may be captured in data and information resources and enable activities to take place. Becoming familiar with how to access this information and knowledge is an important part of being able to undertake common activities, complete tasks, gain recognition, gain resources and possibly contribute to knowledge growth.

One consequence, therefore, of learning, whether conscious or unconscious, in this context is becoming a part of a community of learners. The learner wants or needs (although this may not be either a conscious or explicitly stated goal) to engage with that community, to become a respected and valued member of that community, to be able to contribute to the goals of the community and hence to be valued and accepted as a player and possibly achieve goals associated with gaining access to resources. Resources could be political, economic, a life style, a mind set or a combination of these. This may result in the learner moving from the state of novice to expert. This involves becoming familiar with:

- the language of the community
- the problems that they face
- the solutions to these problems
- the tools that they use to interact with and help understand their environment
- ways of thinking critically about the phenomena they deal with
- communicating with others in the community both to enable learning and to communicate learning.

This knowledge and these skills should develop over time and, generally, this requires the learner to be able to enter a meaningful discourse with other members of that community. This provides an individual with an intellectual home and a sense of belonging, worth and, possibly, a way to get access to resources, to survive and to make a living.

The importance of language

Fundamental to this is, of course, language. Language development takes place in 'shared social and situational contexts because the latter provide information about the meaning of words and sentence structures' (Chapman, 1978: 95). Language is the 'way people act with words to formulate and interpret the world' (Finnegan, 2007: 3). Finnegan talks about oral culture, drawing in particular on examples from the Limba people of northern Sierra Leone, where if people spoke the local language they were deemed to be of that community, a genuine member. Speech, not the written word, was used to make a contract, where education was a 'creative and performance process, involving interaction of specific individuals and specific occasions' (2007: 27). She states that the 'use of storied words must be set within its own complex of practices and ideologies... essential for the subjectivities of the meaning and evocations that they carried' (2007: 51). 'Narrative is truly universal and creates order out of chaos and gives meaning to what otherwise would be uncontrollable and anarchic' (2007: 54). This view should perhaps be qualified in the sense that it is possible to have thought and ideas about the world around one without knowing the 'words' associated with that experience. Literally, one may know about something without having the language to describe it to someone else.

Nevertheless, a shared 'reality' is in a sense a 'product of our use of language which comes into existence through sharing ideas and negotiating meanings with others' (McKillop, 2005), and dialogue (the exchange of language) is 'an indispensable component of the process of both learning and knowing' (Freire, 2007: 49). Freire takes this to another dimension when he states, 'If I do not love the world – if I do not love life – if I do not love people – I cannot enter into dialogue' (2007: 91). This has an echo in the information literacy literature where Bruce (1995) discusses the place of wisdom, which implies thinking about the greater good, as a necessary component of being information literate, in terms of having the knowledge and belief that one should use information wisely.

Using language is an ongoing and active process: 'Thought and language are integrally linked as children learn through socio-cultural means to discriminate, generate ideas, represent, predict, substitute, assemble, classify, evaluate, consider credibility, examine, be critical, design, analyse, anticipate events, empathise, change point of view, transform, parody and invent' (Foreman, 2000: 84). A community of practice is therefore a community that shares, communicates and probably debates using a common language. This language will be used to understand and formulate questions that will be crucial for information seeking as well as for using the information retrieved. In conjunction will be the language associated with information literacy, and information about how knowledge is generated in the domain, which in turn draws attention to the artefacts such as journals, magazines or databases that are used to represent and store the related information. In addition, there will be language that describes the established methods of finding out. To take an obvious example, the phrase literature review has a specific meaning that anyone operating in an academic context needs to be familiar with. At a lower level of granularity, there is language that describes the cognitive processes associated with information literacy and learning such as induction, analysis, synthesis, browsing, narrowing a search, evaluation and authority, and the terms associated with the tools that one is likely to use such as indexes, summaries, abstracts, system functionality, Boolean logic and so on. Language can be used as a means for evaluating information literacy. Walton (2009) found that the language used by first-year undergraduate students who had taken part in an active e-learning process changed. Their new language enabled them to talk more precisely about the process of evaluating information. They appeared to move through four distinct levels on their journey to becoming information literate, which are described below.

Information discernment level 1

Students are unaware or unconcerned about the need to evaluate information and may tend to use information without checking its quality. This is characterised by students making statements such as:

> I didn't really know about what type of things you should look for when you are looking at websites to get references.

> When you first go on a website you don't read all the information.

> I didn't know what the things at the end like .ac and .org meant.

Information discernment level 2

Students show an emerging awareness of the need to evaluate information, expressed weakly through notions of detail, suitability or quantity:

> I have learnt to go into more detail with my work.

> You need to make sure the book is suitable for the task.

> There were so many books it was hard to choose the right ones.

Information discernment level 3

Students are aware of the need to evaluate information for quality but see the process in black and white, true or false, and either or terms:

> When I'm looking at references in the future I'm going to look and see whether it is from a big company where it's very probably going to be factual or whether it's from someone's own personal website or something that's less formal and I'll be able to tell whether to take information from it or not.

[Find out] what references will be real and not real…

I would also make myself aware that these resources may not be trustworthy and the information held in them may not be complete.

Information discernment level 4

Students are now aware that evaluation is not simply a matter of black and white; they recognise the need to judge each source on its merits and talk about balance, deciding and using a range of criteria in the evaluation process:

[I] have learnt how to judge how good a book or journal is.

[The e-learning training] helped [me] decide which resources were reliable and useful and why.

I have learnt a lot of new knowledge from the Berkeley website regarding evaluating information. I know about scope, audience, timeliness, scholarly vs. popular, authority documentation and objectivity.

In addition students are able to talk about the nature and relative value of evaluation criteria in a given setting:

Some of them initially are important like reliability… obviously if you are going to reference something in an essay etc. you need to know that the source is reliable.

… authority, I don't find as important. It could be written by the government or the FA [Football Association] or something and they could make a pretty stand up point, but you could have a third year student from a university make just as good a point.

…relevance as well, you've got to stick to the question or whatever you need to do needs to be relevant to the point you are making.

These level 4 statements exemplify not only a new confidence in information literacy but also a growing ability to become higher order critical thinkers. In effect these are examples of 'breakthrough statements' as they move beyond what was discussed in class. Biggs (1999) regards these kinds of statements as evidence of 'extended abstract' thinking, the highest level of critical thinking identified.

This perspective marries with a broader conception of what it means to be information literate (Hepworth, 2000). Four main components were defined:

- learning how to use information tools (technology, systems and sources) to access, organise and distribute information and knowledge
- learning thinking processes associated with knowledge creation and information management
- learning how to communicate with people to access and exchange data, information and knowledge
- learning the intellectual norms of the subject domain associated with the production of knowledge.

If the purpose, conscious or otherwise, of the learner is to become a part of a community, and part of becoming a part of a community is to become information literate in that community, then the notion of a linguistic and social context has huge implications for the teaching of information literacy. It implies that teaching needs to be situated or embedded in practice (this has also been justified from a motivational perspective as discussed in the previous chapter and would by default be associated with inquiry-based learning) and one objective of being information literate is to enable one to learn about and become a part of a community of practice. However, if this is the case then a liberal interpretation of 'community of practice' needs to be taken that should encompass people whose community membership would be defined as a result of their roles, whether as a parent, a person with an illness, a student, a salesperson, a corporate financier, a store holder, a musician or a chemist. The 'community' is defined by the tasks they perform, the problems they tackle and the set of associated, shared, information needs. A community of practice is therefore not only associated with work-based communities. Specific needs may vary within a 'group' due to personal preferences, including their approach to learning as indicated above, levels of knowledge, their immediate environment and so on. Roles and tasks, in particular, have been seen to be the key drivers of information needs (Leckie, Pettigrew and Sylvain, 1996; Wilson, 1999; Bystrom, 2002; and Ingwersen and Jarvelin, 2005).

Hence, if one takes on board the need to situate information literacy teaching and learning then familiarity with the roles and tasks of the learners is essential, as indicated earlier. Information literacy needs to be contextualised in terms of specific roles, tasks, subject domains and the norms that will be associated with them (particularly in the organisational setting). This means that although common labels can be used to describe common information literacies, common processes, the material that people interact with and the value judgements they make are likely to be different and these need to be understood and made explicit to make the training relevant and engaging. Teaching information literacy in an abstract way without grounding it in the context of the learner and demonstrating how consciousness of information literacy actually contributes to people achieving their objectives, whether work-based, domestic or otherwise, is largely a waste of time. This is because of the reasons already specified but also due to the socially embedded nature of learning. It is of course possible to teach information literacy in the abstract and some aspects will be taught in a way that is disconnected from any particular wider task. However, generally, learning tends to be shallow in the sense that it is not internalised and the knowledge is seldom transferred.

Embedding information literacy

One can therefore envisage that when information literacy is fully comprehended by the educational sector and integrated into the school, further and higher education, it will be fully grounded within the subjects studied. This would be similar to the approach of aiming for 'functional literacy', whereby people's ability to read and write is developed within the context of their work, relating, for example, to the literacy needs of someone who wants to be a plumber or electrician. In school this would imply that when studying a particular subject, appropriate and relevant information literacy will be part and parcel of learning about that subject domain. This would enable learners to be active, independent learners in that domain and help them to become a part of these subject-based communities of practice. This implies that educators need to know how knowledge is generated in the various domains and how information literacy is a part of that subject. It also implies that an inquiry-based or problem-based approach would need to be taken to enable learners to be independent learners in different domains. It also means that in the educational setting an appropriate environment will be needed to support this kind of learning, considering the range of information resources and technologies that need to be made available, as well as appropriate methods for instruction and assessment.

This situated nature of learning implies that the information literacy trainer needs to take note of the information environment, the information landscape, that the community has access to. The information landscape will vary dramatically in form and the content of artefacts that contain knowledge, data and information and the tools that enable access and manipulation of the information. Managing electronic laboratory notebooks may be a key information literacy, for example, in a pharmaceutical company.

The information landscape will vary dramatically due to the subject domain. Sources can be specific to the domain and their form and structure will be determined to some extent by the type of information associated with the domain and how the person needs to process that information. For example, a searchable database of chemical structures, a patents database or a news archive. In a journalistic environment, for example, it may be useful to search by 'byline'. Specific types of information will be associated with role-related tasks, such as a person from an environmental agency determining flood risk prevention strategies using a 'mash up' of topographical map, demographic and flooding data. In these contexts information literacy will need to be developed systematically and embedded within them.

The social, physical and economic environment will also have an impact. To give an extreme example, in a place with low levels of literacy, and because of infrastructure or funding limited access to technological resources (such as telecommunications) or information artefacts (such as published records), then the systematic use of people and networks of people to gain knowledge is essential – what has been called horizontal learning. However, even in a largely oral, people-based information culture a systematic approach can be taken to mapping knowledge, identifying information needs, linking to new sources of information and knowledge, and deciding how to store knowledge in a more accessible form.

Although there are common underlying processes associated with being information literate, common thinking skills, common types of knowledge, and the context-specific nature of information literacy means that supporting information literacy in an organisation needs careful consideration. The information literacy of different staff would need to be considered and related to what they need to achieve. A lobbying organisation, for example, needs to know how to identify appropriate partners using available information about organisations and social networks. This would include thought about the kind of problems they deal with, the information that would be useful, how people are expected to use information, styles for creating information, and policies so that people knew what to keep or discard and where. Different roles may be associated with different information tasks. For example, senior people are likely to be more concerned with defining problems; they tend to need to be aware of the external operating environment whereas junior staff tend to be more inward looking and may be primarily concerned with gathering and processing related information. Individual roles and literacies need to be teased out; information norms and strategies need to be defined and these will have characteristics that are common with those in other contexts as well as some that are distinct.

The important role that language plays in constructing a shared reality also has implications for information literacy interventions. This can be achieved by incorporating into any intervention the opportunity for learners to discuss their learning and the learning process. This requires learners to use the language of information literacy, hence making conscious and concretising this in their minds. Learners need to be asked to collaboratively reflect on their learning, discuss it with their peers and present what they have done and learnt verbally. This helps to foster deeper learning, and from an evaluation perspective enables the teacher to see whether they have genuinely understood what they have learnt. It also provides an opportunity for peer-to-peer learning and helps to reinforce the significance of what has been learnt. Presentation to peers also has a motivational function in that learners generally want to gain the respect of their peers and colleagues and, therefore, put in more effort than is the case if the learning is private and only shared between the teacher and the learner.

An information literacy training course for teachers of information literacy in Tanzania (Hepworth and Wema, 2006) asked the learners to present after each stage in the learning process, explaining the strategies they had taken, the reasons for their choices of, for example, terms or sources and this helped to concretise their information literacy learning. In addition, the better students provided excellent role models and demonstrated what levels could be reached through the sophisticated way they talked about information and processes of finding and using information. It also served to demonstrate whether change and learning had taken place and whether norms associated with that setting were being followed. It also had a side effect of helping students to develop their communicative skills and confidence to present in public. Furthermore, the fact that they were creating knowledge and sharing that with the wider group meant that they were not passive learners but were seen to be active contributors to their community of practice – giving them a sense of self-value and purpose. Active discourse and presentation also helped to map the knowledge of the group.

The situated nature of information literacy is reflected in the models of information behaviour. These models tend to be general and holistic in the sense that they are trying to identify all factors influencing information behaviour. As a result they do reiterate some factors mentioned earlier, such as personal, psychological characteristics. Nevertheless they are worth discussing here, despite an element of repetition, since they provide an excellent description of the significance of the context within which information behaviour takes place. Ingewersen's model, which stems from an interest in information retrieval, highlights factors that are at play when a person is searching for information using an information system. Ingwersen and Jarvelin's (2005) 'Interactive Information Seeking, Retrieval and Behavioural Processes' model indicates that the searcher is driven and influenced by their past and present socio-cultural and organisational context and that 'cognitive actors' interact with 'cognitive manifestations embedded in the IT and existing information objects via interfaces' (2005: 262). Bystrom and Jarvelin (1995) also highlight contextual factors that influence personal action, including subjective task, personal factors, organisation and personal information seeking style. Savolainen (2005) in 'Everyday life information seeking' indicated how 'way of life' (time budget, consumption models, hobbies) and 'mastery of life' (keeping things in order) are interconnected. He shows how this is influenced by 'main types of mastery of life' (optimistic-cognitive and so on) and 'problem solving behaviour' (evaluation of problem at hand, selection of information sources and channels, seeking of orienting and practical information). He indicated how these behaviours are influenced by values, attitudes, material capital, social capital, cultural and cognitive capital, and a person's current situation of life.

Wilson, an influential figure in information behaviour research, developed a generic model of factors that influence people's information behaviour (1999). This included the information need context of the person – some aspect of context that resulted in an information need and how these needs were satisfied depending on factors such as how people cope with stress; their sense of self-efficacy; and demographic, psychological, role-related and environmental factors. He also highlighted how these factors may lead to 'passive attention', 'passive search', 'active search' and 'ongoing search'. This research highlighted an issue that is largely overlooked by people who are involved in information literacy instruction, which tends to assume that access to information is through an active process of information gathering. This is obviously not the case and was evident in Smith's (2009) model of young people's perception of information where one perception of information was that it was something that could be absorbed passively and was not necessarily processed immediately for a specific purpose. Information can be gained through passive listening to the radio or watching TV without any conscious attempt to gather information. A great deal of information is also gained from talking to other people, again not actively seeking information. Information and knowledge can also be obtained by practical tasks and immediate experience that lead to the generation of knowledge and may be codified as information but again were not part of a conscious information-seeking activity.

Teachers of information literacy who give the impression that there is only one way of learning therefore present an unrealistic picture, which is at odds with people's experience. As noted in the workplace study (Hepworth and Smith, 2008), social networking is a fundamental part of being information literate and people need help with this activity not only in mapping the people, organisation and source landscape but also by developing the interpersonal skills associated with this aspect of being information literate. This implies that when teaching information literacy these forms of learning need to be encouraged – suggesting that learners should partake in information-rich experiences within which they should position themselves and facilitate the interpersonal experience of finding out, for example by attending networking events.

As indicated before, numerous studies have been carried out of various groups of people who come from communities that share common information needs, including doctors, nurses, social workers, farmers, small and medium-sized enterprises, children, the public and marginalised groups. The bi-annual Information Seeking in Context (ISIC) conference and the e-journal *Information Research* provide a good way of locating such studies. These studies form a very useful source of material for those who are teaching information literacy to people from these communities. They can help the teacher to understand the context within which the information literacy needs to be embedded and give an indication of the information needs of the community and the information problems they experience. However, if no previous information needs study has been made of the target audience then it is suggested that an information behaviour study should be carried out if possible to ensure information literacy training is relevant and contextualised.

Choo's (2007) study of information seeking in organisations highlights the importance of context and what he calls, in a Kuhnian sense, epistemic communities. He supports the argument that organisations operate as distinct epistemic communities and that this affects what and how they use information and the way they make decisions. Thus if one was delivering information literacy training it would be related to this learning context. This would enable new recruits to become familiar with the information literacy appropriate to their work environment or help experienced staff become more aware of their information literacy and hence more conscious and systematic in their information behaviour. It would encourage thought about and the formulation of information policies and strategies.

One organisation, a venture capital firm, went through a process of assessing opportunities, based on institutionally agreed judgemental guidelines, and made decisions using a range of information sources, including market data, information from customers, competitors, members of the venture fund, and knowledge of comparable business scenarios. Another case study, of the east European development arm of a German bank, describes the process of creating country reports. The reports had a predefined structure that identified the information needed. This structure ('slots') was filled by having access to government and transgovernmental agencies' analyses and reports, and commercial information providers' public and intranet materials, and from contacts and daily news. It would therefore be important to place an information literacy intervention within these scenarios and the effective use of such resources to achieve their corporate objectives. Choo's last example describes how Xerox evolved an effective mechanism for disseminating knowledge from service technicians to other service technicians. This had a big impact on productivity. Part of the process involved technicians sharing useful knowledge they had learnt with an expert. This had the indirect effect of motivating staff who enjoyed the opportunity to talk to an expert and also because they felt their ideas were valued. People came together to think about how they would validate and disseminate information and knowledge. In other words they developed information management strategies. From an information literacy perspective information norms were at play, including valuing the experience and knowledge of technicians plus the notion that this knowledge should be shared and not kept to oneself. The skills and knowledge to do this, we would argue, would need defining and should be supported through information literacy skills training.

Marchand, Kettinger and Rollins (2001) cited six types of information behaviour and organisational values that can predict an organisation's capacity to use information effectively, which should be conveyed to staff through their information literacy training as part of their professional development. These included:

- integrity (using information in a trustful and principled way)
- transparency (openness and reporting of errors) relating to normative values
- control (availability of information about performance) applying information to achieve goals
- sharing
- proactiveness (seeking and using new information to respond quickly to change)
- formality (use and trust of formal and informal sources) again relating to normative values.

Despite this recognition of the importance of taking a conscious approach to people's information behaviour it should not be underestimated how hard it is to get people in an organisation to address such issues, because of the pressures of day-to-day work compounded by the need and desire to produce concrete deliverables in an environment where process is less valued than outcome. It has also proved difficult to get the kind of openness described above in a competitive environment, whereby staff in an organisation are prepared to share their knowledge. More often than not people see their knowledge as something to be accumulated individually and protected since it can give them leverage. People therefore need to be motivated to be conscious and systematic in how they create and deal with information as well as share their expertise. Furthermore, people need support from professionals who can help them with this, partly because they do not necessarily have the expertise or it needs to be brought out, and also because to do it effectively takes time; in cases where the returns are not immediate it can become an irritant, and be seen as a bureaucratic, imposed task. Well-intentioned approaches to capture knowledge in organisations, collecting information about people's experience and what they have learnt, can also be perceived in a negative light and as a form of monitoring and control by management rather than a way to help people in general to be more effective.

Nevertheless positive case studies have been recorded. Snowden (2001), for example, documents a case where systematic approaches to gathering information have succeeded. He describes a situation where tacit knowledge was captured via story telling and people were employed to do this, rather than depending on the existing staff to capture their knowledge. Anecdotes were collected and developed into a 'power story' that encapsulated norms and practice. A cartoon was then produced to help convey this information. This is an innovative example of how information can be captured and communicated and should therefore be a part of the employees' information literacy armoury. This reaffirms our view that our conception of information literacy and the needs of learners should not be confined to the traditional educational ideas of information literacy. Information literacy in the workplace begins with understanding what information staff, experts and communities need access to in order to get their work done. The role of the information professional is to introduce learners to 'tools' and resources that can help them: by fostering information access and processing skills, such as collaboration, listening and presentation; by helping people to develop policies to manage information; and by developing a culture where information and the sharing of knowledge is valued and personalising information provision (Cheuk, personal communication, 2009).

In the educational context, where models of information literacy were originally developed, although these models tend not to be based on learners' conception of the information experience, they do reflect the processes that learners go through when conducting independent research. The SCONUL model relates to a 'competent student' who is able to use basic library and IT skills effectively (Andretta, 2005: 45). These 'study skills' include being able to:

- recognise and information need
- distinguish ways of addressing gap
- construct strategies for locating
- locate and access
- compare and evaluate
- organise
- apply and communicate
- synthesise and create.

These are underpinned by 'basic library skills' and 'IT skills'. The SCONUL model also includes the idea of levels of competence: novice, advanced beginner, competent, proficient and expert. Andretta (2005: 45–46) also highlights the need for an

> awareness and understanding of the way in which information is produced in the modern world, critical appraisal of the content and validity of information, some practical ideas of how information in the real world is acquired, managed, disseminated and exploited, particularly with knowledge of how appropriate professional groups use information in the workplace, in business and in the world of culture and arts.

This reinforces the idea that information literacy needs to be contextualised. The ACRL framework is more detailed and includes specific learning outcomes. As Andretta (2005) points out, the ACRL and ANZIIL frameworks emphasise the recursive knowledge construction process, which is more realistic and echoes the work of Marchionini (1995) discussed previously. Although the overall process has a linear quality – a beginning and an end – the actual experience of learners is likely to be highly iterative and 'messy' as they gradually construct meaning through their interaction with the information environment. In the initial stages of a project, learners become familiar with a topic and the general domain. Then they gain focus and define their information needs more precisely, often requiring access to information sources – artefacts and people; this is not usually a discrete process set outside the 'location and access' activity. Initial sources are most likely to provide general orientation and provide an overview; for example, they are classic texts and encyclopaedias, and more populist sources such as news bulletins, the trade press or magazines, rather than in-depth subject-specific sources such as academic journals. Choice and type of sources depend on the expertise of the learner, so the stylised 'distinguish the gap' followed by 'locate and access' found in many definitions of information literacy over simplifies what tends to happen in practice. In fact if this is conveyed as 'true' to the learner they may be frustrated by the iterative, 'messy', trial and error reality. Nevertheless these frameworks, which stem from the educational context, are useful for teachers of information literacy as they highlight processes.

Returning to the non-educational context, studies that focus on information literacy in the workplace are relatively few. However, studies that fall under the heading of people's 'information behaviour', 'information needs' or 'information seeking' do reveal, albeit indirectly, the information literacy needs of particular social groups. Lloyd's exploration of the information literacy of firemen is one exception. Lloyd sees information literacy as 'deeply connected with peoples' formal and informal meaning-making activities' (Lloyd, 2007: 570). The 'unembodied novice' interacts with the information landscape around them 'to draw meaning from this through engagement and experience with information... from complex contextualised practice, processes and interactions that enable access to social, physical and textual sites of knowledge'. Becoming a part of a community of firefighters involves moving from a position where information literacy is an 'institutionally recognised construct of practice [lessons to be learnt] to an embodied and collective understanding of practice and profession' (2007: 571) – to become a part of that community and possibly an 'expert'. Levels of expertise, as indicated earlier, will have a bearing on the information literacy needs of the learner. The expert is likely to be information literate in their domain. But, they may not be conscious of these skills and knowledge, being what Race (2001a) calls 'unconsciously competent', rather than unconsciously incompetent, and may find it hard to transfer them to or encourage them in others.

Educators, who often have experienced a lengthy education, sometimes undertaking research, have generally become relatively information literate but have not had the opportunity to unpick and concretise these skills to become 'consciously competent'. Yes, they know what they want in learners, in particular, learners who can work independently, identify related material and draw on this previous work to be able to review it analytically and critically and apply new ideas to other related contexts. But they do not necessarily know how to foster these skills nor are they conscious of the individual skills and processes that will enable this to happen. In fact, due to the constantly changing learning and information environment as well as changing norms, the educators need to be able to practise a high degree of information literacy themselves to keep up to date – and probably would benefit from training.

Many activities are associated with an information environment of one kind or another and the ability to access and make use of this landscape is fundamental. The artefacts mediate between the learner and their objectives. These objectives are associated with actions, which are defined by the community (Widen-Wulff and Davenport, 2007). Hence, a fundamental part of teaching information literacy is to enable the learner to become familiar with this landscape. The landscape has physical characteristics and properties. It can be aural, textual or image based. There are tools in the landscape that help to organise and provide access to information such as filing cabinets, and in the electronic domain, databases, which may store indexes to other documents such as HTML documents on the World Wide Web. These resources may be available freely or through subscription. For example, to access the full text of academic journal articles or market research reports requires subscription and hence careful evaluation is required of the often competing resources and services in terms of cost, coverage and functionality before a contract is signed. Increasingly, through the open access initiative a wider range of authoritative sources are becoming available without charge. A similar initiative is happening in relation to software and applications as a result of the open source initiative. However, it should be borne in mind that these services are not really free since time is required to integrate them in one's work environment; support and maybe training is required to use them.

There is a host of information tools, including traditional paper-based items and electronic tools, such as indexes. But they can also include social media such as those that help archive and share resources (such as social bookmarking sites like Delicious), video (such as YouTube), images (such as Flickr), personal diaries (blogs) and places where people can collaboratively discuss and publish (wikis). The most effective 'tool' or 'source' is, of course, other people. In fact people tend to be the most significant source of learning whether formally or informally. This is not surprising since, as we have argued earlier, learning is a social activity and learners are in a sense part of a community of 'fellow travellers' or learners in a shared community of practice. People can filter, synthesise and package information in the most appropriate way for the learner. When we are talking to someone, we govern what we say, and how we say it is likely to depend on our perception of what that person wants or needs to know and their ability to use the information. In other words we can personalise information in 'real time'.

The information landscape gives access to the shared meanings, understandings and thinking that enable learning and the ability to 'do' tasks of importance to the community. One such task is to create new information artefacts that communicate the new information. The features in the landscape also provide the mechanisms by which the individual can communicate to the wider community. Learning what is available and how to use it is a fundamental part of information literacy.

We have of course been aware of these tools and made great efforts to store and make available these artefacts. This has been the role of libraries. Teaching information literacy in the past primarily focused on teaching people how to find the artefacts in the library and has only recently started to address the wider processes associated with defining needs, managing information or communicating information. This often takes the form of creating lists that relate to specific disciplines (in higher education) and other communities of practice such as corporate financiers. Particular emphasis has been placed on the evaluation of sources and the ethical issues surrounding the use of information such as copyright and the dangers of plagiarism. However, teaching has often taken place in an abstract way, focusing on how to use a particular tool rather than on the goals of the community and enabling people to achieve their objectives. This has made it difficult for learners to relate to the teaching and learners are seldom able to transfer these skills into practice.

This is why over recent years we have seen a general consensus that in higher education information literacy teaching should be embedded in the curriculum. Unfortunately the learning institutions and even some academics have not fully understood the nature of information literacy or the role it plays in learning and becoming a member of a profession. This has tended to lead to short, discrete slots being assigned to information literacy, which generally only provide enough time to demonstrate information resources in isolation from the wider learning context. As a result, these interventions tend to focus on the features rather than the benefits of the resource. This may partly be because from the librarian's perspective understanding and evaluating the functionality of information resources is a key part of a librarian's role and their training.

As indicated above, other factors that may affect the information needs of learners and their information literacy include age, wealth and time. Demographic factors such as age and gender have been shown to have an impact on information literacy and information-seeking behaviour (Ford, 2004). Ford, Miller and Moss (2001) showed that although females tend to have a verbaliser cognitive style, associated with a high level of critical thinking, they are likely to be relatively poor in their retrieval performance. However, these issues are not entirely deterministic and the nature of the problem and the context within which these problems arise and are resolved is far more significant. Older people, for example, may be as adept at using technology as younger people and the phrase 'silver surfers' is used to describe older people who are heavy users of the internet.

Demography and information literacy

Demographics may affect information literacy and training interventions. It has been found, for example, that older people tend to prefer to be trained by older people. One of the factors that may be a barrier to learning to be information and e-literate for older people is that older people may not have much previous experience of the current information technologies. As a result they will have little previous knowledge to build on and they may be unfamiliar with the language of ICT or electronic information sources. A consequence is that they tend to have to learn new knowledge by rote, writing down the exact sequence of steps to achieve a goal rather than being able to apply general knowledge to new situations. This leads to feelings of uncertainty and helplessness when the system does not perform as expected.

Wealth may have an impact on a person's information literacy. For example there is a common assumption among some e-learning developers and designers that everyone has access to the internet (Rogerson and McPherson, 2005). In fact this is not the case and the term 'digital divide' has been used to describe the phenomenon whereby some people in the world because of socio-economic disparities between individuals and groups do not have access to technology (or electricity for that matter) and hence cannot make use of ICT (Averweg and Greyling, 2009). In some cases this may coincide with a lack of literacy, which in turn limits the opportunity for individuals to learn independently since they are primarily dependent on face-to-face oral communication. Nevertheless, as mentioned earlier, the processes associated with learning in a literate culture can also be applied to a primarily oral culture; a systematic approach to questioning, seeking and using information can still be enhanced. In fact, a range of aural and visual means of becoming informed are applied in such situations. Radio or social drama have been used to give access to learning from outside the local community. In Africa and other parts of the world plays are used to convey knowledge about a host of topics such as HIV and Aids. In India television 'soaps' are used for similar purposes. The advent of wireless communication is also having an impact in these contexts. For example in Nigeria crop prices are regularly updated and communicated via mobile phones to farmers. This helps to ensure that farmers are not misled by middle men and can command an appropriate price for their produce. It can also help farmers choose where to sell their produce. In southern India people have experimented with using the video facility on mobile phones. Here effective approaches to animal husbandry are captured on video, by the farmer, on a mobile phone. The video is then stored and can be accessed and shared by mobile phone within the community of practitioners. Hence part of being information literate in this context is to be aware of these possibilities and to be able to use the technology to communicate and access information.

Culture and information literacy

Culture can also have an impact on the teaching and learning of information literacy. Culture is used here to encompass the wider set of ideas, attitudes and norms that tend to influence people's information behaviour. The term culture could be used, for example, when discussing a corporate culture or a culture that stems from a specific educational system. For example, in higher education in the UK we find that some students from overseas have experienced a highly didactic, teacher-centred, approach to teaching and learning. These students tend to have little experience of learning independently and in extreme cases they have been actively discouraged to seek alternative sources of learning. They tend to assume that there is one authoritative text, find it difficult to synthesise different views and are very reluctant to make their own judgement and critique texts.

There are of course exceptions where people have, perhaps, attended private schools offering a more liberal education or where the lack of resources has led to students making a huge effort to source material and learn independently. These students have developed their own independent learning skills. In other cases, in response to the great value placed on learning by their parents, students have developed independent learning skills. However, these people tend to be the exception and those coming from these didactic learning environments tend to be passive recipients of learning, expecting all the information necessary for their education to be provided by the teacher. This is exacerbated in situations where information resources, whether paper based or electronic, are limited and class sizes are large. In some cases independent study and critical thinking has been actively discouraged and few opportunities are made for people to pull together, synthesise and critically evaluate information. One PhD student described a situation in his schooling where a fellow student was actually punished for introducing material that had not been provided by the teacher in that school. This makes becoming information literate challenging. The teacher of information literacy therefore needs to be aware of the learning culture that the learner may have come from and its implication for the learner.

In South Africa, information literacy training specifically tried to address this issue (Underwood, 2002). Following the end of apartheid there was a widening in participation in higher education, but the new students to a great extent came from environments where access to information was limited. They were unused to the academic study norms and having to deal with a wide range of unfamiliar sources. Similarly, in the UK (although the situation is obviously less extreme), the government's desire to enrol a larger proportion of the population into higher education has been a major driver behind the information literacy movement, as there are now students going in to higher education from backgrounds where there is less of a culture of using published information resources independently, such as libraries. In fact, during the apartheid years people who were described as 'non-white' by the ruling regime were not allowed access to such services.

Other factors have led to the need for information literacy initiatives in higher education in the UK. Since the 1980s these have included a greater emphasis on assessment (both of the learner and the school) plus the sheer quantity of material in the curriculum that teachers have had to show they have taught. This has led to accusations of spoon-feeding and resulted in pragmatic learning styles. This is supported by a recent unpublished study (Smith, 2009) where it was found that pupils' main perception of information in secondary schools is something that is given to them and associated with facts that they need to know rather than something they seek. This has a negative impact on their information literacy and tends to lead to shallow rather than deep learning. This provides a challenge for teachers who are trying to encourage information literacy and independent learning. This is ironic bearing in mind the current attention paid to human capital and the evolving knowledge-based information society discussed in the introduction.

In organisations similar factors influence information literacy. Hierarchical, authoritarian organisations are less likely to value the ideas and knowledge of people lower down in the organisation, such as those who may have insights resulting from their practical experience and daily contact with products, customers and production processes. This is unlike the Japanese industrial practice where factory floor knowledge is valued, or the Xerox example mentioned earlier.

Another cultural aspect of learners that has received much publicity in the UK, relevant to the teaching of information literacy, is the 'nature' of young learners. Various terms have been used to describe them, including the 'digital natives', the 'net generation', the 'Google generation', the 'nintendo generation', the 'Y generation' and 'millennials'. The 'new' learners have been characterised (Howe and Strauss, 2000; Prensky, 2001; Windham, 2005) as being pragmatic (only doing what is necessary to achieve reward or concrete outcomes); being unable to concentrate for long periods of time; wanting an active learning environment where they can access learning when they want to, in a form they want (brief, colourful, little text, to the point, using multimedia); liking multitasking; and expecting learning to be entertaining. The learners are also characterised as highly gregarious, enjoying social interaction and being part of a social cohort. The latter may have always been the case; however, expertise in branding associated with the consumer society and its attendant effective marketing may have exaggerated this feeling of alliance with a group, driven perhaps by the commercial need to segment and create new markets. This is evident in the transient fashions for applications such as Facebook, Beebo and MySpace, which tend to correlate with specific age groups. Whether or not the characteristics of the young learner are genuinely new, as teachers we should make sure our interventions relate to these learners.

Most people, whatever their age or background, get bored and lose attention after 20 minutes of listening to a speaker who uses the old-fashioned lecturing style that many of us were used to in our school and university days. We would argue that the characteristics of the learner have probably not changed as much as is claimed. Zipf's (1949) law, which has been cited for many years, states that people's information seeking is governed by the least effort it will take them to achieve an expected result. In other words people will put in the minimum effort to achieve an outcome. It has been claimed that in the past we were different. The difference is that we knew no different and had no choice but to use what was standard practice. Teacher centred and often dull, single media delivery was the norm. Nowadays younger people have choice in how they learn and are presented with information and learning in a variety of forms and media – video, animation, music, printed text, web text, chat etc. via phones, the internet, television, theatre and magazines, with increased professionalism; so expectations are high.

A recent study, known as the CIBER report (UCL, 2008), attempted to predict the nature of researchers of the future and provided an indication of current behaviour of students through logging their use of electronic resources and interviews (Rowlands and Fieldhouse, 2007). It was found that young people scan online pages rapidly, and click on hypertext links rather than reading sequentially. They make little use of advanced search features, assuming that search engines 'understand' their queries. They tend to move rapidly from page to page, spending little time reading and digesting information, and have difficulty making relevance judgements. When making judgements, they are based on the presence or absence of words exactly describing the search topic.

To what extent these observations are specific to the Google generation, as implied, is debatable. To some extent they reflect the environment within which learners operate – the learner is doing what the technological environment allows. Therefore one cannot help wondering whether previous generations were really so different and if the implied beliefs about how they were more engaged and rigorous in their use of information and learning are idealised. It may have been true that higher education learners were willing to sit and listen to lectures where the lecturer read from notes and made no use of other media, but this was not because learners were fundamentally different then from the learners of today. This method of teaching was accepted because learners had experienced little else – it was the norm that they accepted. Perhaps learners of previous generations scanned and flicked through sources just as commonly as learners today scan online pages, only occasionally reading any text at length. Today, lengthy reading may also take place offline using printed hard copy.

The CIBER report monitored what people did and not whether fundamental changes in learning style had taken place or would take place in the future. The high use of links in the document is to be expected since this is a function of the system and a way of navigating to other potentially relevant material. In the past it would have been far more laborious – for example, physically searching out works referenced in the physical text. In fact the CIBER report did throw doubt on a number of common, negative, perceptions about the Google generation. The authors found that these learners were impatient about delays and did not necessarily learn computer skills by trial and error, a popular myth. It is likely that the way people learn, for example through trial and error, formal instruction, or the use of tutorials, is more likely to vary according to their learning style rather than their 'generation'.

The CIBER study also found that learners of the Google generation were not expert searchers, as might have been expected of people who have had a long exposure to search engines. From the perspective of a teacher of information retrieval and information literacy this was not surprising. These learners are used to the apparent and much advocated simplicity of finding information via search engines and have not been taught search methods in their education. The learners in the study did cut and paste, which is hardly surprising since it is so easy to do in the electronic domain. This 'cut and paste' behaviour was evident in Smith and Hepworth's (2007) study, which found that 49 per cent of the young learners who were surveyed cut and pasted material into their study report without reading it. The root cause of this was not that they were inherently lazy or duplicitous but because of a lack of engagement with the independent research task. As topics were imposed on them, they took little time to engage with the task, such as by discussing a topic and identifying research questions. In addition there was little support while learners searched for information. This meant that they were not made aware of key aspects of the search process, which led to them feeling insecure about the process as they did not understand how to go about it. This cut and paste behaviour was also exacerbated by the learners only being rewarded for the content and layout of the final report and not for the information literacies associated with carrying out independent research. They were not rewarded for the way they defined the topic or the clarity or appropriateness of the questions they chose to investigate, or whether they had chosen their sources wisely or used them in the most effective way.

One difference between the behaviour of current learners and learners in the past is that the majority of information seeking today takes place in the electronic domain and simple-to-use search engines tend to dominate the information-seeking process. OCLC's (2006) study showed that 89 per cent of college students used search engines to begin an information search. This is not surprising since a high proportion of students have access to the internet and this is a tool they were familiar with. This is not necessarily a bad thing, but these findings imply that students do not use other sources such as hard copy publications, and it leads one to wonder how they used the search engines. They may have used them effectively to find a broad range of electronic sources. The impression given from this kind of research is that learners take whatever they find that seems to answer the question they are considering and do not consciously think about the range of sources they could obtain via the internet. For example, learners could consciously decide to use Wikipedia to orientate them to a subject but then use a more detailed and authoritative source to get more reliable depth. The general implication of the CIBER and OCLC studies and other related work is that younger people (probably like the majority of people in society) are not highly information literate.

The need for information literacy training is therefore evident. This is particularly the case because of the information-intensive nature of today's society and the exponential increase in available information. Recently we have also seen an increase in 'non-traditional outlets for research such as institutional repositories, blogs, wikis and personal websites' (Rowlands and Fieldhouse, 2007), which have led to more opportunity for independent learning. This could be useful in the teaching context since the glut of information of varying quality could be used to show learners the need to appreciate the value of putting more effort into looking for 'good' information. However, Rowlands and Fieldhouse recognise a significant challenge: 'They [the Google generation] simply do not recognise that they have a problem' (2007: 24).

Another cultural phenomenon in the UK is that learners are increasingly perceived and perceive themselves as consumers of education, particularly in higher education where they now have to pay tuition fees. They expect the learning experience to meet their needs, wants and desires. In addition they have high expectations, expecting learning to be challenging, exciting and possibly fun. They do not expect to learn passively. This trend is likely to continue as educators in primary and secondary schools in the UK gradually introduce more active forms of learning, use materials presented in a more imaginative way, and draw on the available ICTs and, in general, create learning and teaching that relates to the needs of the learner, including, for example, their individual learning style. It is likely that, bearing in mind our comments about the current tendency to 'spoon-feed' secondary school children, resulting in pragmatic learners, that there will be a shift away from assessment-driven learning in schools to a more flexible approach where independent learning is encouraged. In fact, this is already taking place. A combination of these factors will lead to even greater emphasis on the need to create appropriate information literacy learning environments. On a positive note, the tools that we have available, particularly the Web 2.0 technologies, also provide an opportunity to make the learning of information literacy fit the profile of the learner. This is evident from Godwin and Parker's (2008) book, which discusses the role of Web 2.0 in the information literacy teacher's armoury.

Cultural and social norms that may span generations, geographical areas and organisational contexts can be seen to influence learners and their information literacy. Teachers of information literacy therefore need to be aware of the information landscape, the information norms and attitudes of the people they are helping, and the roles, goals and tasks that underpin their need to become information literate whether in the educational, commercial or civil society context.

Conclusion

Trainers, teachers and facilitators of information literacy have a lot to take on board if we wish to develop effective learning interventions. We need:

- to be aware of the embodied nature of learning and how the physicality of learners can have an impact on learning
- to be aware of the behavioural and cognitive aspects of their learning experience and of how they make sense of reality
- to understand the significance of cultural and social contexts and how they influence learning.

Figure 6.1   The learning spectrum

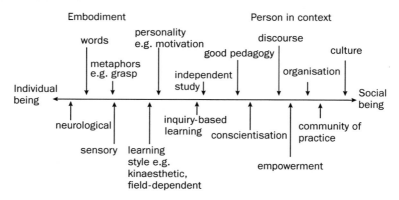

Each of these dimensions enables us to view learners and the learning intervention from different perspectives and should give us ideas about how to design effective learning interventions, and relate them to the needs of the learner and their capacity to learn.

There is therefore a spectrum of ideas that bear on our perception of the learner, and a range of explanations for what motivates learning. Figure 6.1 represents this spectrum, which is populated with keywords that imply different ways of viewing the learner. The middle line implies that there is a continuum of ideas. On the left-hand side the learner is viewed primarily as an individual, a learning organism. Here the learner is seen as a physical being and learning is an embodied experience dependent on the physical aspects of learner. Emphasis is therefore given to the neurological and sensory nature of the learner, aspects of which can have a bearing on the way people learn and the learning environments we create. On the right-hand side the learners are perceived primarily as social and cultural beings. Here the social nature of the learner and the need to be a part of a learning community is given importance. Communication, discourse and the impact of different environments on learning are seen to be fundamental. The relationship between knowledge, the capability to learn independently, and power also reside here. At this end of the spectrum the cultural context of the learner, including the learning norms associated with a particular community or society, are given more significance. We therefore believe that becoming aware of the continuum illustrated in Figure 6.1, and the factors that impinge on it, is a first step towards designing effective information literacy learning and teaching interventions.

Part 2:
Teaching interventions

7

Introduction

Part 2 describes the ways in which the theories of how people learn can be applied to teaching and learning interventions that foster information literacy. These interventions address, to varying degrees, the implications of the knowledge of learning discussed in Part 1. They have been chosen because they reflect good practice and the ideas that were elaborated in Part 1. Ideally all aspects of how people learn and effective pedagogy outlined in Part 1 should be considered if not incorporated in any information literacy intervention. These interventions should therefore provide a guide that can be used to develop teaching and learning, but will need to be adapted to different contexts. Ideally they would be embedded within other teaching and learning interventions, for example, integrated within a specific inquiry-based task, such as preparing a presentation on a topic in school or conducting research at university. Alternatively, they could be adapted to workplace human resource capacity-building exercises, such as improving people's ability to scan the business environment or identify new opportunities. Or, they could be applied to situations where people are dealing with life situations. Note that the communication of information is not addressed here – how to design posters, write reports and so on. These skills are amply covered in study skills guides.

There are four interventions, each relating to how people perceive their interaction with information and information literacy. This division of interventions is expedient and driven by the need to break down the overall process into chunks that have some internal consistency and can be taught. In real life it is likely that aspects of each of these interventions will take place at the same time.

Each intervention is structured along similar lines identifying the purpose, context, underlying pedagogy, learning outcomes and specifics of the learning intervention. A brief description of other related learning interventions is included. As each intervention is treated in isolation, there is some repetition between the various interventions, but not too much. In fact, it was hard to separate the different interventions and to some extent the success of any one intervention may depend on learners having experienced the other interventions. The divide between different aspects of information literacy such as identifying need, and locating and accessing material (as has been stated in Part 1) are high-level abstractions of the learning process and do not necessarily relate to how the learner experiences 'finding out'. These abstractions tend to be intertwined, highly iterative and relatively 'messy', whereas in the past most information literacy teaching tended to be a compartmentalised process. In fact the overall process of finding out may have a linear structure at a high level, but elements within it are iterative, especially in the early stages. Learning is also a continuous process and the same material may have a different meaning or impact at a different time. A novice is unlikely to appreciate the nuances that someone who has spent a lot of time thinking and doing in a particular domain, an expert, does. There is therefore a tension between teaching and learning information literacy, that is, between finding a practical way to encourage information literacy and relating this to the actual experience of the learner.

Three broad terms – 'behaviour', 'cognitive' and 'constructivist' – are used to tease out how people are being encouraged to learn. 'Behaviour' is used to encompass sensory aspects of learning (sight, touch, feelings), and characteristics of learners, such as learning style and learning through doing. The latter implies a behaviourist emphasis – learning through experience, reflection and practice. 'Cognitive' relates to the cognition of the learner in terms of thinking skills and what they need to know. It tends to incorporate reflection and the development of metacognitive knowledge. 'Constructivist' relates to both cognitive constructivism – whereby people make sense and build up a cognitive map of a subject, system and so on – as well as social constructivism. Social constructivism emphasises the social and cultural aspects of learning. It tends to involve discourse, discussion, cultural and social values, and norms and systems associated with experiencing the world as a social being and where meaning is socially constructed.

Again it is sometimes difficult to distinguish one term from another. Is cognitive constructivism not an aspect of the cognitive? People who label themselves as one or the other would probably react strongly to being lumped under another heading – specifying their epistemological grounding as very different. Cognitive constructivists tend to assume an interpretivist orientation, and sometimes call themselves social constructivists, where cognitivists who focus on mental constructs may assume a positivist stance. Cognitive constructivists tend to allude to the individual process of sense-making and how thoughts, meanings and 'mental maps' are an individual response to experience. In contrast, purely cognitive perspectives tend to focus on what are assumed to be underlying cognitive processes and structures that are common to all people and in a sense 'hard-wired' in the brain. When the word behaviour is used people tend to assume that one is taking a behaviourist orientation to teaching and learning, but this is not necessarily the case.

These confusions and complexities are compounded by the vagaries of language. In the area of people's information behaviour and studies of information seeking the same words are sometimes used to refer to different things. For example 'browsing' is used to talk about the physical process of moving one's eyes across a collection. It is also used to talk about the mental process of recognising items of interest or relevance out of many. The same terms tend to be used for both the cognitive and behavioural aspects of the process.

Figure 7.1 identifies the different ways people learn. From a practical point of view the diagram should help teachers or facilitators think about learning interventions. For example, we need to consider whether the learning is primarily sensory, focusing on how we interact physically with an information system, or social, focusing on the norms and values associated with information use. The diagram has implications for how interventions are implemented. For example, an intervention may require 'hands-on' exercises so that the physical mechanics of use become embedded, or might require reflection so as to develop metacognition. The emotional

Figure 7.1 How people learn

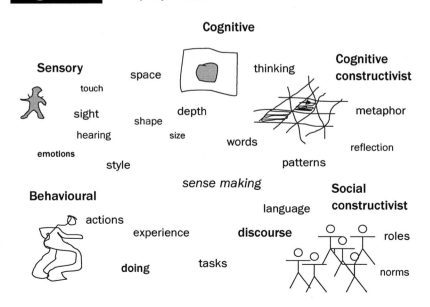

dimension may be important, for example recognising the feelings of uncertainty and confusion associated with starting to research an unfamiliar topic. Or discussion may be the key activity, where a consensual understanding of definitions and shared values is achieved.

The following part of the book provides examples of teaching interventions that cover key aspects of information literacy. The information literacy interventions are clustered under broad headings or aspects of information literacy:

- *Learning intervention 1*: knowledge of learners' information needs and identifying that aspect of their knowledge base learners want to develop. This section enables the teacher to develop learners' ability to 'map' and define their information needs, identify the subject domain and the language and key concepts associated with the domain, and think about what would be appropriate for the tasks they are undertaking and the purpose of their learning.

- *Learning intervention 2*: knowledge of the 'information landscape'. This section enables the teacher to develop learners' knowledge of the range of sources of information that are available (people, information artefacts), their characteristics and the ability to choose appropriate sources.

- *Learning intervention 3*: knowledge of the acquisition of information or what could be termed 'connecting with information' in both a 'passive' and an 'active' way. This section enables the teacher to develop learners' knowledge of tools and places that give access to information, showing how to use them effectively and strategically, including describing their functionality and processes they need to be aware of.

- *Learning intervention 4*: knowledge of the application of information or use of information that has been found. This section enables the teacher to develop learners' ability to interact with, use and store the information they find.

- *Learning intervention 5*: The last 'intervention' differs from the previous four in that it combines aspects of knowledge of the 'information landscape', the 'acquisition of information' and the 'application or use of information'. This example provides an insight into incorporating information literacy in the workplace. Due to the nature of the workplace this is a highly integrated and holistic approach.

Each section is introduced with a discussion of the problems and challenges that learners commonly experience. Within each broad section suggestions are provided to help a teacher design a specific learning intervention. Each teaching intervention is structured in the following way:

- *Title and introduction*: the aspect of information literacy that is covered and the overall rationale for the intervention
- *Purpose*: an indication of what should be achieved
- *Context*: who will be involved in the learning and an overview of the setting plus the expected level of knowledge of the learner
- *Physical environment*: the characteristics of the learning environment (electronic, paper based, blended electronic and paper based, neither electronic nor paper based); the equipment and other physical resources required, including information resources
- *The underlying pedagogy*: whether the teacher is taking a behavioural, cognitive or constructivist (cognitive or social) approach, and specific pedagogic techniques such as scaffolding, peer-to-peer learning or reflective practice. A behavioural approach incorporates the 'sensory' nature of learning, for example, by paying attention to the look and feel of an interface, the layout and design, and considering whether it recognises the emotional state of the learner and whether it is accessible by people with different abilities. This approach highlights the physical process of interacting with information. The cognitive approach focuses on thinking processes, such as understanding search strategies that enable the broadening and narrowing of a search, and the critical thinking skills associated with evaluating and processing information, such as synthesis or induction. The cognitive constructivist approach emphasises the 'sense making' and building of mental maps that help orientate learners to the domain and information resources. The social constructivist approach dwells on the social nature of learning and information, such as who constructed it and why, and the values attached to it.
- *Levels of complexity*: the implications of different levels of knowledge and experience. For example, distinctions are made between what can be expected of young learners and older learners, and challenges they are likely to experience.
- *Methods of assessment and learning outcomes*: what the learner should be able to do and has learnt as a result of the intervention (although where a participative, action research approach is taken the outcomes may not be exactly what the teacher envisaged). Ways of assessing outcomes are included.

- *Main example of the intervention followed by other alternatives in different contexts*: a description of how the training takes place, the sequence of events, from the scaffolded introduction to the final stages of reflection; suggested timings may be given, which can be shortened or lengthened depending on the situation.

Although the structure of interventions may vary, from previous experience, we have found that the more time spent discussing a task, encouraging learners to reflect on their previous relevant knowledge, generating their own questions and critically reflecting on the process, highlighting and discussing problems and solutions, the better. Peer-to-peer learning through presentation of the overall experience and learning further deepens learning and the development of metacognitive skills that can be applied in similar situations.

The learning environment

Before any information literacy intervention takes place a learning 'space' should be set up with the learner. This would be a space or portfolio where the learner would keep material associated with the learning experience, including lists of key terms, vocabulary, search strategies and sources (artefacts, organisations, people, places; text, moving and still images, figures, audio, notes, mind maps or visualisations, articles, web pages and references). In a paper-based environment this would mean creating folders, files or card catalogues (to index material). In the electronic environment this would mean creating a 'desk top', perhaps personalised using a system like iGoogle to embed useful sources such as news feeds (RSS feeds) and links to useful information sources (databases, websites). Within this space a structure (reflecting the tasks of the learner) of electronic folders and sub-folders to store information would need to be created. The labels used to organise this personal library would evolve, to a great extent, as the domain is mapped.

Systems for storing and locating information should be developed that enable efficient use of what is found and learnt. How this would be done would depend on the context. Orna and Stevens (2000) provide a good overview of information management techniques in the formal learning and academic research environment. Learners should be familiar with information management tools such as databases (that provide access to information and can be used to store information such as references, notes and so on), and information processing tools such as word processing, mind mapping, social bookmarking, annotation and collaborative software.

Ideally a basic personal information management environment would be created initially. Familiarity with the range of tools ('digital literacy') and artefacts would be incorporated in the information literacy interventions. This would mean that learning about these tools would be contextualised and purposeful.

The reflective practitioner

The practice of teaching does not stop when the interventions have been delivered and the session comes to an end. We, as practitioners, still have work to do. We will come away from the session, as do our students or trainees, with feelings about how the session went: what worked well and what did not, what should be expanded and what might to be left out next time. In effect, what begins to happen in our own minds is the process of reflection. Indeed, to learn anything the process of reflection is a necessity and we need to harness it and turn it to our advantage. In doing this we can address the questions: are our learning outcomes satisfying institutional demands?, are we developing and improving our own practice? and, last but not least, are we having an impact on our learners?

From an institutional perspective we need to show that our teaching aims are being achieved and provide evidence to show this. We need to know our teaching strengths and weaknesses, and how to evaluate innovations (Hounsell, 1999) such as those recommended in this book. This process is difficult because there does not appear to be agreement on what constitutes a good teacher. However, Trigwell (2001) helpfully argues that good teaching is carried out in a holistic, dynamic, reflective and constantly evolving manner. There are many methods we can adopt in order to achieve this approach, for example, by evaluating feedback from a number of sources: self-generated (teaching diary), from colleagues (as peers or mentors), from students (incidental feedback during a teaching session and/or from questionnaires), and/or from management (annual review and appraisal). Evaluation of teaching should be developmental and involve others (Bell, 2001).

To realise this aim we suggest a reflective process, which Schon describes as 'a dialogue of thinking and doing through which I become more skilled' (Schon, 1987: 31), and envisage it as a cycle as recommended by Gibbs (1998a: 7) (Figure 7.2).

Like information literacy and models of learning this is only an abstract structure and there are a number of things that we must do in order to make this a real reflective experience. It must become an integral part of

Figure 7.2 Reflective practice cycle

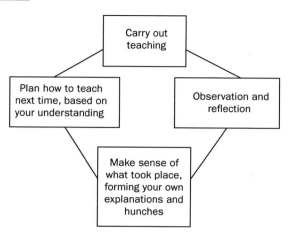

our work as recommended by Gibbs (1998b), where we move round the cycle many times and use a number of mechanisms (student, incidental, peer observation and self-generated feedback) to make it work. This process should take place within the wider learning context and combine teachers' thinking, planning and teaching strategies to make the students they teach the primary focus of their reflections (Trigwell, 2001).

In some of our teaching we use feedback sheets devised by faculty and it is important that teachers spend some time interpreting and responding to this feedback rather than simply gathering it. However, we must be mindful that student ratings do not always reflect teaching effectiveness or quality (Shevlin et al., 2000) and may depend on lecturer characteristics (Worthington, 2002).

Bearing this in mind, we suggest that practitioners engage in peer observation to assist their development as reflective practitioners because we argue that this will improve their reflective process. Informal peer observation can aid reflective practice and improve teaching interventions. There are many examples of the peer observation process; we recommend the approach put forward in Fry, Ketteridge and Marshall (1999). It is also worth considering keeping a teaching diary to enable you to produce self-generated feedback to aid reflective practice. This is particularly helpful when swift changes to delivery are necessary, for example, when a number of repeat sessions are timetabled to follow each other immediately, a frequent occurrence for information professionals teaching on core modules with many students.

8

Learning intervention 1: Understanding learners' information needs and identifying the knowledge base that the learner wants to develop

Without developing this aspect of information literacy and the ability for learners to understand their information needs and identify that aspect of their knowledge base they want to develop, subsequent independent learning is difficult and often frustrating. Learners need to define what they want to find out about in the subject area and the language associated with it. Where relatively information-intensive decisions need to be taken, if they do not define their needs, people tend to reinvent the wheel and miss relevant knowledge, information and data that may inform them and aid the completion of a task. To define their needs, learners should have in their minds either purposefully stored and structured and related knowledge of a domain, or a general awareness of the domain that they are working in. In some situations this would be useful even if this knowledge is only consciously applied later in the learning process as a kind of general awareness that aids serendipity and recognition of new ideas.

Purpose

- Mapping the subject domain, gaining an overview of areas of knowledge that are important in that domain and how they relate to each other.

- Knowing the words and phrases (the language) used to describe the subject domain (language related to the domain in terms of subject matter where people are working and trying to resolve problems and achieve certain objectives).

- Identifying a focus for research and learning.

- Determining information needs, areas to be aware of and gaps in knowledge.

- Becoming familiar with the sources of information that help them get orientated to the topic and help map the domain.

Context

This intervention could be carried out with people of almost any level of ability or age and in any subject domain. It could use an electronic or paper-based environment. It could also be undertaken using physical objects such as plants, stones, artefacts and scenery, where types of objects and their characteristics are clustered and given descriptions, and patterns and gaps in knowledge identified. Similar exercises could be carried out in any of these environments.

Physical learning environment

General

Flip charts; whiteboard, blackboard or smartboard; Post-it notes; coloured pens and pencils.

Electronic learning environment

Personal computer (ideally a maximum of three people to one PC). Where access is very restricted access time needs to be planned and the intervention should take place over a more extended period of time. In the education sector ideally every learner will have their own device such as handheld or netbook devices or even a mobile phone with World Wide Web access. There should be access to a communications network and applications, including virtual learning environments, word processing, mind mapping, and internet access to the World Wide Web or local information stores. The WWW is used to access encyclopaedias, dictionaries, thesauri, databases and organisations that either host or provide links to information and people. The sources accessed tend to be those that can provide a good overview and orientate the learner to the subject. Radio or mobile phones can play a role in facilitating access to information.

Paper-based learning environment

The same as above excluding the electronic tools but including paper-based encyclopaedias, dictionaries and thesauri if possible.

Blended learning environment

A combination of the two described above.

Non-electronic or paper-based learning environment

Physical objects need to be provided or collected by the learners or observed in the environment. People need to be identified for learners to contact and help map the domain.

The underlying pedagogy

The learning intervention focuses primarily on the cognitive and constructivist nature of learning. However, there is a behavioural component. As you will see from the description of the teaching intervention, the intervention will draw and build on prior knowledge. It will be scaffolded and incorporate reflection.

The learning intervention tends to include a facilitator, people working individually and in groups, possibly with some organisational structure, such as team leaders, scribe and so on. Discussion and presentations take place.

Useful metaphors include: 'mapping', 'mapping the domain', 'charting', 'inside or outside the domain', 'the flow of ideas', 'pools' of knowledge, 'the sea of information', 'cast adrift', 'lost' and 'not knowing where one's going'.

Initial stages of mapping a topic and identifying what we are interested in or the precise question we are trying to answer is often very difficult and associated with feelings of uncertainty and frustration, particularly for the novice. Exploring and bringing to the foreground previous knowledge and showing how the new knowledge builds on this aids confidence.

Behavioural learning

The behavioural learning in this intervention includes the ability to visualise a domain using either a mind map, a hierarchical tree structure, Venn diagrams or a concept table, tag cloud or scatter diagram. Different ways of visualising the domain are likely to appeal to learners with different learning styles. They will learn about the orientation sources available (World Wide Web search engines, subject gateways, subject portals, encyclopaedias, organisational sites and so on), and how to access such sources and structure simple searches, as well as to browse retrieved items and use the structure of the information sources such as contents pages and indexes to get an overview of the domain.

Learning outcomes stem from this, including knowledge of those sources that aid orientation, such as encyclopaedias and thesauri, and being able to search these sources using broad terms and, possibly, controlled vocabulary with an emphasis on search techniques that lead to 'casting a wide net', such as the Boolean OR. Alternatively, a search could be limited to the title of documents and only the titles may be read, just to get an indication of the extent to which a topic is covered.

From an emotional or affective viewpoint, starting to become familiar with a new domain is daunting and associated with feelings of uncertainty. Not being able to see the wood for the trees is often a frustrating experience. Identifying a focus for research is difficult and determining the aims and objectives, the research questions, of an independent study ('what exactly am I trying to find out about') and being able to define them succinctly is notoriously difficult even for people who are relatively knowledgeable about a subject. Ill-defined questions are a common source of subsequent problems, such as using inappropriate sources or overlooking relevant areas.

Cognitive learning

Cognitive learning includes thinking of terms related to the domain; identifying new terms through information seeking and using information resources; analysing, classifying and categorising and synthesising, as well as identifying relationships and distinctions between topics; and being able to apply labels to the domain in a systematic way. The learner should also develop metacognitive skills associated with understanding their information needs and identifying that aspect of their knowledge base that they want to develop.

Learning outcomes stem from this, as evidence of these skills is expected – the application of these thinking skills and a representation of this thinking, for example, a mind map. The complexity of the mind map and the number of sub-topics and terms depends on the breadth, depth and complexity of the topic – a simple topic may result in a simple mind map.

Constructivist learning

Cognitive constructivist learning, from an individual perspective, relates to building a mental map of the domain – making sense of the subject. Explaining and presenting this 'map' helps the learner concretise and internalise this world view. From a social constructivist perspective the learner is becoming aware of the socially accepted ontology of the domain. This develops through communication, including the learner presenting and discussing their conception of the domain, exchanging and defining meaning using the language and possibly reaching a consensus about how the topic can be defined and the appropriate sources of information. The learner works with others involved in the community of practice, whether other learners, the teacher or the wider academic or practitioner community – possibly via social media – to reach this consensus.

Learning outcomes stem from this, for example, the 'map', but also an appreciation of the value of the collaboration and learning from others and understanding how this may help to complete a task and, in this case, to see the world in different ways. In addition, an appreciation of the areas that concern the community of practice is gained.

Levels of complexity

Levels of complexity about learning expectations depend on three main factors: the depth of learners' knowledge of the subject domain; their knowledge of the related technology and systems for facilitating access to knowledge, data and information; and the extent and quality of their social networks.

Although a similar learning intervention could be applied to learners with different levels of expertise, a learner with limited knowledge of the subject domain has limited vocabulary to describe it. This applies to novices or young learners. Young learners have a limited vocabulary and are likely to produce a smaller network of terms. They may find it easier to identify vocabulary from lists of terms than independently thinking of terms, and make fewer distinctions between sub-topics. These learners have limited knowledge of information resources, and the extent of their social networks makes it more difficult for them to gain different perspectives.

The impact of having a limited number of terms that describe a topic will tend to limit the information the learner can find, especially when searching with electronic search tools that only retrieve information that mention the terms they ask it to look for.

Methods of assessment and learning outcomes

A fundamental choice needs to be made when designing methods of assessment: whether the assessment is carried out by an 'expert' or by peers. Peer assessment has been shown to lead peer-to-peer learning and can result in deeper learning – partly because the assessor is forced to reflect critically on the activity.

Quantifiable outcomes include:

- ability to complete a mind map and use a mind map, fishbone, hierarchical tree, Venn diagrams etc.
- identifying terms relevant to the domain
- ability to provide a comprehensive map of the domain
- ability to identify primary, secondary and tertiary topics within the domain and sub-topics
- listing a number of alternative terms or synonyms
- ability to use orientation 'tools' – number, appropriateness (relevance, coverage, authority) and orientation search techniques
- ability to work collaboratively (participation, co-operation and teamwork)
- ability to present (confidence, clarity and efficiency)
- ability to reflect and communicate what and how they have learnt and describe strategies that were useful, and how they would apply this knowledge to other situations.

These areas of assessment could be applied in the electronic or paper-based learning environments. Where neither is available emphasis is given to oral presentation and the collection and classification of physical objects according to their properties and relating these to the topic of inquiry. In this context visualisation of ideas can be carried out using the material world (soil, chalk, stones). The use of reference tools that enable orientation to a topic is not possible due, perhaps, to a lack of resources. However, other people would be likely to be an important source of 'orientation' information.

Examples of interventions

1 Example with Master's students

This case formed part of an information literacy intervention for students undertaking a Master's in Participation, Power and Social Change at the Institute of Development Studies in Brighton, UK. Students came from a mixed background. All were working in the development context either as a part of a non-governmental organisation (NGO) actively involved in helping to improve the wellbeing of people in a community or acting as a consultant to NGOs or working in government designing and implementing development programmes. They came with experience of development work but did not necessarily have an extensive knowledge of participation, power and social change. The group was very varied in their knowledge of formal information resources having tended, in the past, to depend on local knowledge. However, most had used Google but the majority were unfamiliar with electronic information retrieval systems found in UK academic libraries.

The course started with an explanation of the information literacy programme, identifying what we would do and what was expected, hence scaffolding the intervention. This progressed into a discussion of information literacy, knowledge and power as well as indicating how the programme would help the students to do well in a forthcoming assignment. This was intended to show the relevance of the task and this intervention, and to gain motivation. It was also intended to show that this was a participative learning session rather than passive teacher-centred learning, and that the students' ideas were valued. Figure 8.1 gives an indication of the 'engagement' discussion.

The structure of the three-hour session can be seen in Figure 8.2.

Figure 8.1   Engagement topics for intervention 1

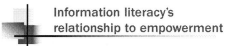

Information literacy's
relationship to empowerment

- **What are the PROS and CONS of the following statements:**
    - Independent, self directed, learning leads to empowerment.
    - Knowledge gives power.
    - Data, information and knowledge enables greater control over one's life.
    - We listen to all voices.

Figure 8.2   Structure of intervention 1

Agenda

- 2.00 Introduction
- 2.10 Information literacy and empowerment – students present
- 2.40 Mapping the information landscape – orientation tools
- 2.50 Mapping the PP&SC subject – students present
- 3.30 Break
- 3.40 Mapping your topic for the Analytical Paper – students present
- 4.15 Reflection – discussion – consolidate learning
- 5.00 Close

Prior to starting the task a metaphor was used to introduce the activity. This was to show that this was part of a wider process of discovery. Hence the 'journey' metaphor was used and a further geographic metaphor 'mapping the subject'. Students were asked to imagine the subject as a 'landscape' which was inhabited by clusters of knowledge, in a sense 'villages' that represented the interests of the community of practice.

The flip chart was used to draw the landscape (Figure 8.3). The journey metaphor set expectations showing that there was no direct route, and that students were likely to experience dead ends, retrace their steps – it was an iterative process – and that the task would be associated with feelings of uncertainty and frustration.

Figure 8.3   The landscape of intervention 1

Flip chart

- Flip chart
  - Journey of discovery
    - Different routes, dead ends
  - Iterative nature
    - Redefining, refining, retracing one's steps
  - Associated with thinking (cognitive skills), behaviour (doing skills), emotion (uncertainty, frustration, confidence)

Having set the scene students were introduced to orientation tools that would help them to start to get a feel for the general domain and their specific sub-topic (Figure 8.4). Prior to this, however, their previous knowledge was elicited. This indicated that their previous knowledge was valued, helped to build on existing knowledge and led to peer-to-peer learning.

Figure 8.4   Orientation tools for intervention 1

Introduction to orientation tools –
'mapping the information landscape'

- Physical locations:
  - IDS Library (BLDS – catalogue, subject guides)
  - Participation Resource Centre
  - University of Sussex Library
- Books (reading lists, Amazon, shelves)
- Journals, e-journals (African journals online)
- 'Tools'
  - OECD macrothesaurus (English, Spanish, French, German)
  - Databases (see BLDS list), portals (ELDIS gateway, R4D, Global Development Gateway)
  - Search engines (Google, SCIRUS)
  - Websites
- People (supervisors, experts – IDS participation team, colleagues, community)
- Organisations (FAO, GDN, DfID, IIED, OED, WHO, World Bank, ILO, IMF, Futures Group, OECD, ActionAid, IDRC, SIDA, CIDA, NORAD, USAID, Manchester School of Environment & Development, Overseas Development Group UEA etc.)

  - See Flip Chart – the 'Information Landscape'
    - See subject guides to library resources
      - See 'Participation databases'
        - See 'Participation team'

Again the 'journey' and 'travelling through a landscape' metaphor was used and drawn on the flip chart to indicate how the students would be 'travelling' through and trying to identify sources of information in the information landscape. The concept of 'tools' that would help them explore this landscape was introduced, including people and organisations.

The mapping of the domain then took place. The students were shown a mind map that gave an indication of what was expected (Figure 8.5).

Initially students were expected to create a 'map' of the participation, power and social change domain in general and then create a mind map of the topic they had chosen to research for their extended essay – their 'analytical paper'. Participative visualisation techniques were introduced as possible alternatives to mind mapping. On reflection it would have been good to explore the use of these techniques to represent knowledge and where it originated. Students had prior knowledge of these techniques and could have used them to present their 'map'.

The general mind map was produced in groups, but the mind map relating to each student's topic was carried out individually. The final product was presented to the whole group and led to discussion. Presentation and discussion meant that students had to use the language of the domain and consciously verbalise connections and define in their own minds what it was they were interested in. An example of a broad subject domain mind map was introduced to help students reflect on what they had included or left out, and on the extent of the domain (Figure 8.6). An example of an individual topic mind map is shown in Figure 8.7.

Figure 8.5   **Mind map task for intervention 1**

Activity

- Create a mind map of terms used to describe the Participation, Power & Social Change domain
  - use the orientation 'tools' described above that provide definitions, explanations of key topics
  - use the flip chart paper to document your thoughts
- Are there techniques from PRA/PLA that could be applied?
- be able to present and discuss your thoughts – what was difficult, how was the process useful?

         - See flip chart – showing 'subject journey'
           - See PP&SC mind map

Figure 8.6 Participation, power and social change mind map

As shown above, orientation resources, although not strictly a part of the domain mapping process, were also introduced at this stage (Figure 8.4). Searching for information exposed students to new words that defined the domain and helped inform them about the boundaries of their topic.

Figure 8.7 Individual topic mind map for intervention 1

Activity

▨ Create a visualisation (mind map, tree structure etc.) of the topic, identifying key terms, concepts etc. that you have chosen for the **Analytical Paper** (you may only have a vague idea – this activity and the subsequent program should help you to define your topic more precisely).

▨ Indicate on the general mind map where your topic fits in.

▨ Create a table/list of search terms

   ▨ What do you need to cover for your Analytical Paper?

Figure 8.8 Student mind map 1

The overall process:

- encouraged peer-to-peer learning, working in groups, agreeing on the overall domain and understanding this bigger picture
- enabled students to develop and refine their thoughts about their individual topic and to place it in a wider context
- helped students develop their communication and presentation skills
- helped the students, the majority of whom did not speak English as their first language, to become familiar with the language of the domain. The latter would be fundamental for searching the electronic

Figure 8.9   Student mind map 2

sources for related information as well as enabling them to have dialogue with the wider community about their topic.

Figures 8.8 and 8.9 show students presenting their mind maps to the wider group. Two very different styles for visualising and presenting information are evident.

This intervention proved popular with the students primarily because it helped them with a daunting task – choosing a topic for research. Through reflection (Figure 8.10), they were able to develop the metacognitive skills associated with this information literacy and a skill that they would be able to apply in other learning contexts.

As they had access to orientation sources of information, the students started to become familiar with the information landscape, and the use of simple search techniques and those tools and information resources that provided an overview and orientation to the subject domain. The latter included organisational WWW sites, internal reports, development portals and so on.

The questions posed in the reflection slide helped the students to identify and concretise the process they had gone through. They were able to recognise common challenges, identify strategies and processes as well as specific techniques that were useful – often by pooling experience and knowledge through peer-to-peer learning and direction from the facilitator.

Figure 8.10   Reflection on intervention 1

Reflection

- What have you learnt today?
- How important is it to map the domain? Processes, barriers, strategies?
- How important is it to map the Information Landscape? Processes, barriers, strategies?
- Has it helped you to define your Analytical Paper topic?
- Has it helped you to define what information you need?
- Is this a process you can apply to other tasks?
- Would this be useful in the workplace? Processes, barriers, strategies?

Figure 8.11 Example information science mind map

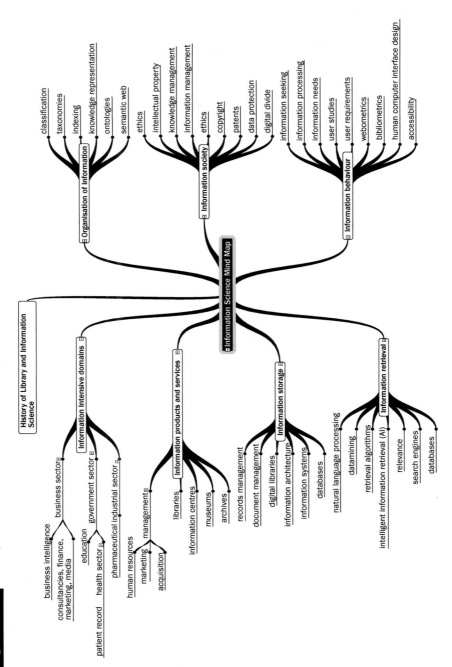

2 Example with undergraduates

A similar approach was taken with first year, first semester undergraduates. This was a part of a module that enabled them to develop 'academic' information literacy. This included enabling them to become familiar with the domain of information science; the information landscape associated with information science; information retrieval techniques; and the norms associated with academia, such as referencing and how to avoid plagiarism, group work, handing in and electronic submission of assignments and so on.

A mind map that stemmed from this activity is shown in Figure 8.11.

9

Learning intervention 2: understanding the information landscape

People's ability to learn is inhibited if they do not know where to go for information or what learning contexts to use to help them become informed. In a situation where relatively information-intensive decisions need to be taken, without this knowledge, people tend to reinvent the wheel, miss relevant knowledge, information and data that may inform them and take longer to complete a task. It is important for learners to become aware of sources of information (people, books, articles, databases, organisations and so on) and ways of becoming informed. This includes knowing about the tools that enable them to identify sources of information, such as indexes, catalogues, search engines, information retrieval systems, portals and so on. The information landscape also provides a physical representation and maps the extent of knowledge within a domain. Different types of source indicate the knowledge generation process within a domain (primary information such as data sets, secondary information such as articles, and knowledge such as experience found through social networks and contacts). Different value is placed on specific sources by the community of practice and normative criteria of content and functionality will be evident. Knowing these criteria helps learners choose information that is appropriate to situation and social context.

Purpose

- Mapping the information landscape, gaining an overview of sources of information that are important in that domain and how they relate to each other.

- Knowing the names of sources and the language used to describe and think about them.
- Being able to evaluate the design and appropriateness of sources for undertaking the learning task.
- Being able to relate personal knowledge, gaps and information needs to sources in terms of their content, character (e.g. eye witness, subject expert, depth, level), form (e.g. text, image) and functionality.

Context

This could be carried out with people of almost any level of ability or age and in any subject domain. Teaching interventions could use an electronic or paper-based environment. In the educational environment a flexible study space is ideal, where people can work in groups or individually and have access to information resources and the means to capture information, and discuss and share their findings. It could also be undertaken where people identify physical spaces or places that lead to becoming informed, such as markets, conferences and clubs. A mutual support group for people who have the same medical condition could provide a context where people focus on sources, and undertake and become familiar with this process and sources of learning. Similar exercises would be carried out in either of these environments.

Physical learning environment

General

Flip charts; whiteboard, blackboard or smartboard; Post-it notes; coloured pens and pencils.

Electronic learning environment

Personal computer (ideally a maximum of three people to one PC). Where access is very restricted access time needs to be planned and the intervention should take place over a more extended period of time. In the education sector ideally every learner will have their own device such as handheld or netbook type devices or even a mobile phone with World Wide Web access. They will also have access to a communications network and applications, including telecommunications, word processing and mind mapping, and internet access to the World Wide Web or local information stores such as databases. The WWW would be used to access orientation sources, such as subject specific, encyclopaedias, dictionaries, thesauri, databases, RSS feeds, organisations (that either provide information or links to information) and people (via organisations, discussion lists and blogs), as well as in-depth sources, such as e-books, electronic journals, portals, online databases or organisational websites. The sources accessed should orientate the learner to the subject, keep people up to date, and give in-depth information, such as academic articles or case studies of practice. Radio and mobile phones could also provide access to information.

Paper-based learning environment

The same as above excluding the electronic tools but including paper-based sources, such as books, academic or newspaper articles, conference papers, market research reports, encyclopaedias, dictionaries and so on. These could be accessed via public, institutional or personal libraries or collections, bookshops, publishers or organisations (such as government departments).

Blended learning environment

A combination of the two described above.

Non-electronic or paper-based learning environment

Physical objects, available to the teacher and learner, need to be provided, collected or observed and thought about in terms of what can be learnt from them. Learning through experience is important; for example, observation of nature may be informative. Observation of the layered nature of the natural forest, for example, has informed permacultural methods of farming.

Media such as drum, dance, theatre or story telling may be important sources of information and knowledge.

The underlying pedagogy

Learning about the information landscape has sensory, behavioural, cognitive and social constructivist elements. Sensory elements include appreciating the physical construction of the source, for example, the human computer interface design, and its 'look and feel', purpose and audience. This might be done by appreciating that ways of presenting information at the interface may be designed to appeal to the holist, such as tag clouds or hyperbolic trees that use three dimensional representations of sources and information such as Kartoo, Webrain or Quintura. Another example is to illustrate how design may relate to an emotional state that the user is likely to be experiencing, such as isolation, e.g. the young carers' website or Mencap's site. The behavioural aspect of learning relates to the physical use of and interaction with sources, searching, using functions and features and becoming familiar with how they can be applied.

From a cognitive constructivist viewpoint emphasis should be given to learners building a mental map of the information landscape from an individual perspective and relating sources to their needs, which are likely to be informed by the social context. As you will see from the description of the teaching intervention it is important to build on previous knowledge and experience, possibly drawing analogies and knowledge from other contexts, for example sources of information in the home, such as tools that help keep in touch with people, including telephone directories or mobile phones; and reference sources such as recipe books, which can be used to think about the new information landscape. From a social constructivist viewpoint learning focuses on the socially defined relationships and distinctions between artefacts and the processes and infrastructure associated with the social construction of knowledge either generally or within a particular domain. This includes reflection on whose voice is being heard, and the values attached to information artefacts and their origin, such as authority or credibility.

The intervention will be scaffolded and incorporate reflection on the process of 'mapping the information landscape'. The learning intervention usually includes a facilitator and people working individually and in groups, possibly with some organisational structure, such as team leaders and scribes. Discussion and presentations take place. The form teaching and learning takes depends on the social and physical context of the learners.

Behavioural learning

The behavioural learning in this intervention includes the experience of using information sources and the ability to navigate sources effectively to find information. This depends on learners' knowledge of the sources (cognitive learning). Unless learners apply this knowledge relatively frequently this knowledge will not be embedded.

Learners will find out about external sources outside the personal or organisational context that are available (databases, World Wide Web search engines, including subject specific search engines, such as Scirus, subject gateways, subject portals, encyclopaedias, organisational sites and so on), and internal sources such as organisational databases, repositories and the intranet, and efficient ways to access such sources. This includes knowledge of the content, form and structure and functionality of sources and how they can be used. Less emphasis is given to the latter aspects of information literacy in this intervention, but it will be dealt with when discussing use of information in later descriptions of teaching interventions.

The emotional context needs to be borne in mind. For example teachers need to be aware that the early stages of research, especially for the novice, are likely to be associated with a high degree of uncertainty since they will not know where to find information and become informed. The incorrect choice of source will lead to frustration because learners do not find relevant information. This should be recognised and appropriate support provided.

Learning outcomes stem from this, including knowledge of the features and benefits of the sources that enable access to information. The ability to organise the information landscape is a part of this activity. For example, a learner might create a personalised desktop that includes links to preferred sources and bookmarks of web-based resources using the browser or social bookmarking applications such as Delicious or Connotea (the latter is specifically aimed at researchers) and CiTuLike, which enables the sharing of information resources.

Cognitive learning

Cognitive learning includes having knowledge of the range of sources and their characteristics (coverage, functionality and so on), and being able to categorise them. In addition it encompasses knowing how to analyse and evaluate sources by applying appropriate criteria, and to think strategically about when to use certain sources.

Learning outcomes stem from this – evidence of these skills is expected – learners need to apply these thinking skills, be aware of the range of sources available and be able to justify their choice of them.

Constructivist learning

Cognitive constructivist learning, from an individual perspective, relates to building a mental map of the information landscape. Presenting, explaining and justifying this 'map' helps the learner concretise and internalise this view. From a social constructivist perspective the learner is learning about the information artefacts and tools that a specific 'community' uses and values. Learning involves learners presenting and discussing their conception of the information landscape, exchanging and defining categories of sources and information either face to face or via social media such as e-mail, discussion lists or blogs. They learn to use the general language of sources, such as 'portal', 'full text', 'open access' or 'creative commons', or those specific to the domain. Discussion and possibly consensus could be reached with others in this community of practice about what is valued and how to evaluate such sources.

Learning outcomes stem from this, for example the 'map', and an appreciation of the value of the collaboration and learning from others and how this may help complete a task and see the world in different ways. Another outcome is to appreciate the types of knowledge, data and information that relate to the domain and the community of practice.

Levels of complexity

Levels of complexity about learning expectations depend on three main factors: the depth of learners' knowledge of the subject domain; their knowledge of the related technology and systems for facilitating access to knowledge, data and information; and the extent and quality of their social networks.

Although a similar learning intervention could be applied to learners with different levels of expertise, learners with limited knowledge of the subject domain are likely to have limited knowledge of the range of sources available or the vocabulary to talk and think about them. This applies to novices or young learners, who are likely to be familiar with fewer sources and to make use of people as their predominant source of information. These learners have limited knowledge of information resources, and because their social networks are small it is more difficult for them to access and gain different perspectives.

Methods of assessment and learning outcomes

A fundamental choice needs to be made when designing methods of assessment: whether it is carried out by an 'expert' or by peers. Peer assessment has been shown to lead peer-to-peer learning and can result in deeper learning – partly because the assessor is forced to reflect on the activity.

Quantifiable outcomes include:

- ability to create visualisations of sources, such as a source scattered landscape, a list or mind map; Venn diagrams could be used to indicate where the most information originates, with larger circles for more important sources and so on (a process that helps learners to think about the relative merits of sources); flow charts could be used to indicate how knowledge is generated, where and how it becomes accessible, ownership and so on

- ability to provide comprehensive coverage of relevant sources in a domain or location

- ability to be able to identify appropriate sources for a particular task

- ability to be familiar with and apply evaluation criteria (relevance, coverage, authority, functionality and so on)

- ability to demonstrate collaborative skills (participation, co-operation and teamwork)

- ability to demonstrate presentation skills (confidence, clarity and efficiency)

- being able to reflect on what and how learners have learnt and strategies that were useful, and how they would apply this knowledge to other situations.

These areas of assessment could be applied in the electronic or paper-based learning environments. Where neither is available emphasis is given to oral presentation and the identification of useful people who hold information and knowledge. Even in this context visualisation can be carried out using the material world (soil, chalk, stones) to map and indicate sources of information and learning.

Examples of interventions

1 Example with undergraduates – orientation to sources

This case formed part of an information literacy intervention for students undertaking an undergraduate degree in information management at Loughborough University. Students, generally, came straight from school. They had very little experience of independent learning in the academic context and were unfamiliar with the range of sources available to them. In their school environment they were either given or pointed to the information they needed. They may have used a school library or public library but generally used Google to find web-based information resources.

For their first semester a module was developed to orientate them to learning in the academic environment and to the discipline, information science. It focused on the students' information literacy and involved seeking information independently, and making use of and communicating information (via a poster) effectively and ethically. A poster was chosen as the final 'product' because it forced students to synthesise and distil their knowledge and to communicate it effectively.

The final poster session took place in a large, public exhibition hall and enabled peer-to-peer learning; it showed that the students were valued as active producers of knowledge; and created a social event. The students were given a broad remit for the poster: to describe an area where information science – in its broadest sense, using any context that involved knowledge, data and information management – was systematically being applied (previous work necessitated that they had charted the remit of information science). Students identified various areas that interested them – such as space exploration, the armed forces, the police, the health service and business – and where information was available. This served to orientate them to the relevance of information science (a domain where they had no previous formal knowledge) through guidance, discovery and choice. It required them to become familiar with the academic and domain specific information landscape that they had access to. Through the intervention they were sensitised to the norms of academic work, for example the issue of plagiarism and academic practice, such as electronic coursework submission. A series of lectures, interspersed with practical tutorials and small assignments, scaffolded the learning.

The learning about the information landscape was placed in context using the slide shown in Figure 9.1, which shows the focus of the learning.

Figure 9.1 Connecting with information (adapted from Markless and Streatfield, 2007)

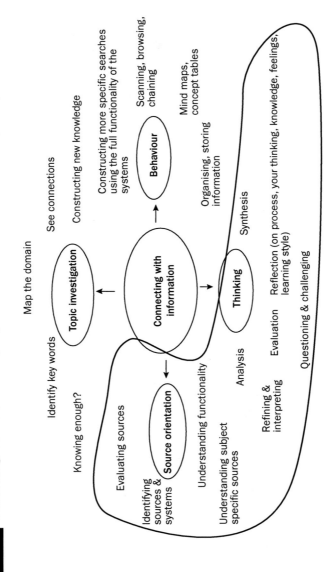

Previous sources of information that the students had used for personal or study reasons were discussed, and common problems were identified, such as the difficulty of identifying relevant and appropriate information. The relative merits of sources the students had used were identified and the evaluation criteria highlighted. New sources were introduced and an overview given of the information landscape, including the library catalogue and the library gateway to electronic information sources (Metalib).

The students were then introduced to the content and functionality of the electronic information gateway and individual online databases that the university subscribed to. They were shown how to access supporting material such as help systems (which people seldom think to check). A brief demo preceded a practical session showing the students how to identify appropriate databases, find out about their content and access them. They were then asked to identify ways to search the sources effectively and efficiently on their topic of information management to try to find articles that would help them in their overall assignment – creating the poster as described above. Once students had had time (with the help of a roving facilitator), they were asked to reflect on the process and identify what was difficult and what helped, hence sharing expertise through peer-to-peer learning.

This was designed to prepare the learners for an assignment that would encourage further reflection and reinforce this learning. An outline of the assignment is shown below:

> Provide a list of information retrieval tools you have found useful for finding out about information science. It is possible you will already be deciding on a subset of information science that will become the focus of your final piece of coursework – the group poster.
>
> Choose three information retrieval tools that you have used. These should include:
>
> - a database (such as ABI or Emerald)
> - a portal (such as Intute or R4D)
> - a search engine (such as SCIRUS or Google or iBoogie).
>
> In each case describe why you chose these sources in terms of their:

- authority (quality of material)
- coverage (subject matter, geographical coverage, up to dateness, type of material, e.g. full-text articles)
- functionality (how the tools allow you to search, e.g. can you limit your search to specific fields such as the title? Do they enable Boolean logic or searching for multiple alternative terms, the output, etc?).

Although students did the assignment independently, a discussion list was used to support them and to share learning. A response to an e-mail from a student asking 'Why Metalib?' (an electronic gateway to electronic sources including databases of academic articles) gives an indication of how the teacher can provide ongoing support remotely:

A student said: 'I don't really understand what "database" means. Is there any difference between the information that we search by using the normal search engine and the databases that we found via Metalib?'

The tutor's response was to state that the main difference is the quality of the information and the organisation of the information. In a way Google is also a database – a database of words, terms that 'point' to information that can be found via the internet. However, the library *pays* for databases such as Nexis and Emerald that you can search via Metalib (Metalib provides a 'gateway' or 'front end' to different databases).

Why does the library pay to get access to these databases? Basically because they are put together by e-publishers who either own the publications or have paid for the right to put the publications on a database and then sell access.

They are worth paying for (companies do this, not just university libraries) because most of the publications are of high quality. All the academic journal sources have had to go through a peer review process before they are published. The database companies (e-publishers) themselves work hard to build up a collection of top publications that relate to a subject. Often these sources are only available on subscription.

However, some (and only some) of the publications, articles and so on can be found free because they are published via Open Access or by an individual. The down side of this is that there is little quality control and you have to go to lots of different places to find the recent articles on, say, e-publishing, whereas a database via Metalib should enable you to locate good, recent, articles via one search. Plus the interfaces of the databases allow you to be very specific in your searching – so you don't get snowed under.

For example, a search on ABI Proquest (via Metalib) for e-business articles (related to coursework in another module), limiting the search to articles that mention e-business in the title of the article and those published within the last year, found 29 relevant articles from reputable sources.

Feedback from the students showed that they appreciated how this learning enabled them to find material that was relevant to other modules and courses they were taking.

2 Example with Master's students – evaluating sources

The following slides stem from a lecture to Master's level information science students. They give an indication of the depth that can be covered in relation to an online database:

Slide 1: Who are you evaluating?

- data owner or information provider (source)
- the database producer (may supply it to various vendors)
- publisher, host or vendor (maintaining databases and providing access – may well be the software developer).

Slide 2: Consistency: any database should follow rules [about]:

- editorial policy
- indexing
- same field labels and data elements.

Slide 3: Coverage: comparative questions on:

- subject coverage
- type of material
- [if it is] considered authoritative

- strengths and weaknesses
- [if it] covers major journals
- omissions
- time span.

Slide 4: Timeliness:

- frequency of update
- currency of material
- priorities.

Slide 5: Accuracy:

- typographical errors
- mis-spellings
- data in wrong fields
- incorrect figures or citations
- oddly formatted records
- what quality control there is in source selection as well as processing.

Slide 6: Accessibility and ease of use:

- connecting to the service – agreements, concurrency, software and hardware
- [for] expert or novice, basic or advanced
- disabled access
- functionality and interface design
- added value – indexing, related terms, spellings, saved searches
- integration with other systems.

Slide 7: Interface design:

- purpose, audience
- intuitive – know what to do; uncluttered, 'white space'
- ease of navigation – consistent; easy to get back, forward, exit
- response time.

Slide 8: Functionality:

- command line, drop-down menus, forms
- Boolean logic
- field searching
- proximity searching
- display options
- use of controlled vocabulary.

Slide 9: Documentation:

- availability and cost
- usability
- thesauri supplied
- help systems (problem-based, FAQ, A–Z, context sensitive)
- useful error messages
- updates.

Slide 10: Customer support and training:

- well-trained, responsive customer support staff
- hours of access
- toll free numbers
- workshops
- tutorials
- discussion list.

Similar criteria can be applied to the evaluation of search engines, and students should discuss the different types of search engine (metasearch engines, single search engines and so on) and how they work. Professionals who select or use such services need to understand how they generally work. The next slide introduced the concept of ranking and how search engines rank the information they find:

Ranking is based on:

- the concepts of 'relevance', 'nearness', 'aboutness' … rather than matching associated with Boolean logic

- statistical analysis and weighting by the number of terms matching, frequency, words in the title etc., in fields, 'freshness' and by popularity (links to the page, whether it has been reviewed).

3 Example with Master's students or undergraduates – exploring a source

The following is an intervention that encourages learners to analyse a specific source in more depth and compare it with others:

Objective: Describe the structure of records in one of the following databases: Emerald, ABI, LISA or FAME.

Procedure:

1. Split into groups (4–5 people in each).
2. Each group will be assigned one database: Emerald, ABI, LISA or FAME.
3. Decide who is going to be:

   a. team leader

   b. time keeper

   c. scribe

   d. speaker.
4. Access the database.
5. Identify a record.
6. Identify the fields in the record (searchable and non-searchable).
7. Determine the purpose of these fields. (Why are they useful? What is their value?)
8. What is the purpose of this product?
9. Who is the target community for this product and why would it satisfy their needs?
10. Present your findings to the rest of the tutorial class (this will take place next week).

Remember to use the help systems.

Learners presented their findings at a later date. This enabled discourse, the sharing of knowledge and peer-to-peer learning. A competitive element was introduced in some interventions whereby learners had to make a case for their source being 'better' than the others. This proved successful and motivational, and required the learners to investigate how the features of the database could benefit the learner.

4 Example with undergraduates – evaluating search engines

A similar exercise to the one above was conducted with undergraduates but in this case the sources were search engines:

> The purpose of the tutorial is to encourage you to apply your critical evaluation skills to a number of search engines and appreciate the design features of these services.
>
> Questions you may ask:
>
> 1. Who is the service aimed at: the general public, specialists or another group?
> 2. In terms of ease of use (both basic and advanced search interface) what do you think of the design?
> 3. What functionality is offered? What can you do?
> 4. To what extent does the service address the information-seeking needs of the user?
>   a. Does it help them identify good resources?
>   b. Does it help them identify useful search terms?
>   c. Does it help them define the subject area?
>   d. Does it help them narrow and broaden the search?
>   e. Does it help them manage the results and information retrieved?
> 5. What information does the service give access to? Consider the following questions:
>   a. Is it primarily commercial or academic?
>   b. Is there any quality control?
>   c. Is it up to date?
>   d. Is it comprehensive?

The services you will evaluate are: Exalead (exalead.com), Surfwax (surfwax.com), Scirus (Scrirus.com) – and [also consider how] these services compare with Google.

Although the interventions described above are from the higher education context there is no reason that they could not be applied in other contexts such as school or even the workplace.

10

Learning intervention 3: using information retrieval tools and techniques to locate information

The effective acquisition of information involves 'connecting with information' in both a 'passive' and an 'active' way. If one can use the full range of tools and sources effectively, in a conscious and critical way, then the learners are more likely to be informed quickly. This section enables the teacher to develop learners' knowledge of tools and places that enable access to information, including knowledge of their functionality and how to use these tools effectively and strategically, considering specific techniques and broader processes that they need to be aware of. This complements learning intervention 2.

If learners do not know how to use information location tools they can become frustrated, as they tend either to find too little information, or too much that is irrelevant or inappropriate. They are not necessarily familiar with what features to expect and often lack knowledge of how to use the functionality of e-tools, such as search engines (like Technorati, which indexes blogs), databases (like Eldis, which indexes material on work relating to developing countries) or compact disks that provide health and medical information. Learners tend to be particularly frustrated when they assume the search process is straightforward and relatively linear – a simple sequence of choose search tool, enter search term, receive results, read, end search – rather than a 'messy', iterative process. Even those who have grown up with the internet and the World Wide Web, but who are not necessarily expert searchers, can be frustrated.

The systematic use of sources can also include placing oneself effectively in an appropriate physical environment (library, gallery, exhibition and so on) or social context (performance, market, meeting, e-social networking site and so on) where the learner can actively seek information or be informed or passively and indirectly add to their knowledge base. Often information will be encountered, absorbed but not necessarily processed or applied immediately for a specific purpose and may be recalled and used at a later date. This can be planned, as can access to information tools.

Purpose

- Understanding the nature of information tools and places and how they differ in look, feel and functionality.
- Being able to use this knowledge to access and use these tools and places effectively to find or be alerted to information that helps people learn.

Context

This could be carried out with people of almost any level of ability or age and in any subject domain. Teaching interventions could use an electronic or paper-based environment. In the educational environment a flexible study space is ideal, where people can work in groups or individually and have access to information resources and the means to capture information, discuss and share their findings. It could also be undertaken where people think about how to use physical spaces or places that lead to becoming informed, such as e-social networking sites, chat rooms, markets, conferences, clubs, performances and so on. Similar exercises can be carried out in any of these environments.

The emphasis in this intervention is on how to use tools to find information in the electronic domain, for example, using search engines, portals, online indexes to academic papers and so on. These may have a specific purpose such as to find a blog, to index a library collection or newspaper articles, or to find information on a specific geographic area or topic. They may be specific to age or purpose. In this intervention prominence is therefore given to how to use tools or sources effectively, rather than to what is available, which was the purpose of intervention 2.

Physical learning environment

General

Flip charts; whiteboard, blackboard or smartboard; Post-it notes; coloured pens and pencils.

Electronic learning environment

Personal computer (ideally a maximum of three people to one PC). Where access is very restricted access time needs to be planned and the intervention should take place over a more extended period of time. In the education sector ideally every learner will have their own device such as handheld or netbook devices or even a mobile phone with World Wide Web access. There should be access to a communications network and applications, including telecommunications, word processing, mind mapping, and internet access to the World Wide Web or local information stores such as databases. The WWW is used to access orientation sources, such as subject-specific encyclopaedias, dictionaries, thesauri, databases, RSS feeds, organisations (that provide information or links to information) and people (via organisations, discussion lists and blogs), as well as in-depth sources, such as e-books, electronic journals, portals, online databases or organisational websites. The sources accessed tend to be those that orientate the learner to the subject and keep people up to date, and have in-depth information, such as academic articles or case studies of practice. Radio and mobile phones can also provide access to information. Choosing sources to search depends on the context of the learner.

Paper-based learning environment

The same as above excluding the electronic tools but including paper-based sources, such as books, academic or newspaper articles, conference papers, market research reports, encyclopaedias and dictionaries. These could be accessed via public, institutional or personal libraries or collections, bookshops, publishers or organisations (such as government departments).

Blended learning environment

A combination of the two described above.

Non-electronic or paper-based learning environment

Physical objects, available to the teacher and learner, need to be provided, collected, observed and thought about in terms of what can be learnt from them. Experiential ways of learning are important. For example, observation of nature may help learners to identify problems associated with crops.

Knowing how to access and understand media such as dance, theatre or story telling may form a part of this aspect of becoming informed. Access to appropriate people needs to be a possibility either individually or through meeting places.

In addition, physical information-rich places, such as exhibitions, museums, libraries, personal collections and community meeting places, are important for learning.

The underlying pedagogy

The tools we use to search are but artefacts, made by people, to be appreciated as one would any other artefact, such as an axe with its various features, for example, its weight, size, shape of head and purpose. They help us with thinking tasks and enable us to learn and act. These tools can be more or less reliable and useful, depending on the expertise of the user.

Knowing how to use sources is of course related to knowing what is available, that is mapping the information landscape (intervention 2). A knowledge of the functionality of sources is intertwined with the process of distinguishing the different types of source that are available. This intervention emphasises how to use the source and its broader characteristics rather than what is available.

From a learning perspective there is a sensory component about appreciating the look and feel of a tool or information product. This is related to learners being familiar with using these tools, experiencing what happens, and understanding that design aspects of tools may relate to the user. Tag clouds, for example, may be preferred by the holist;

spending time planning a search may be uncomfortable to the kinaesthetic learner. There is a cognitive component of knowing a search tool's character and how features and functionality can be used to achieve search and retrieval goals, such as the breadth or specificity of the search. A cognitive constructivist makes sense of the character of information tools by considering the range of their functions and how they can be used. A social constructivist emphasises the value attached to style, function and content, and how the design of systems is related to the socio-cultural context.

Metaphors implied by terms such as 'overload', 'panning for gold', finding 'the needle in the haystack', 'refining', 'filtering', 'narrowing', 'broadening' and so on can be useful.

Behavioural learning

The behavioural learning in this intervention includes the experience of using information sources and the ability to navigate them effectively to find information. This depends, of course, on people's knowledge of the sources (cognitive learning). However, unless learners apply this knowledge relatively frequently it will not be embedded. Repeated use of information tools helps to connect and embed the behavioural and cognitive experience.

The intervention emphasises the internal design of sources and search tools, and the importance of being familiar with using their features and functionality (the search of e-tools, advanced or simple interfaces, command-driven interfaces, the Boolean operators, truncation commands, proximity searching and output or capture options).

The emotional context needs to be borne in mind in the sense that teachers need to be aware of the emotional states associated with the discovery process. For example, unfamiliarity with tools and sources of information may be daunting and frustrating. Familiarity with and the ability to handle these tools can lead to a sense of efficacy and is linked to the ability to take control and exploit them effectively. Learners need to be supported in this.

Cognitive learning

Cognitive learning relates to the learner's knowledge of the design and structure of these tools, of how they work and how they can be used; their relative merits; and how they can be applied and used to resolve problems.

Lack of knowledge of functionality and how it can be used systematically and strategically is likely to lead to poor results, such as irrelevant hits, or too many or too few of them. In addition, learners need to know how to use language (words, phrases, 'terms', 'concepts') to retrieve information that relates to a specific question or domain. The decision whether to use more terms or alternative terms and how to combine them depends on whether learners appreciate the internal mechanics of search tools.

Constructivist learning

From a cognitive constructivist perspective learners are developing a mental map of sources and their features and functions in this intervention. Understanding ontologies that are used to describe content is important not just to understand the extent of the subject but to be able to use this language to find information. An example is when people use recognised terms to classify content, such as medical information, which may be coded by drug, chemical compound, intervention, relevance to age group and so on. These 'labels' can be agreed as a form of controlled vocabulary, and used by a community to map a domain. For example, in the business domain, codes and terms can be agreed to indicate the industry, company, business activity (acquisition, annual report and so on), geographic location and aspect of content, such as market share. Different types of labels are determined to some extent by the information-processing tasks of the community of practice, such as identifying an appropriate company for acquisition or tracking the competition. Hence knowledge of these combined with knowledge of retrieval functionality and an understanding of the task will lead to the successful use of appropriate information resources.

Levels of complexity

Levels of complexity about learning expectations depend on three main factors: the depth of learners' knowledge of the subject domain; their knowledge of the related technology and systems for facilitating access to knowledge, data and information; and the extent and quality of their social networks.

Although a similar learning intervention could be applied to learners with different levels of expertise, a learner with limited knowledge of the subject domain is likely to have limited knowledge of its language, processes and associated norms, or of the tools or places used to find information in that domain.

Novices with less experience of a range of sources can be helped to think in an abstract way about information tools by drawing on their knowledge of related experiences. For example, young people may be familiar with using mobile phones and can discuss functionality in terms of what they do and how, and their usefulness for learning or the process of learning from different people, including how this is done and the characteristics of people as sources. This thinking can then be applied to an information tool.

Very young people find it easier to browse categories of information than to think of terms. They perform better with subject indexes where they can browse and recognise relevant terms or topics. They may have more difficulty thinking about the logical connections, in the electronic domain, between search terms and what impact this may have on searching.

Advanced searchers would be expected to exploit the full functionality of systems, such as advanced and command interfaces, and to use them in a strategic way to broaden and narrow the search, retrieving specific types of material to fulfil a broad range of tasks. They should also be able to evaluate the functionality of a system and how it relates to achieving their learning tasks. The extent of searchers' knowledge of these tools and their use is reflected in their ability to use language that enables them to think in greater detail and precision about them.

Methods of assessment and learning outcomes

A fundamental choice needs to be made when designing methods of assessment: whether the assessment is carried out by an 'expert' or by peers. Peer assessment has been shown to lead peer-to-peer learning and can result in deeper learning – partly because the assessor is forced to reflect on the activity.

Quantifiable outcomes for a learner include:

- understanding how information retrieval tools index information
- being able to apply knowledge of indexes and the structure of tools to individual learning and socially defined tasks
- being able to resolve cognitive issues associated with information processing, such as narrowing and broadening the search and balancing precision and recall

- developing a broad conception of the functionality of tools, for example, simple and advanced search interfaces, Boolean logic, relevance ranking, truncation, proximity and so on
- being able to evaluate features (look and feel, structure, functionality) in comparative terms and to assess their usefulness for finding information
- being able to engage socially with people who will aid learning both in terms of using technology and interacting with people
- being able to identify and place themselves in learning places.

Examples of interventions

1 Example with new undergraduates – searching e-resources

This intervention was developed for first semester new undergraduates. It started with reflection on the ways learners learnt and tools they had previously used. They discussed these and their relevant merits, such as use of Google and reference tools. This included discussion of tools used outside the academic context, for example, the use of mobile phones, use of music or video download sites, their functionality, and how they find out what is going on.

Common problems were identified, including too much information, too little information and irrelevant items; and inappropriate results (wrong level, lack of credibility or detail). Strategies and techniques discussed included '…', use of advanced interfaces and alternative sources. Those who had studied ICTs were sometimes able to contribute relevant knowledge about databases, but had not always used this knowledge to think about information retrieval in general.

Learning from this was consolidated and presented in the following way:

Too many hits?

1. Go back to the terms you have chosen and see whether you can be more specific.

2. Choose a term or terms that are not going to be common in many records in the database. Use more specific words.

3. Link terms using AND or ask for them to be near each other (if the database enables this).

4. Restrict your search to the title field.

5. Restrict your search to fields that ensure that the records retrieved will have been indexed as about that term, such as the descriptor or keyword field.

6. Reduce the number of items by limiting the search by date, for example, only getting material published in the last year or by author or type of publication.

Too few hits?

1. Go back to the terms you have chosen and see whether you can think of more terms that could be used to search, such as synonyms or related terms.

2. When you are searching for several alternative terms OR them.

3. Don't restrict your search to any field; just search for any occurrence of the term(s) anywhere in the database records.

4. Check to see what the database covers and whether there are other databases with more relevant content.

A basic overview of the information retrieval process was presented to provide a conceptual framework. An overview was given to orientate learners to the focus of the intervention and how it related to other activities by placing it in the wider context and other learning interventions. The emphasis in this case was the bottom and left side of the slide shown in Figure 10.1.

Aspects of the search process were highlighted, for example, the iterative nature of the search, especially when orienting oneself to the topic, and how information retrieval tends to become more specific as one learns more – often resulting in searches that check information rather than seek information (Figure 10.2).

An abstract representation of the information retrieval was introduced (Figure 10.3). The purpose was to provide a structure that learners could follow, a framework; also it makes it easier for learners to reflect, and go back and think about whether they have worked through each stage effectively. This is particularly important if learners were getting poor results. Had they really defined their search topic and created a concept map of search terms? Had they chosen an appropriate source? Were they using effective search strategies and techniques? Strategies must take into account the breadth and depth of the search. Whereas techniques tend to relate to the use of specific functions or features, such as use of proximity operators (to search for words near each other), field searching, such as

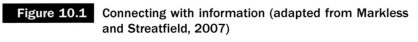

Figure 10.1 Connecting with information (adapted from Markless and Streatfield, 2007)

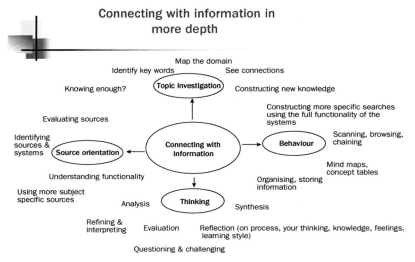

Figure 10.2 An iterative search process

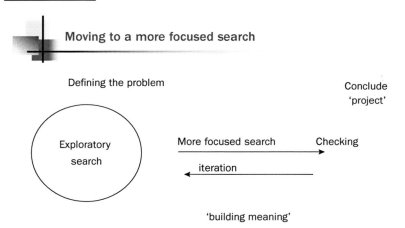

limiting a search to the title of records that are available in search systems, improves the precision of the search. Most search engines allow this kind of searching.

In Figure 10.3 the 'faces' try to convey that there is an emotional component to the search process and indicate the frustrations that learners often experience.

Figure 10.3 The overall search process

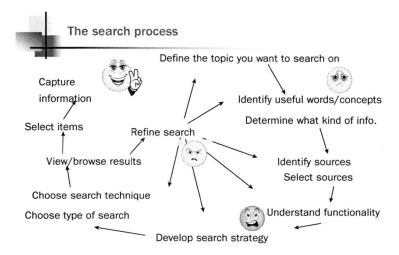

The search process

Define the topic you want to search on

Capture information

Identify useful words/concepts

Select items

Determine what kind of info.

Refine search

View/browse results

Identify sources

Select sources

Choose search technique

Choose type of search

Understand functionality

Develop search strategy

Information about the structure of electronic sources and how learners can use them to improve their search was introduced (Figure 10.4).

An example of how to search an information retrieval tool was given to help learners apply the theory previously discussed (Figure 10.5). An

Figure 10.4 Record structure

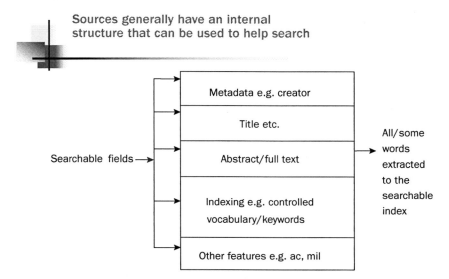

Sources generally have an internal structure that can be used to help search

Metadata e.g. creator

Title etc.

Searchable fields →

Abstract/full text

All/some words extracted to the searchable index

Indexing e.g. controlled vocabulary/keywords

Other features e.g. ac, mil

Figure 10.5 The Emerald search interface

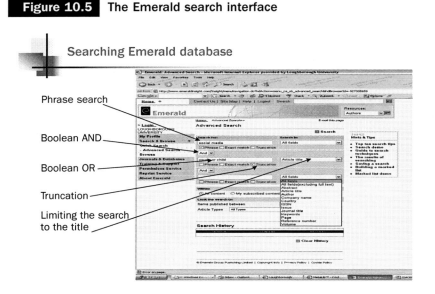

Searching Emerald database

Phrase search

Boolean AND

Boolean OR

Truncation

Limiting the search
to the title

introduction to what exactly they are searching – an index (whether this tool is a database or a search engine) – can be useful to help explain how Boolean logic actually works. It can be used to alert people to the topic of currency – even a search engine may not be up to date if its index has not been updated. It also provides an opportunity to discuss what exactly is indexed, by whom and whether there are any consequences of this in terms of who we get to read or not read – the social dimension of information retrieval.

The strategic nature of searching was introduced. The aim was to start learners thinking about how they can use the features of an information retrieval system in a strategic and tactical way – so that they can be in more control of the process. Here searching is placed on a continuum between a narrow, well-defined search, perhaps for a known item, and those that are broad, possibly for orientation purposes or where the topic is less known or broad (Figure 10.6).

In discussion learners recalled situations where they had used such techniques, how it helped, how they dealt with problems, how to aid peer-to-peer learning and the use of information literacy language and deeper learning. Exceptions were identified, for example when they would limit a search to the title field of records in the database just to find out how the topic is being covered by authors to orientate the learner to a topic rather than a specific search.

Figure 10.6   Narrowing and broadening a search

 Search techniques

- Narrower/specific/known item
  - known author
  - controlled vocabulary within an index field
  - within the title field or other searchable field
  - using proximity or phrase searching
  - using the Boolean AND
  - 'free text' term
  - using the Boolean OR
- Broader/unspecific/unknown item

A practical session was then run where students worked individually searching online sources (a database, a portal and a search engine) for information relating to their final piece of coursework, the poster, and applied their theoretical knowledge. Students were asked to analyse the characteristics of the source (purpose, audience, content, currency and functionality). They were asked to report back verbally on the characteristics they had noticed, useful search strategies stimulating reflection, discourse and peer-to-peer learning, and how they would apply this knowledge to other learning situations.

An alternative approach is to throw learners in at the deep end. First, try to persuade them to use the help system (an information literate strategy to educate themselves – after all they will be exposed to new systems in the future that may work differently). Ask them to search for topics and then through discussion reflect on how they searched, what worked, the problems they encountered and how they dealt with them. This can be very effective and leads to peer-to-peer learning, although learners who are used to a more teacher-centred approach, rather than this relatively unstructured, explorative one, can find this method unsettling. Instructions for this type of activity are shown below:

> Objective: Describe the structure of records in one of the following databases: Emerald, ABI, LISA or FAME.

Procedure:

1. Split into groups (4–5 people in each).
2. Each group will be assigned one database: Emerald, ABI, LISA or FAME.
3. Decide who is going to be:
   a. team leader
   b. time keeper
   c. scribe
   d. speaker.
4. Access the database.
5. Identify a record.
6. Identify the fields in the record (searchable and non-searchable).
7. Determine the purpose of these fields. (Why are they useful? What is their value?)
8. What is the purpose of this product?
9. Who is the target community for this product and why would it satisfy their needs?
10. Present your findings to the rest of the tutorial class (this will take place next week).

Remember to use the help systems.

The outcomes of this type of intervention can be captured, expanded if key features have been overlooked, and then presented to the learners to reinforce and help embed the learning, and provide a guide for future use. Another approach is to ask learners to identify and possibly debate evaluation criteria, gradually reaching a consensus. However, most learners at this stage tend to prefer to have some instruction first, then to search independently and then to reflect and share.

Second, learners can be given tasks, which can be marked, to assess their learning, stimulate reflection and further consolidate learning, as illustrated in the assignment below. (The poster was the final piece of work that learners, working in groups, were to produce. This task was therefore integrated into a wider process, helping learners achieve a longer-term goal, hence providing motivation.)

Choose a database, a portal and a search engine (not Google) that has helped you find information for your poster on an area where information science is having an impact.

- State why you have chosen these sources, their strengths and weaknesses in terms of purpose, content, format, authority and currency.

- Analyse their functionality in terms of searchability (use of Boolean logic, ranking, truncation, proximity searching, field searching and presentation of results) and interface design (simple, advanced interface; layout, navigation; accessibility and help system).

- Document your search strategy and why you have taken this approach; discuss how you broadened and narrowed the search.

2 Example with Master's students – a participative approach to fostering information literacy

The following intervention took a participative action and learning approach. Learners were asked to design the interface of an electronic information retrieval system that would meet their learning needs. To do this they were asked to observe a partner from the point of formulating a topic, choosing and searching for information on the topic to capturing information. The searcher was asked to verbalise their thoughts. The observer filled in a pre-designed form that helped record the thoughts and feelings of the learner, what they did and the environment within which they were acting. This took place over several weeks. However, it could be condensed into an activity that takes place over a short period of time.

Table 10.1 illustrates the different types of data a learner might use when searching through electronic sources. Positive and negative situations are evident. Needs are apparent such as speed of service, help with thinking of key terms and language, help with using search techniques, and the need to browse to determine relevance. This helped to make explicit cognitive and behavioural processes and raised consciousness of the knowledge and skills to use e-sources effectively.

Table 10.1 Participative action research information seeking intervention 1

Cognitive and personal data	Behavioural data	Environmental data
Type in internet address	*http://www.digilib.org.sg*	TIARA
Why is it taking so long?		
Go to choose Social Science database (have searched before)		Couldn't access
Go to Library Services	'Library Services'	
Thinking of a word that appears in the title of a book is harder	'commodity' scroll next page	Headlines ... investment, shares, stock...
Browse Not relevant Want to give up this search	'information + price'	... information bill of rights...
Possibly relevant but would have to look at the book and flip through to see whether relevant	information + (fee or 'price or commod* or merchandise or charge)'	
Try new strategy	Write down subject descriptors	... public library and charge... ... (dissertation) fee-based information services...
Look for assigned subject descriptors None assigned Find the subject		...information services – fee... ...fee-based library services... ...commodity exchanges...

The process of finding physical artefacts in the library was also recorded (Table 10.2). Again certain behaviours and needs are apparent, for example, to be able to browse and identify key terms; the use of call numbers to search; the need to browse contents pages; the difficulty of determining relevance; and the need to be able to take away information. All these activities highlight what needs to be known and therefore identify information literacies.

Going through this process the learners exchanged roles and both analysed the transcripts. This enabled them be active researchers, a skill

Table 10.2	Participative action research information seeking intervention 2

Cognitive and personal data	Behavioural data	Environmental data
Look for book title using call number Found relevant book	Checked shelves	Library Library shelves Book ... *The future development of libraries and information services...*
Look for next document (book)	Browse shelves for related books	Books on shelves
Find relevant book Verify by checking words in title with 'master list' of keywords		Title of book List of key terms
Look for book... the changing role of the special librarian in industry, business and government... via call number.		OPAC Headline/record
Not available in NTU, found in NL central reference library		Library shelves
Look for book via call number... information superhighway, role of the librarian, information scientist and intermediaries... (conference paper)		Book Contents page
Difficult searching the shelves by call number	Check table of contents	
Found book Some of the articles are relevant. Decide to photocopy. Can't find photocopier. Decide to take out and renew via the internet.		Facility closed ... the emerging and future role of the chief information officer...
Look for video	Move on to search for other titles	
Feel that the books found are too general and will need to narrow/refine the search. Relevancy based on interpreting the headline	Search call numbers on shelf Scan 'abstract' Put back on shelf	... career perceptions of American librarians...

Table 10.2 Participative action research information seeking intervention 2 (*Cont'd*)

Cognitive and personal data	Behavioural data	Environmental data
Look for a book with a known title. Might be too generic. Difficult locating but found after some time.		
	Use automatic checkout. Put problematic books to one side. Tried again.	Books
Browse for relevance Find not relevant after reading		
Decides to borrow the books that were found.		
Had a problem checking out some books		
Borrowed		

they may need in their future career, and importantly enabled them to observe the searching process and through analysis, reflection and discussion understand and become conscious of it. They were able to highlight the problems experienced and the knowledge and skills required to be information literate. The tone of this intervention implies that learners and their abilities are valued rather than seen as passive recipients of information.

Learners were then asked to share their findings in a larger group. This enabled them to learn from others and identify common characteristics (generalities) across data sets. They then designed an ideal interface that would help other learners undertake the information retrieval tasks and finally presented their ideas to the cohort.

3 Example with undergraduates – accessing e-resources

This was the first part of a workshop session on accessing e-resources delivered to second-year undergraduates in psychology. These students had received an e-resources intervention in their first year. The purpose of the session was to build on their prior knowledge and the first session began with a question to establish what this was.

This was very much a student-centred approach and activity based, so it was essential that students understood at the outset what was required of them. To facilitate this it was important to spend some time outlining how the session was to be run and how the students would make their contributions. The activities were group based (apart from the final reflection) and took place in a lab with PCs available.

All students were given a relevant topic to search – ideally set by the module leader or one of the module tutors – which gave the session a situated feel that was explicitly anchored within the subject area. Students were required to reflect on their learning and then write a reflective statement using the e-portfolio software PebblePad. This reflection could have been completed equally well by e-mail, VLE discussion board or paper.

The structure of the session is shown in Figure 10.7.

This constituted a cognitive and situated approach where students were required to reflect on their previous experience and use it to inform their discussions. They then negotiated with fellow students what was to appear on their list for sharing with the whole class. We have found that students often report having used a wide range of resources at this stage. Therefore this activity was an opportunity to tease out students' prior

Figure 10.7 Plan for session on using e-resources

Using e-resources plan for today

✏ **Introduction**
   ✏ Learn how to use Web of Science
   ✏ Group work throughout

✏ **Activity 1**
   ✏ We know about PsycArticles – what else do you (or would you) use to find information?

✏ **E-resources Essential Guide – how to use it**

✏ **Activity 2**
   ✏ Find out how to use Web of Science

✏ **Mini-presentation**
   ✏ Show off your new skills

✏ **Reflect on your learning using PebblePad**

knowledge and experience to create a positive atmosphere, and to harness these experiences to illustrate similarities and differences between the e-resources the students use. It was necessary to issue health warnings if the e-resources being used were of poor quality or inappropriate for the subject. This activity enabled the tutor to show that all of the full-text e-resources such as PsycArticles and Swetswise can be accessed by searching top level databases like Web of Science. This neatly led in to distributing the in-house *Essential guide to e-resources*.

The way the session was carried out is described below.

Introduction (10 minutes)

Discussed what students were to do: have an activity-based workshop where they worked together to answer the questions. There was group work for all activities – students worked in groups of four. Each group contributed an answer at some point.

Activity 1 (20 minutes)

Think about finding quality information, to which e-resource would you go to find it? You know about PsycArticles. Use the guide to find subject-related information. What else do you use or have you heard about?

Take 10–15 minutes to discuss together and come up with a list of quality resources. (During this activity the tutor toured the room and had a look at the lists being drawn up, encouraging students to come up with ideas. It was surprising to see what they already knew.)

Essential guide – What is it? (10 minutes)

The teacher worked through the guide and explained to students that, in groups, they would use the guide to find subject-related information and in the process learn how to use Web of Science. Time was allowed to explore one resource only; students were invited to investigate the other resources listed in their own time.

Activity 2 – Find out how to use Web of Science (25 minutes)

The class was told that at the end of the activity they would be asked to come to the front, in their groups, and demonstrate one or more of the skills listed below in a mini-presentation. This enabled students to show that they could not only apply their new knowledge but also communicate it to their peers.

The skills that the students were required to demonstrate to the rest of the class were:

- how to get to Web of Science
- how to combine keywords
- how to use truncation
- how to use wildcards
- how to do a phrase search
- how to obtain full text
- what to do if full text is not available.

These skills were written out on the flip chart or whiteboard and constantly referred to during this activity to make sure that students remained on task.

This task was cognitive in nature in that students had to engage with both the *Essential guide to e-resources* and apply the principles shown, such as combining keywords and so forth. It was also behavioural in that they needed to read the guides, cognitive in that they needed to comprehend what is written, behavioural again in that they needed to use the resources and cognitive in that they applied new knowledge to find information. They then had an opportunity to analyse the outcome of different searches and the quality of the information retrieved. The group work allowed students to negotiate and create new meaning regarding which database was the most appropriate for their topic and their search techniques, and which articles they had retrieved would be useful in their assignments.

Mini-presentation (15 minutes)

Each group in turn came to the front and talked the rest of the class through one or more of the skills listed. The tutor needed to be ready to dive in and help students out if they got into difficulties. To clarify any points, the tutor made comments and/or asked questions as the students progressed through their mini-presentations.

This activity further demonstrated students' ability to apply their new knowledge and synthesise it into a mini-presentation.

Reflection (15 minutes)

Every student was asked to log on to PebblePad and write a reflective statement identifying what they had learnt in the session. They were then asked to share this reflection with the tutor. In effect this promotes metacognition, allowing students to evaluate their learning and realise for themselves what they had learnt.

Here are some examples of students' reflections:

Student 1

This seminar covered finding quality information, accessing relevant journals and articles and evaluating website articles.

This seminar was helpful in showing me a more logical method of searching for articles rather than the hit and miss method I currently use, which should make the process easier and quicker in future.

I have always found it frustrating when I find an article only to realise there is no full text available and this seminar showed me where to go when this happens. It also clarified some points such as how to use wildcards and truncation and how to combine phrases etc.

I am going to practice using the new skills I have acquired in preparing for assignments and research this semester, starting with finding information for Children in Context and Workbook Activity 1 for Identities and Groups.

This was a really useful seminar. It showed me that I still have things to learn about literature searching and gave me some direction and new skills that I am going to use in preparing for assignments this semester. The information on evaluating articles and websites will be particularly useful for the Children in Context workbook activities.

Student 2

I learnt about using the e-resources in a professional way, how to access Web of Science and found out about wildcards and truncation.

Found it ok, learned quite a lot from fellow students and it was interesting in parts.

I need to read up on how to further my experience on using e-resources.

Wasn't a bad session, lecturer was helpful and pushy... got us off our backsides as I think most of us were half asleep until then!!

Student 3

Learnt how to use Web of Science and Psycinfo.

Being able to use Web of Science and knowing how to find available paper copies of journals will be useful for assignments.

I'll keep the booklet on how to use the databases, highlight key areas to help research for assignments. Having to complete our own searches rather than just using the ones in the booklet will help remember how to do them.

Student 4

Searched using Web of Science and used wildcards, truncation, Boolean 'AND'. Very important to look at the essential keywords to make the search more precise.

Difficult to get to grips with and need to use more often and practice to gain experience but will be very useful when planning essays and finding journal articles.

11

Learning intervention 4: interaction with and use of information

Introduction

Interaction with information and using information is fundamental to learning. Learners experience two common situations: where they are overwhelmed with too much information from a variety of sources, and when they are unable to sort or manage it systematically, including making judgements about its relevance, reliability, currency and so forth.

Purpose

- Assisting learners to understand and comprehend the structure of sources so they are able to navigate them.

- Applying this knowledge to the use of the structure or character of information sources to evaluate and judge relevance or worth of information under consideration. In other words enabling learners to answer these questions in their own minds: is it the right stuff?, why is it the right stuff? and how is it the right stuff?

- Developing thinking skills to be able to make balanced decisions about content and create knowledge through induction and deduction. It is envisaged that learners will become aware of methods for managing, organising and storing content.

- Through a variety of methods, depending on the context, communicating and/or sharing new knowledge with others, for example, in the academic context, via a poster, essay or report; in the professional context, via an executive summary; or in the media context, via a newspaper article or video.

Context

This could be carried out with people of almost any level of ability or age and in any subject domain. Teaching interventions could use an electronic or paper-based environment. It could also be undertaken using physical objects such plants, stones, artefacts and scenery, where types of objects and their characteristics are clustered and given descriptions. Similar exercises would be carried out in either of these environments. The subject focus needs either to be provided by the tutor or taken from one of the earlier interventions mentioned above. Additionally learners may bring examples such as blogs, wikis, organisational websites, books, articles or other artefacts that they would like to work with. Access to an environment where learners can manage content they have retrieved or found is required. Avenues for communication need to be facilitated either in person or virtually.

Physical learning environment

General

Flip charts; whiteboard, blackboard or smartboard; Post-it notes; coloured pens and pencils.

Electronic learning environment

Personal computer (ideally a maximum of three people to one PC). Where access is very restricted access time needs to be planned and the intervention should take place over a more extended period of time. In the education sector ideally every learner would have their own device such as handheld or netbook devices or even a mobile phone with World Wide Web access. There should be access to a communications network and applications, including word processing and mind mapping, and internet access to the World Wide Web or local information stores. For purely electronic delivery a suitable environment is required, for example, a VLE discussion board, a social networking site, a blog or wiki, Google docs, YouTube, or a social bookmarking site such as Butterfly, along with access to e-resources such as databases, software such as Word, bibliographical reference databases or box files for hard copy.

Paper-based learning environment

Learners require access to a records management or filing system to organise references, articles, ongoing work and tools such as a highlighter.

Blended learning environment

In essence both the virtual and face to face combined; it is preferred that a social networking device is used – either a discussion board via VLE or freely available tools such as Ning, Elgg or Facebook.

Non-electronic or paper-based learning environment

Face to face involving direct conversation and contact with the physical world – in other words primary research, which is beyond the scope of this text.

The underlying pedagogy

At the sensory level there is, in the individual learner, cognisance of the form and structure (in other words the 'look and feel') that relate to the learning style of the learner (visualiser, verbaliser and so on). This is followed, at the cognitive level, with an appreciation of ways to evaluate content (which could be learned in a behaviourist or mechanical fashion) and the thinking skills associated with processing and organising information. In turn, at the cognitive constructivist level, the learner may critically reflect on the task and make sense of content. However, this is set within a social constructivist framework that highlights normative values about how information is evaluated and what criteria might be used to achieve this, for example, how authority might be defined in this context. It is envisaged that the interventions will be scaffolded and incorporate reflection. The learning intervention tends to include a facilitator, and people working individually and in groups, possibly with some organisational structure, such as team leaders and a scribe. Discussion and presentations should take place.

Behavioural learning

The behavioural learning in this intervention includes using artefacts such as web pages, books and articles to familiarise learners with the physical structure of the artefact. For example, a book has a contents page, chapters, headings and sub-headings, diagrams, tables, an index and a list of references. A web page might have a URL, a title metadata, links, a search facility, a site map, a 'bread crumb trail', other navigation buttons and features, white space and balance between text and pictures, which may or may not relate to the learning style of the learner. These structures are similar in other artefacts or applications, for example e-journals packages such as ScienceDirect.

Cognitive learning

At one level, in terms of Bloom's taxonomy for instance, the cognitive approach is concerned with applying evaluation criteria in order to analyse content in order to judge the merits of a piece of information. In other words, applying critical thinking to describe, analyse, critique and eventually synthesise the information to complete a task. This outcome probably involves creating a new piece of information, for example a report or presentation for communication, and it may include genuine new knowledge in the form of 'breakthrough statements' as identified in the SOLO model by Biggs and Collis (1982) (Table 4.1). This thinking influences what is done with the information associated with this activity and may be reflected in any output, whether written, aural or visual.

Constructivist learning

From a cognitive constructivist perspective the emphasis here is 'making sense' and building a knowledge base. From a social constructivist point of view learning highlights the relative value that is placed on certain types of content – authority, relevance, reliability, scope, currency and so on. For example, in the commercial domain information is often deemed to be out of date and of little value after six months; an extreme form of this is in the trading environment where information that is more than four seconds old is considered historical. Conversely, the importance of academic information is measured through the process of peer review, which can result in research taking as long as two years to reach publication. In tandem with this are the norms associated with the context. For example, in the academic domain referencing other people's ideas and avoiding plagiarism are seen as important goals for learners. Online social networking tools have been shown to be effective ways of facilitating the discourse required to realise the higher order thinking engendered by a social constructivist approach.

Levels of complexity

Learners come to the learning situation with varying levels of understanding about the nature and structure of content. For example, many first-year undergraduates are unable to distinguish between an e-book chapter and an e-journal article. As students progress, the distinctions become more refined so second and third-year students begin to understand the difference between peer-reviewed articles and articles for a specific profession. At post-graduate level students need to be more aware of the relative soundness of the methodology and any data analysis within the research reported in the article.

From a thinking skills perspective a lower level of achievement is characterised by learners having less expertise in independent thinking and learning through work that is descriptive rather than analytical or critical, with only a degree of synthesis. Learners find it difficult to digest and/or apply their learning to the situation(s) they are dealing with, relating other people's opinion to their research topic. At the undergraduate level less original thought is likely because of the students' lack of knowledge. Intermediate levels of achievement are characterised by the descriptive element found at the lower level plus some aspects of application, analysis and synthesis, but no evidence of the 'breakthrough statements' found when learners operate at the highest level. High levels of achievement are characterised by learners demonstrating lower and intermediate levels of evidence with significant amounts of application, analysis and synthesis of their work. They use many 'breakthrough statements', evidencing new knowledge or viewing existing knowledge in a novel way, and are able to evaluate or reflect on their learning process in a meaningful way.

Methods of assessment and learning outcomes

A fundamental choice needs to be made when designing methods of assessment: whether the assessment is carried out by an 'expert' or by peers. Peer assessment has been shown to lead to peer-to-peer learning and can result in deeper learning – partly because the assessor is forced to reflect on the activity.

The learning outcomes should determine whether the purpose (see earlier section) has been achieved. For example the learner should:

- be familiar with the form and content of different types of information
- be able to use the structure of information or content to navigate it effectively
- be able to analyse and evaluate content critically
- be able to make balanced judgements regarding the relative merits of individual information sources using a range of criteria derived either via discourse or from extant guides relating to evaluating information, or both
- be able to synthesise content
- be able to choose appropriate mechanisms, tools, formats and media to communicate information effectively.

Examples of interventions

1 Example with undergraduates – evaluating information using online collaborative learning

This example takes place entirely online and involves online collaborative learning (OCL). The intervention was delivered to a group of first-year undergraduate students in sport and exercise science as part of their study skills module Effective Learning Information and Communication Skills. Each week students attended a 50-minute workshop. The assignment used a problem-based approach with a scenario in which students had to find information for a fictitious presentation to A-level students. Students were expected to find six good-quality information sources – two books, two journal articles and two web pages – and provide a short evaluation for every item. This is an extract from the assignment handbook:

> A local PE teacher asks you to do a talk about soccer violence (also known as football hooliganism, or stadium violence) to class of 'A' level sports students. Please provide two web sites for your audience along with a reading list to allow them to conduct further reading on the topic.

Students had received a face-to-face session on finding information using e-resources the previous week. The OCL activity spanned five weeks in all, with four weeks devoted to evaluating information sources and one week to referencing them. The evaluation of information OCL activities was divided into two sub-tasks; each took approximately 25 minutes to complete.

In the first activity students were instructed to log on to Blackboard (Figure 11.1) and complete the activity. In essence they were expected to devise their own evaluation criteria by considering the question posed, reading a web page and posting a reply to the discussion board outlining the criteria they would use. The beauty of this exercise is the fact that the tutor did not tell the students 'the answer' but they found it out for themselves by reading a web page resource on evaluating information (a sensory activity). Then they extracted what they regarded as relevant from the information given (a cognitive activity involving comprehending the text and constructivist in that students, in deciding their own evaluation criteria, are creating their own meaning before posting what they regard as relevant to the discussion board) and

Figure 11.1   Discussion board forum

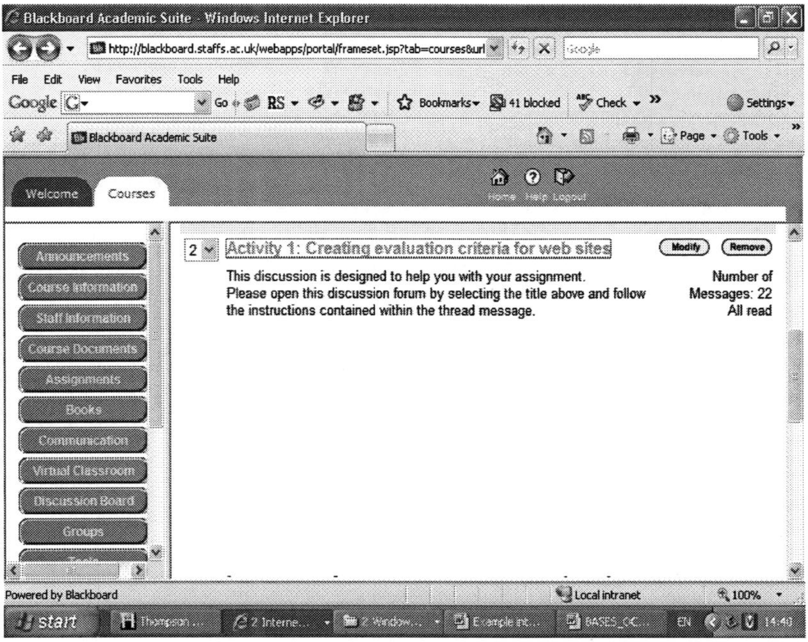

through online discussion came up with a set of criteria. (This is a situated activity regarding negotiating meaning and students sharing their new knowledge in a nascent community of practice.)

Thread of discussion plus student statement 'seed' and instructions to students to complete the activity

The instructions gave the activity its scaffolding and the tutor summary provided a sense of ownership and participation, which promoted metacognition and reflection. Each stage of the activity is shown below, with student examples.

The thread, seed, student postings and tutor summary are shown below exactly as they appeared on the Blackboard discussion board.

> **Thread and seed text**
> For your portfolio assignment (Section E) you need to provide web pages or sites and give reasons (also known as evaluation criteria) why you think they are good.
>
> For this activity last year a student commented that she, 'always ensures that a web page is reliable before using any information on it'.
>
> So, how would you decide what makes a reliable, good quality web page?
>
> To find out follow the instructions 1–9 below:
>
> 1. Have a look at this example: *http://news.bbc.co.uk/hi/english/static/in_depth/programmes/2002/hooligans/*.
>
> 2. Evaluate this web site using a set of detailed criteria – go to this webpage for help: *http://www.lib.berkeley.edu/TeachingLib/Guides/Internet/Evaluate.html*.
>
> 3. Read it carefully and make some notes.
>
> 4. Once you have read this resource go back to our original message.
>
> 5. Select the **reply** button.
>
> 6. State briefly what the web page is and paste in the address.
>
> 7. Write down how you would evaluate this web page.
>
> 8. Write a brief statement about the website under each question as suggested by the Berkeley help site.
>
> 9. Select **submit** to post your reply.

Examples of student postings

Example 1

http://news.bbc.co.uk/hi/english/static/in_depth/programmes/2002/ hooligans/

The web page is a bbc [sic] news page with links to hooligan interviews and reports.

You could evaluate the web page by looking at other pages with the same topic and compare. You could also look through and see how relevant it is to the information you are after.

What can the URL tell you? It informs you that it is from a popular and reliable source, BBC. It also gives you the date and the subject topic. It tells you it is not somebody's personal page.

Are sources documented with footnotes or links? Yes they are. There are links to reports and interviews.

Does it all add up? it [sic] looks like a decent web site with all of the relevant information around the subject. It is well supported and linked to reliable interviews.

Example 2

http://news.bbc.co.uk/hi/english/static/in_depth/programmes/2002/ hooligans/

The web page highlights football hooliganism interviews and reports with links to look deeper into the articles.

You could evaluate the web page by looking at other football hooliganism webpages and compare them to see how they are set out and how they get their information across. You can also look at how relevant the information in the web page is.

What can the URL tell you? It tells the user [it] is from a well known and is a reliable source that could be user friendly. It also tells you the date in which the programme took place telling you how old the information is.

Is the page dated? Yes within the URL.

Example 3

When looking at a website it is important to check the author or who it was created by. You can check if it is a government website by looking at the web address. Some websites have headings saying, 'Background' or 'who am I [sic]?' this enables somebody to look for reliability.

Example 4
I would evaluate a web page by; looking at the ULR address and seeing weather [sic] it is e.g. a government source, which would mean the source is reliable. You can also look at the author and find out whether they have a good reliable background and you should also be able to find any related links and other sources used. Finally look at the last time when the web page was updated especially when stats are involved.

Text of the tutor summary which brings together salient comments within the activity

Well done to all those who contributed! You have identified some excellent evaluation criteria. Jamie and Geoff have summarised your work below.

SUMMARY
Woody stated that he would evaluate a web site by giving 'a quick overview'.

Jamie and Geoff agree and suggest 5 headings for organising this 'quick overview'. We have also put some of your recommendations under each of these headings.

Authority
John argued that 'it is important to check the author or who it was created by'. George mentioned that you can do this by finding out 'whether they have a good reliable background'. Ozzy pointed out that the author could be 'a major company like Microsoft'. **Jamie and Geoff would argue that company or organisation size does not necessarily guarantee information free from bias. Ask yourself – why is the information there?** Finally, Ringo mentioned that when looking at personal pages 'look at their reputation and what they study and research'.

Currency
Paul pointed out that we need to be able to work out 'how old the information is' and George recommended that we 'look at the last time the web page was updated especially when stats are involved'.

Relevance
Sandy recommended that when viewing a web page you need to 'look through and see how relevant it is to the information you are after'.

Reliability

Jody advised that, 'you could evaluate the web page by looking at other pages with the same topic and compare'.

George also identified that valid links are a good indication of reliability. Daniel made the point that you should be able to find 'other sources used' in writing the web page.

Sandy, George, Lemmy, Maddy, Ozzy and Ringo all mentioned the importance of the URL in working out a web page's origin and reliability.

Ringo mentioned that a good way of judging a web page can be done by 'looking at the URL address and seeing whether it is for example a government source'.

Ozzy mentioned that you can get clues from a URL to see whether it is a 'personal website and (therefore) the information may not be a reliable source'.

Jamie and Geoff agree with Ringo and Ozzy regarding URLs BUT stress that we need to be more systematic in the way we analyse their structure.

TASK: To practise analysing a URL follow the instructions 1–5 below:

1. Here is an example web address: *http://www.le.ac.uk/football research/resources/factsheets/fs1.html*.

2. Read the information source BELOW on analysing URLs to break down the sample address into its components, *http://www.vts.intute.ac.uk/detective/urlclues.html*.

3. Do a breakdown and post your answer by replying to this message.

4. If you have time have a look at a fellow student's posting.

5. Discuss their answer by posting a reply.

The tutor summary gave ownership to students by making their output from postings the bulk of the content. Their contributions were personalised and tutor comments were woven in to provide a continuous and logical narrative. It also provided what we call a reflective bridge between week A and week B etc., continuity of learning where by reading the summary students were reminded of what took place the previous week. The task was iterated by focusing on URLs, which enabled the tutors to facilitate the exploration of this issue in more detail. Hence, the iteration is scaffolded. We could have chosen a number of areas to iterate based on students' contributions, such as any one of the four evaluation criteria mentioned in the tutor summary. However, the URL comment provided the opportunity to lead students to the Internet Detective website, which we felt gave a greater opportunity to take their learning deeper.

Finally, the important issue to note here is that these activities were highly participative and cognitive, and involved learning by doing where the learner was reading, comprehending, applying, analysing and synthesising knowledge in order to make a contribution. Student feedback indicated that the students found these activities enjoyable, motivating and rewarding. Diagnostic tests and assessment data showed that students exposed to OCL performed significantly better than those who did not experience the intervention (Walton, 2009).

2 Example with undergraduates – evaluating information using blended learning

This intervention was delivered as part of a first-year information skills elective. It involved a face-to-face seminar with access to the Blackboard discussion board, in effect a blended learning session. However, it could be delivered without any recourse to the technology if necessary. In summary the tutor very briefly set the scene; then students were asked to log on to Blackboard and write down on the discussion board what they looked for when judging the worth of a website for inclusion in an assignment. They then received a mini-lecture and did some group work, after which they returned to Blackboard and wrote down what they would look for in a web page in the light of discussions. Finally, students were asked to share one thing they had learnt in the session. It can be seen from the notional times given below that we had allowed 70 minutes all together, but it would be useful to schedule up to two hours for this session to allow extra time for discussion.

This intervention uses 'the pedagogy of the question' technique where students have to engage immediately with the subject area and first demonstrate their prior knowledge. This in effect creates a participatory atmosphere where students are more likely to ask questions and, more importantly, contribute. By its very nature this session is first and foremost cognitive, in that students have to think about what they know and write it down. It is a sensory activity in that students use visual and auditory learning during the mini-lecture. Task 2 is constructivist in that students take the information they have received and via group work negotiate and agree what it means. Finally, it is cognitive as students synthesise this new knowledge into a second posting for the discussion board.

This gives students the opportunity to see in a very direct way how their knowledge has changed, become more detailed and indeed more critical through attending the workshop. By using a VLE such as Blackboard, where students post their 'before' and 'after' answers, a record is kept, which can be revisited by tutors or students in the future.

Figure 11.2 shows how the tutor structured the session and what was covered.

Figure 11.2   Introduction to evaluating information

Plan for today

- Introduction – setting the scene
- Task 1 how do you evaluate information?
- Mini-lecture evaluating information effectively
- Task 2 re-appraising your approach to evaluating information
  - Group discussion
  - Individual activity
- Plenary

Introduction – setting the scene (notes) (10 minutes)

This was a very brief overview without giving too much away to students, because we wanted them to have their own thoughts about this topic!

These are our notes for the introduction:

'Evaluate' means the following: value, appraise, weigh up, judge worth or quality, assess, gauge.

In my view evaluating information is the most important information literacy skill.

Implications of not being able to evaluate information correctly might be:

- By using poor quality information you end up with a lower mark than if you had taken care to examine your information sources carefully

- Life threatening certainly in some professions such as the NHS
- Disastrous for the economy; poorly understood consequences of sub-prime mortgage lending and associated risks of over-lending led to a banking crisis, compounded by misinformation which in turn was misunderstood by the public leading to panic and a worse situation!

Task 1: how do you evaluate information? (15 minutes)

This was put to the students verbally and in roughly the following way:

> This is an individual exercise – to get the most out of it please don't discuss this task with your colleagues just yet. Cast your mind back to your most recent assignment. Imagine you are trying to find some information on the web to support your work. You probably would do a Google search (or whatever) and find a web page that you think is just right for the job.

> So how do you decide that the web page is just right? What do you look for and what are the issues that you consider?

> Do the following:

> 1. List all your ideas on paper.
> 2. Log on to Blackboard.
> 3. Go to the discussion board.
> 4. Go to Forum Evaluating information.
> 5. Reply to the posting 'Put your ideas here'.
> 6. Leave your PC open and return to your seat.

Mini-lecture on evaluating information effectively (15 minutes)

The tutor moved on to talk about evaluating information using a questioning approach as illustrated in figures 11.3 and 11.4. Figure 11.3 shows the critical and analytical manner in which students should approach their evaluations.

Of course this is the ideal! The focus for individual criteria is illustrated in figure 11.4.

Figure 11.3 Approaches to evaluating information

What should our approach be...?

Define and apply criteria for evaluating information:
- Examine and compare, in a critical manner, information from various sources.
- Analyse the structure and logic of supporting arguments or methods.
- Recognise and question prejudice, deception or manipulation.
- Recognise the cultural, physical, or other context within which the information was created and understand the impact of context on interpreting the information.
- Recognise and understand own biases and cultural context.

Figure 11.4 Criteria for evaluating information

What criteria should we use?

- **Academic context:**
  - Authority (e.g. .gov .edu .ac .mil .co author, organisation)
  - Time (how up to date, when published, period)
  - Coverage/relevance (geographical, subject, information contribution, primary/secondary)
  - Accuracy (errors, corroboration)
  - Audience (age, specialised, general, level)
  - Format/style (logically organised, readability)
  - Documentation/reliability (explanations of origin, bibliography)
  - Point of view (opinion, objectivity, emotional content, bias)

The mini-lecture then turns to the CIBER report (UCL, 2008) (Figure 11.5) and then our own research (Figure 11.6) to look at the reality of students' approaches to evaluating information.

The terminology used to describe types of learner is explained in Figure 11.6. Figures 11.7–11.10 give examples of comments about searching that someone in each of these categories might make.

Figure 11.5 **What people do when searching for information (based on UCL, 2008)**

What people actually do...?

- ✒ Users pay 'little regard to the document content'.

- ✒ 'Speed of young people's web searching indicates that little time is spent in evaluating information for relevance, accuracy or authority...'

- ✒ 'Many teenagers thought that if a site was indexed on Yahoo then it had to be authoritative.'

Figure 11.6 **Different types of learner**

User experiences: examples from research (evaluating web pages)

- ✒ **Information agnostic:** Unaware or unconcerned regarding need to evaluate – copies and pastes large chunks without checking quality.

- ✒ **Information novice:** Aware of need to evaluate information for quality but sees it in black/white, true/false, either/or terms.

- ✒ **Information critic:** Aware that it isn't simply black and white; need to judge each source on its merits. Talks about balance, weighing up, using range of criteria.

- ✒ **Information sceptic:** Can talk about the nature and relative value of evaluation criteria in a given setting, aware that all information is biased to some extent.

Figure 11.7 **Comments that an information agnostic might make about searching**

Information agnostic

- ✒ I didn't really know about what type of things you should look for when you are looking at websites.

- ✒ Really when you first go on a website you don't read all the information.

- ✒ [Before] I didn't know what the things at the end like .ac and .org meant.

Figure 11.8 Comments that an information novice might make about searching

Information novice

- ◁ I'm looking at references. In the future I'm going to look and see whether it is from a big company where it's very probably going to be factual.
- ◁ You don't want to be writing stuff in your assignments that's not true.
- ◁ You didn't realise how many websites could be frauds.

Figure 11.9 Comments that an information critic might make about searching

Information critic

- ◁ You can, like, judge websites for their stature... basically how reliable information is going to be and whether it is worth putting in your essay or assignment. I look for where it comes from now.
- ◁ I look at other universities' pages, they are always good to look at. Obviously people like the BBC, then if you look at one from a really random place I tend to look again.
- ◁ When looking at a website it is important to check the author or who it was created by. You can check if it is a government website by looking at the web address. Some websites have headings saying 'Background' or 'Who am I?' This enables somebody to look for reliability.

Figure 11.10 Comments that an information sceptic might make about searching

Information sceptic

- ◁ Some of them initially are important like reliability and relevance, obviously if you are going to reference something in an essay you need to know that the source is reliable.
- ◁ Currency as well, to be honest, it needs to be up to date, opinions and things change. People thought the earth was flat but things get updated.
- ◁ It could be written by the government or the FA or something and they could make a pretty stand up point, but you could have a 3rd year student from a university make just as good a point and just as relevant.

As a very quick interactive activity the tutor asked students to say where they would place themselves against these four levels of information discernment. From our experience, students in class often place themselves between novice and critic (and this is borne out by the Task 1 student statements shown below). Thus this quick activity enabled the tutor to engage the students in reflecting on their current knowledge and to find out how confident they feel about this particular skill.

The tutor then looked at evaluating information using different metaphors to illustrate the point further (figures 11.11 and 11.12).

Figure 11.11 simply takes the 'mine of information' a little further to give visual form to a common idea.

Figure 11.12 uses another more obscure metaphor to illustrate the need to evaluate information. Figures 11.11 and 11.12 are intended to engage visual learners and challenge students' existing outlook.

Figure 11.13 illustrates how new knowledge can be disseminated in a straightforward way in a number of different information sources.

This use of the 'food labelling' metaphor (Figure 11.14) struck a chord with students from first year to postgraduate; there is an immediacy to this which students find engaging. The 'very low' box is green (represented here

Figure 11.11 The mine of information

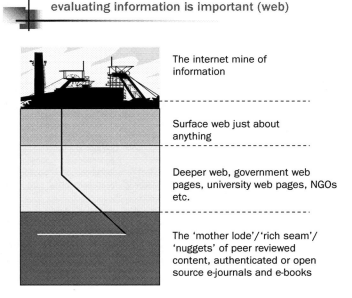

Some ways of thinking about why evaluating information is important (web)

The internet mine of information

Surface web just about anything

Deeper web, government web pages, university web pages, NGOs etc.

The 'mother lode'/'rich seam'/ 'nuggets' of peer reviewed content, authenticated or open source e-journals and e-books

Figure 11.12 Information as another way of thinking

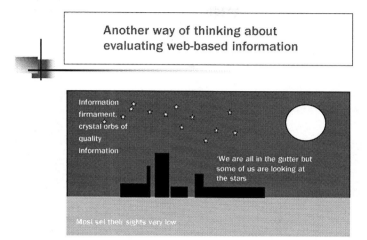

Figure 11.13 Reporting scientific research

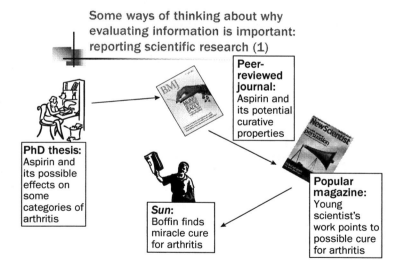

with vertical stripes), the 'low' box is yellow (represented here with horizontal stripes), the 'medium' box is orange (represented here with diagonal stripes) and the 'dangerous' one is red (represented here as a chequer board).

Figure 11.15 is taken from the ANZIIL information literacy model (Bundy, 2004: 17) and neatly encapsulates how we should go about evaluating information.

Figure 11.14 'Pinch of salt rating'

Some ways of thinking about why
evaluating information is important:
reporting scientific research (2)

☞ **PhD thesis**	Pinch of salt rating: very low	
☞ **Peer-reviewed journal**	Pinch of salt rating: low	
☞ **Professional magazine**	Pinch of salt rating: medium	
☞ **Newspaper**	Pinch of salt rating: dangerous!!	

Figure 11.15 Conclusion to evaluating information session

Conclusion: ideally we should all
do this...

- ☞ Examine and compare information from various sources in order to evaluate reliability, validity, accuracy, authority, timeliness, and point of view or bias.
- ☞ Analyse the structure and logic of supporting arguments or methods.
- ☞ Recognise prejudice, deception or manipulation.
- ☞ Recognise the cultural, physical or other context within which the information was created and understand the impact of context on interpreting the information.

Having provided more detail regarding the need to evaluate information the next step was to get students to discuss the issues themselves.

Task 2: re-appraising your approach to evaluating information (20 minutes)

1. Now discuss in groups of four the concept of evaluating information and make a list of all the criteria you would now use to judge the worth of a website.

2. In the light of this discussion go back to Blackboard and reply to your own first posting noting what you might add to your original list.

Plenary (10 minutes)

There was then a plenary where the tutor asked each student to say in what way they had changed their views on evaluating information in the light of the session they had just experienced. This gave a chance for students to reflect again on what they had learnt and for the tutor to check that they had understood the main ideas. Finally, students received a handout that outlined how to evaluate information systematically for their assignments.

Examples of student postings

Some examples of student postings gathered after the latest delivery of this session are shown below. These postings illustrate what to expect from students and, in this instance, show how their information discernment might change to become more detailed and critical as a result of the intervention. As you can see there is a step change between task 1 and task 2 in the way that students reported how they would evaluate a web page.

Student 1
Task 1

- See if I know of the website or have used it before, if it's a reputable source.
- Scan through the information for keywords or phrases.
- Check when it was written and who by to check the relevance and reliability of the information.

Task 2

- Check quotes used, if they too are a reliable source.
- Check the reliability of the source, if the information contains relevant theories, if it's established, the validity of the information.

- Note the website, if it ends .gov, .ac, .edu and so on.
- Look into background of the author, is it a professor? academic? blogger?
- See if the website has contact details, e.g. web master.
- Check the presentation and layout of the website – spelling errors, broken hyperlinks, headings, relevant photos/graphs.

Student 2
Task 1

- Search through for keywords.
- Look who's produced information and when it was written to see if it's reliable.
- Read it through to see if it is relevant for the information I need.

Task 2

- Reliability/validity of the source quotes and references; is it established?, consistency.
- Check who's produced the resource; find out their background.
- Scan through for keywords; check relevance of the source to information needed.
- Contact details – organisations, web master – check end of web address.
- Presentation and quality – pictures, spelling errors, overall design – easy to access?
- Check when the information was published.
- Is it someone's point of view? Check opinion, emotional content, bias.

Student 3
Task1

- Look at the titles displayed on the web page and check their relevance to your essay.
- Read any abstracts if applicable.
- Click any links on the page if they are relevant.
- Reference any information.

- Check the source of the information and its date.
- Check out any reviews.

Task 2

- How up to date is the website?
- Look at the authority of the information, which is the author, and check their background
- How relevant is the information?
- Look at different points of views and opinions of people that have accessed the website.
- The format of the web page, which is its layout and accessibility, e.g. hyperlinks.
- How accurate the information is? Looking at its original source and how accurate that is.
- What audience is the information directed to and whether or not you will find it useful.
- The reliability of the information and the references people have given it.

Student 4
Task 1

- Is the site up to date?
- Who wrote the information?
- Check for references/quotes to support the information –> reliability?
- Is the information useful for the topic? –> check for keywords.

Task 2

- Validity?
- Consistency? How long has the page been there?
- Presentation? (pictures, spelling, page design).
- Webmaster?
- Point of view? (opinion, objectivity, bias, emotional content).
- Audience? (age, specialised, general).
- Documentation? –> reliability (explanations of origin, bibliography).
- Is it established? –> theories.

- Who wrote it? (author, contact details, background).
- Authority? (.gov, .edu, .ac, .co, and so on).

3 Example with any learners – finding information in a book

The following intervention was aimed at learners who had not developed strategies for identifying relevant information in a book. The need for this was suggested by a lecturer who had had the experience that when he suggested that a book might be relevant to students they would read it from cover to cover without determining its relevance or picking out the relevant bits. They were slow to identify useful material from it.

Initially learners were asked to brainstorm methods they used to identify quickly whether a book was relevant and contained useful material. These methods were discussed and good techniques were listed on a flip chart. The following text formed a handout that summarised useful strategies.

'SMART' READING

Do you have a lot to read? Does it take you a long time? Do you want to:

- Quickly judge the relevance of a text (document, book)?
- Speed up your ability to get an overview of the main ideas in a text?

If so, the following techniques will help.

DON'T immediately read the whole text from beginning to end.

To help you absorb the new information take 2–3 minutes to: First think about what you want to find out (maybe an overview, explanations, examples). What do you already know? Who is the author? What is their background? What is the author likely to say?

Read the reviewer's comments.

READ the **Contents** page – to get an overview of content and structure.

BROWSE the **Index**. Does it cover the topics you need?

MAKE BRIEF NOTES **– active reading helps you concentrate and remember**
IF RELEVANT CONTINUE

SCAN the **Chapter headings**

LOOK for **diagrams, figures or tables** – these condense the message, provide an overview. What do they show?

MAKE BRIEF NOTES **– key terms, ideas, names, page numbers**
IF RELEVANT CONTINUE

SKIM the **Abstract, Introduction, Preface or Foreword** – what is the document trying to cover and what are the key arguments?

MAKE BRIEF NOTES
IF RELEVANT CONTINUE

READ the **introduction or first paragraph** for each relevant chapter – what is the author about to discuss?

READ the **conclusion** to the chapter(s) – what are the main ideas? note: the section before the conclusion often debates the alternative ideas/conclusions.

MAKE BRIEF NOTES
GOT ENOUGH? STOP or CONTINUE!

READ the relevant **Chapter(s)** or the text in full.

MAKE BRIEF NOTES
GOT ENOUGH? STOP. FIND ANOTHER SOURCE.

Remember:

- Texts tend to follow either **introduction – main arguments/ topics/describing a process – conclusion OR problem – proposed solution(s) – evaluation, OR problem – previous knowledge (literature review) – research method (methodology) – results (findings) – discussion (implications) – conclusion.**

- Italics indicate *important point*. Words in (brackets) provide examples.

- Check the references to help identify other related texts.

4 Example with primary school children – evaluating a book

This intervention was delivered to Year 1 primary school children, though it could equally be delivered to those in year 2. The session focused on establishing whether a book presented by the teacher to the class was fiction or non-fiction. This was achieved by working with the whole class to decode the source and judge its content, in effect evaluating an information source. Hence, from the information literacy perspective the information source needed to do the task was already selected by the teacher (this is why there are no antecedents to this example). Pupils then used the information book to create their own glossary entry. In information literacy terms this was using and communicating information.

The teaching intervention was group based and required a non-fiction resource as an example; in this intervention it was a book on plants.

The first activity was carried out by the whole group. It was followed by small group work and then another plenary. The whole session took one hour.

In essence the first part of the session was concerned with guiding children to look for clues as to what kind of book it was. Therefore, this session was heavily scaffolded, and the teacher offered a great deal of structure to children's individual answers and group discussions. Hence, this part of the session began as a sensory activity and then moved towards a cognitive approach. First of all the teacher addressed the whole group, showed the children the book resource and asked them to look at the front cover. The first question was, 'Is the front cover picture an illustration or a picture?' (Often non-fiction books have a photograph rather than an illustration – not always though.) This was a cognitive exercise, which involved the children drawing on their prior knowledge of non-fiction books and comparing this example against it.

Second, the teacher asked the pupils to see whether there was an author and illustrator (often a fiction book has both author and illustrator; sometimes a non-fiction book has neither). Next the teacher turned to the back cover to what is called the 'blurb', the description of what the book is about. After this the teacher turned to the contents page and asked pupils to say what kind of contents page it was. From the contents page the teacher guided children to see that the contents page was not in chapters and that they could go to a specific page for information rather than read from cover to cover (as in a story book).

Turning to the back of the book, the tutor looked for an index and asked the children through whole group discussion to explain its form: that it was a list of words in alphabetical order with numbers beside them. Through discussion the teacher established that words in the index were references to particular points in the text. In this set of activities, by asking questions the children were engaging their cognitive abilities, then through discussion the learning situation became social constructivist. The teacher was guiding children, through discussion, to negotiate a common agreement on whether the example book was fiction or non-fiction.

Finally, the teacher examined the glossary and asked pupils to comment on the form – a list of words with a short description. Once the teacher had used elements of the book to determine what it was and how to use it she turned to the content and pointed out that the book was in sections rather than chapters. The pupils examined the content of the book; the teacher asked them what they noticed about the photographs and illustrations – she wanted them to notice that they all had captions explaining what they were. Hence, by examining a book in this way pupils where shown that they could judge a book to see if it was a good information book or not. This was further exemplified by looking for a specific piece of information in the book to see if it gave them what they were looking for. At this point the teacher guided pupils to the various ways in which they might find the information they needed, via the contents page, index or glossary.

The small group activity was to look at the book *Plants* and agree on some keywords to look for in the book. Once they had found the information on the keyword, pupils were asked to write an explanation of it in the form of a glossary entry. This was a cognitive approach in that pupils were showing that they had comprehended what a glossary item was by applying their knowledge, analysing an example and then synthesising this into new knowledge – their own glossary entry. The task also had a social constructivist dimension in that pupils did this cognitive work together as a small group.

This activity was 'differentiated' in that different words were given to different groups depending on their ability:

- The more able were given subject-specific words like 'vein', 'root' or 'stem' to look for.

- The middle ability children were given words such as 'seed', 'leaves' and 'food'.

- The least able group were given more general words, for example, 'sun', 'water' and 'flowers'.

In the plenary session each group was asked to read out their glossary entry so that the teacher (and the group) could discuss how successful they were. This last activity allowed pupils to reflect on what they had learnt through communicating their work to others and peer reviewing others' work in the class.

12

Learning intervention 5: enhancing information literacy in the workplace – a holistic approach

This intervention provides an excellent example of how information literacy can be integrated and delivered in a holistic way in the workplace. Furthermore, it helps to indicate how the theory of information literacy learning discussed in Part 1 can be applied. It stems from the work of Bonnie Cheuk (Cheuk, 2008) in an organisation called Environmental Resources Management (ERM), one of the world's largest environmental consulting firms.

Fostering information literacy in the workplace has to be fundamentally linked to helping the organisation and the people in it to achieve their objectives, otherwise it will fail. In fact this is true wherever it is learned. However, in the educational context projects and 'finding out' can follow a relatively linear path (although within the overall process, from a learning perspective, it is highly iterative) from problem definition to delivery of the final product – whether essay, poster, report or presentation. The task of finding out also tends to be performed by an individual or possibly a small group, and everyone needs to be information literate. The teacher has control over this environment and the learning process, so information literacy can be introduced in a relatively structured way. Nevertheless, it still needs to be integrated into the task of the learner.

In the workplace people tend not to spend time learning formally about managing information or information literacy. Some organisations, such as the Community Development Resource Association (CDRA) in South Africa, take a more conscious approach about how they learn, spending time 'harvesting' their experience.

However, they are unusual and generally the onus is very much on getting on with the task at hand. Hence there is even greater necessity to integrate information literacy into the day to day completion of work tasks. The information environment is likely to differ from the educational environment, although in higher education one would expect the resources to emulate the workplace information environment to some extent. In ERM the materials, systems, roles, tasks and information norms are very different from those in the educational environment and this is reflected in the approach taken to foster information literacy described below.

As indicated in Part 1 of this book, to inform an effective information literacy intervention in-depth research needs to be carried out by the facilitator, in this case the knowledge management team. The team spent three months identifying the issues that ERM staff were facing in order to access information and expertise to support the sales and marketing effort, and for developing more innovative client solutions.

Problems experienced by employees included:

- the use of outdated information (because it was convenient)
- a lack of awareness of existing resources
- unfamiliarity with the tools that would help make best use of information
- the assumption that Google is the best search engine to look for information
- the inability to manage personal e-mail box 'overload'
- an unwillingness to share information.

Staff's information literacy needs fell into the second, third and fourth intervention categories: 'knowledge of the information landscape', 'knowledge of the acquisition of information' and 'knowledge of the application and use of information'.

To develop an information literacy strategy Bruce's (1997) seven faces of information literacy were used to focus information literacy interventions. This included using information wisely; organising and controlling information for it to be retrievable; the skills to use existing information and systems; and an increased consciousness of the information seeking and use process.

Ways of achieving information literacy

Help senior leaders to see the value of using information wisely

A knowledge management strategy and budget to invest in a global knowledge sharing programme were used to help senior leaders in the organisation to see the value of 'using information wisely for the benefit of the organisation', through organised discussions. This resulted in a knowledge management strategy and budget to invest in a global knowledge sharing programme. Without the involvement of senior managers it is unlikely that the strategies to strengthen information literacy that were identified would have been effective.

This participation would be necessary in any context where figures of authority need to sanction and condone new practice, and tends to be the case even in the non-commercial world. In schools, for example, the systematic integration of information literacy tends to stem from a proactive school librarian but with the support of an enlightened headteacher! This is partly explained by the day-to-day pressures people experience in the workplace where people have to manage their time and balance the various demands placed on them. Senior or more experienced figures can help encourage people to shift that balance. In a sense, from a social constructivist perspective, managers were becoming conscious of and helping to concretise the significance of 'knowledge' to the community of practice.

Develop and make use of a new knowledge management system

The newly developed knowledge management system Minerva was developed and used: 3,000 staff were asked to find ways to reduce ERM's carbon footprint by using Minerva. This served to engage staff with a question that they could relate to and required them to make use of a system designed to help communicate knowledge and information. Hence the 'pedagogy of the question' sparked people's interest and gave them a purpose and motivation for getting to grips with the information system that enabled them to share and discuss their ideas.

Recruit knowledge champions

Prior to the launch of Minerva 50 staff members were recruited to become 'knowledge champions', which presumably appealed to various personal motivations. These staff were introduced to practical ideas about how knowledge sharing and using 'information' can reduce proposal time and increase sales opportunities. This expanded their knowledge of the purpose of information literacy and how it would benefit them, and of the organisation as a whole. The staff were given in-depth training on Minerva and became advocates to inspire other consultants. In a behavioural sense, this training helped to develop information literacy skills in the staff, which enabled them to use the available information tools. Within any community of practice, the advocates of the training create and disseminate the information norms by encouraging aspiring members to conform. As noted in Chapter 6, where 'the learner as a social being' was discussed, tapping into this aspect of the 'social' learner is a necessary aspect of developing information literacy.

Give training

To enable them to develop their knowledge of the information landscape, 3,000 staff were given 60-minute training, face to face and via webconferencing and teleconferencing. This enabled them to learn about the information resources that were available and how to use them via Minerva.

Maximise the use of Minerva external contacts

To maximise the use of Minerva external contacts, newsletters and e-mail communication with external vendors and internal information resources were incorporated into the knowledge management system. This showed an appreciation of the information reality of the staff – again recognising that information solutions and information literacy must address the 'reality' of the learner, and not confine itself to the environment managed by the internal information professionals, such as internal databases or a corporate library.

Use Minerva to support the consultancy process

Once they were familiar with using Minerva, employees were asked to consider how it could support their work and, in particular, the specific stages of the consultancy process. In this way information literacy was further embedded in the roles and associated cognitive tasks of the staff. This provided a relevant context for staff to think about information literacy (although this phrase was never used) and served to enable staff to become more conscious of the role knowledge and information plays in their day-to-day tasks and hence become more information literate. In addition the onus was placed on the staff to determine how Minerva could be used, ensuring that solutions were user driven, related to their reality – their 'sense-making' – rather than imposed.

Educate site managers

Every month site managers were educated in ways to create and present content on the intranet and how to design and index this information, further enhancing and embedding the skills to manage information and help them to achieve their role as communicators in the organisation. It can be seen that information literacy incorporated the ability to manage information and the skills and knowledge to communicate information effectively. Hence the intervention moved beyond the information access conception of information literacy that tends to predominate in the literature.

The complexity of incorporating information literacy

This approach to fostering information literacy reinforces the point made earlier that it is a complex activity to incorporate information literacy in any environment. If it is to lead to a shift in motivation, thinking and behaviour, it needs to be resourced, and involves a great deal of work. In this case four information professionals were employed full time to facilitate this activity. There is no 'quick fix' to fostering and supporting people's information literacy. Providing condensed, abstract, information literacy interventions that are not integrated into the work context or that do not explicitly enable people to achieve their objectives will fail. Furthermore, the process is both incremental and ongoing. Cheuk (2008) recognises that the knowledge management team has to continue to find a way to motivate and enable employees to learn from the information available and to learn from one another.

Part 3:
Conclusion

13

Concluding comments

For us, writing this book has been a learning process. In trying to understand how to teach, facilitate and foster information literacy it has been necessary to find out more about how people learn and what affects people's learning and information behaviour. It has also involved us reflecting on what we do as teachers. We are, in effect, the independent life-long learner that we seek to foster. This is not entirely through choice but as a consequence of the constantly changing environment and the need to adapt to the learners and colleagues we work with and the technologies available.

The examples given in the learning interventions described in Part 2 are tried, tested and based on a sound bedrock of learning, pedagogical and information behaviour theory, but they are not set in stone for all time. As noted, we too are on a journey of discovery and our ideas have developed over time and continue to do so. Although we feel that the approaches described here have enabled students to gain a greater degree of information literacy, our future interventions will try to find even better ways to incorporate what we have learnt and design accordingly. We also realise that certain interventions may not work in every part in all institutions and settings. The thing to do is to try them out or try parts out and modify the interventions to your teaching style and the needs of your learners in your specific context.

Reflecting on the content of this book it is evident that to enable someone to become information literate takes time and any training needs to be underpinned with knowledge of how people learn. There is no quick fix. It involves the learner bringing to the forefront of their mind the processes and knowledge associated with how they learn and viewing the world from an information perspective. Thus, it is challenging because this is not a natural process for most people. The role of information in the learning process is largely unconscious; people are often relatively good at it, but have absorbed the norms, knowledge and techniques in an unconscious way, and do not appreciate the complex nature of this knowledge. Therefore they may be reluctant to spend time and effort developing their information literacy. As a result, they may not see the necessity of spending time developing information literacy in others. This is evident in higher education where faculty are reluctant to spend time incorporating information literacy in their programmes and tend to perceive information literacy only in terms of becoming aware of the subject specific sources available to the student. Alternatively, people are not information literate, are not conscious of their lack of information literacy, are unaware of the benefits of being information literate and hence find it difficult to understand the need to learn to be information literate.

It is essential that we recognise the learner's sensory capabilities, cognitive thinking skills and capacity for social learning. In so doing, we can begin to construct our interventions accordingly. We must also take more care to recognise the person in context, in other words, what people bring to the learning situation, and begin to see learners positively; after all, learning is a two-way process and as tutors we can learn a great deal from learners if we are prepared to listen. A lack of understanding of the full meaning of information literacy and relevant teaching and learning theory often leads to teaching abstract behavioural and cognitive processes associated with aspects of information literacy such as searching a database. Although this is useful it tends to have little long-term impact on the behaviour of learners and even when learners take on board new skills it does not lead to an information literate independent learner. As indicated in parts 1 and 2, information literacy needs to be contextualised and integrated into the day-to-day role and tasks of the learner. As we have stressed, different aspects of the learner and learning – individual and those that stem from the social context – need to be taken into account.

We would argue that although information literacy interventions in higher education can be highly successful they are, in essence, remedial. We would therefore like to see information literacy supported and incorporated in all learning environments, starting in primary school, developing into secondary education, then built on in higher education and eventually transferred into the work place and active citizenship. This would mean placing a greater emphasis on inquiry-based learning throughout the learner's educational experience. We would like to see information literacy taught and fostered in such a way that the subject is internalised so learners have the motivation and ability to learn independently and in a critical fashion. This would benefit learners, helping them to resolve problems and deal with situations by systematically drawing on existing knowledge and managing information as any other resource. This would also enable learners to take part in and contribute to any activity that requires access to knowledge, data and information.

It is our earnest view that information literacy is not just a functional tool to becoming better qualified but really is a means for people to become engaged citizens who can, through the lens of information literacy, become informed and constructively critical of the world around them. We predict that the teaching of information literacy to support inquiry will grow and expand into different contexts. We will probably start to see employers placing increasing value on their employees' information literacy skills and broader knowledge, data and information management skills, and investing time and money to develop the staff's knowledge and skills in this area. This would be a move from narrowly focusing on digital literacy or investing in technology to recognising that people's capacity and ability to access, use, manage and communicate knowledge, data and information is essential.

We would like to know from anyone directly involved in this area who tries out some of the examples illustrated in this book, whether you are successful or not. Many of you will have already developed information literacy practices that work well. We would welcome hearing from you about successful information literacy interventions, especially those that have worked in contexts other than higher education.

We would like to wish good luck to those who have been involved in facilitating information literacy for some time (often dealing with a lack of understanding and institutional or 'turf' barriers) and to those who have recently become involved in this important endeavour. Enjoy the opportunity of being in a position to help empower individuals, organisations and society as a whole, promoting egalitarian access to knowledge and contributing to a better place for all.

References

ACRL (2000) *Information literacy competency standards for higher education*, Association of College & Research Libraries. Chicago: American Library Association.

Andretta, S. (2005) *Information literacy: a practitioner's guide.* Oxford: Chandos.

Andretta, S. (ed.) (2007) *Change and challenge: information literacy for the 21st century.* Adelaide: Auslib Press.

Armstrong, C., Abell, A., Boden, D., Town, S., Webber, S. and Woolley, M. (2005) Defining information literacy for the UK, *Library and Information Update*, 4 (1–2), 23–25.

Averweg, U. and Greyling, E. (2009) A survey of information and communication technologies and information needs in the eThewkwini Municipality in South Africa. In: Leaning, M. (ed.) *Issues in information and literacy: education, practice and pedagogy.* Santa Rosa, CA: Informing Science Press, 227–256.

Baker, L. (1994) Monitors and blunders: patient health information seeking from a different perspective, *Bibliotheca Medica Canadiana*, 16, 60–63.

Barranoik, L. (2001) Research success with senior high school students, *School Libraries Worldwide*, 7 (1), 28–45.

Beardon, H. (2004) *ICT for development: empowerment or exploitation?* London: Action Aid International.

Belkin, N. J. (2005) Anomalous state of knowledge. In: Fisher, K. E., Erdelez, S. and McKechie, L. E. F. (eds), *Theories of information behavior*, Assist Monograph Series. Medford: Information Today, Inc., 44–48.

Belkin, N. and Robertson, S. (1976) Information science and the phenomenon of information, *Journal of the American Society for Information Science*, 27 (4), 197–204.

Bell, M. (2001) Supported reflective practice: a programme of peer observation and feedback for academic teaching development, *International Journal for Academic Development*, 6 (1), 29–39.

Big Blue Project (2002) *The Big Blue: information skills for students, final report*, *http://www.leeds.ac.uk/bigblue/finalreport.html*, accessed 19 March 2009.

Biggs, J. B. (1999) *Teaching for quality learning at university: what the student does*. Buckingham: Society for Research into Higher Education/Open University Press.

Biggs, J. B. and Collis, K. F. (1982) Evaluating the quality of learning: the SOLO taxonomy. New York: Academic Press. Cited in Moseley, D., Baumfield, V., Higgins, S., Lin, M., Newton, D., Robson, S., Elliot, J. and Gregson, M. (2004) *Thinking skills frameworks for post-16 learners: an evaluation*, a research report for the Learning and Skills Research Centre. Trowbridge: Cromwell Press, 21.

Biggs, J. B. and Moore, P. J. (1993) *Process of learning*, 3rd edn. New York: Prentice Hall.

Bloom, B. S., Engelhart, D., Furst, E. J., Krathwohl, D. A. and Hill, W. H. (1956) *Taxonomy of educational objectives: the classification of educational goals: handbook 1: cognitive domain*. New York: David McKay Company Inc.

Bordieu, P. (1986) The forms of capital. In: Richardson, J. (ed.), *Handbook of theory and research for the sociology of education*. New York: Macmillan.

Borgman, C. L., Gallagher, A. L., Hirsh, S. G. and Walter, V. A. (1995) Children's searching behavior on browsing and keyword online catalogs: the Science Library Catalog Project, *Journal of the American Society for Information Science*, 46 (9), 663–684.

Boud, D. and Feletti, G. (1997) Changing problem-based learning. In: Boud, D. and Feletti, G. (eds), *The challenge of problem-based learning*, 2nd edn. London: Kogan Page, 1–14.

Bransford, J., Brown, A. and Cocking, R. (eds) (2000) *How people learn: brain, mind, experience, and school*, Commission on Behavioral and Social Sciences and Education. Washington, MA, National Academies Press.

Bruce, C. (1997) *Seven faces of information literacy in higher education*, *http://sky.fit.qut.edu.au/~bruce/inflit/faces/faces1.htm*, accessed 17 April 2009.

Bruce, C., Edwards, S. L. and Lupton, M. (2006) Six frames for information literacy education: a conceptual framework for interpreting the relationships between theory and practice, *ITALICS*, 5 (1), *www.ics.heacademy.ac.uk/italics/vol5iss1.htm*, accessed 17 April 2009.

Bruce, C. S. (1995) Information literacy: a framework for higher education, *Australian Library Journal*, August, 158–170.

Bundy, A. (ed.) (2004) *Australian and New Zealand Information Literacy Framework: principles, standards and practice*, 2nd edn. Adelaide: Australian and New Zealand Institute for Information Literacy.

Bystrom, K. (2002) Information and information sources in tasks of varying complexity, *Journal of the American Society for Information Science and Technology*, 53 (7), 581–591.

Bystrom, K. and Jarvelin, K. (1995) Task complexity affects information seeking and use, *Information Processing and Management*, 31 (2), 191–213.

Case, D. O. (2007) *Looking for information: a survey of research on information seeking, needs, and behavior*, 2nd edn. New York: Academic Press.

Catts, R. and Lau, J. (2008) *Towards information literacy indicators*. Paris: UNESCO.

Chambers, R. (2002) *Participatory workshops: a sourcebook of 21 ideas and activities*. Brighton: Institute of Development Studies.

Chapman, R. S. (1978) Comprehension strategies in children. In: Bransford, J., Brown, A. and Cocking, R. (eds) (2000) *How people learn: brain, mind, experience, and school*, Commission on Behavioral and Social Sciences and Education. Washington, MA, National Academies Press.

Cheuk, B. (1998) Modelling the information seeking and use process in the workplace: employing sense-making approach, *Information Research: An International Electronic Journal*, 4 (2), *http://InformationR.net/ir/4-2/isic/cheuk.html*, accessed 17 April 2009.

Cheuk, B. (2008) Delivering business value through information literacy in the workplace, *Libri*, 58 (3), 137–143.

Cheuk, B. (2009) Personal communication from Bonnie Cheuk in 2009 regarding her work at ERM.

Choo, C. (2007) Information seeking in organisations: epistemic contexts and contests, *Information Research*, 12 (2), *http://informationr.net/ir/12-2/paper298.html*, accessed 19 March 2009.

Cornwall, A. (2008) *Democratising engagement: what the UK can learn from international experience*. London: Demos.

Cowan, J. (2002) *Facilitating development through varieties of reflection*, Higher Education Academy Resources on Reflection, *http://www.heacademy.ac.uk/resources/detail/id481_facilitating_development_through_reflection*, accessed 19 March 2009.

Dervin, B. (1983) An overview of sense-making research: concepts, methods and results to date, paper presented at the International Communication Association Annual Meeting, Dallas, Texas, May, *http://communication.sbs.ohio-state.edu/sense-making/art/artabsdervin83smoverview.html*, accessed 19 March 2009.

Dervin, B. and Nilan, M. (1986) Information needs and uses, *Annual Review of Information Science and Technology*, 21, 3–33.

Ellis, D. (1989) A behavioural approach to information retrieval design, *Journal of Documentation*, 45 (3), 171–212.

Engestrom, Y. (1999) Innovative learning in work teams: analysing cycles of knowledge creation. In: Engestrom, Y., Miettinen, R. and Punamaki, R. (eds), *Perspectives on activity theory*. Cambridge: Cambridge University Press.

Finnegan, R. (2007) *The oral and beyond: doing things with words in Africa*. Chicago: University of Chicago Press.

Ford, N. (2004) Towards a model of learning for educational informatics, *Journal of Documentation*, 60 (2), 183–225.

Ford, N., Miller, D. and Moss, N. (2001) The role of individual differences in internet searching: an empirical study, *Journal of the American Society for Information Science and Technology*, 52 (12), 1049–1066.

Foreman, M. (2000) Email: 'the new way to write a phone call – perspectives of an ICT novice'. In: Gamble, N. and Easingwood, N. (eds), *ICT and literacy: information and communications technology, media, reading and writing*. London: Contunuum.

Freire, P. (1974) *Education for critical consciousness*. London: Sheed-Ward.

Freire, P. (2007) *Pedagogy of the oppressed*. New York: Continuum.

Fry, H., Ketteridge, S. and Marshall, S. (eds) (1999) *A handbook for teaching and learning in higher education: enhancing academic practice*. London: Kogan Page.

Gagne, R. M. (1985) *The conditions of learning and theory of instruction*. New York: CBS College Publishing.

Gamble, N. and Easingwood, N. (eds) (2000) *ICT and literacy: information and communications technology, media, reading and writing*. London: Contunuum.

Gardner, H. (1993) *Frames of mind: the theory of multiple intelligences*, 2nd edn. London: Fontana Press.

Gaunt, J., Morgan, N., Somers, R., Soper, R. and Swain, E. (2007) *Handbook for information literacy teaching*, Cardiff University, *http://www.cardiff.ac.uk/insrv/educationandtraining/infolit/hilt/index.html*, accessed 19 March 2009.

Gee, P. (2003) *What video games have to teach us about learning and literacy*. New York: Palgrave.

Gibbs, G. (1998a) *Reviewing and improving your teaching*: H851 *Teaching in Higher Education*, Practice Guide 7. Milton Keynes: Open University.

Gibbs, G. (1998b) *Teaching in higher education: theory and evidence: H851 Teaching in Higher Education*, Chapter 4: Marking and Giving Feedback. Milton Keynes: Open University.

Gibbs, G. and Coffey, M. (2004) The impact of training of university teachers on their teaching skills, their approach to teaching and the approach to learning of their students, *Active Learning in Higher Education*, 5 (1), 87–100.

Gibbs, G., Morgan, A. and Northedge, A. (1998) *Teaching in higher education: theory and evidence*, Chapter 6: How Students Learn. Milton Keynes: Open University.

Godwin, P. and Parker, J. (2008) *Information literacy meets library 2.0.* London: Facet.

Griffiths, R. (2004) Knowledge production and the research-teaching nexus: the case of the built environment disciplines, *Studies in Higher Education*, 29 (6), 709–726.

Gross, R. D. (2005) *Psychology: the science of mind and behaviour*, 5th edn. London: Hodder and Stoughton.

Healey, M. (2005) *Linking research and teaching: exploring disciplinary spaces and the role of inquiry-based learning.* In Barnett, R. (ed.), *Reshaping the university: new relationships between research, scholarship and teaching.* Milton-Keynes: McGraw Hill/Open University Press, 67–78.

Healey, M. and Jenkins, A. (2009) Case studies of linking studies discipline based research and teaching in disciplines, departments, institutions and national systems; handout for research-informed teaching seminar: Issues, Developments and Opportunities, 14 January, Staffordshire University.

Heinstrom, J. (2003) Five personality dimensions and their influence on information behaviour, *Information Research*, 9 (1), http://InformationR.net/ir/9-1/paper165.html, accessed 17 April 2009.

Hepworth, M. (2000) Approaches to providing information literacy training in higher education: challenges for librarians, *New Review of Academic Librarianship*, 6, 21–34.

Hepworth, M. (2002) A conceptual framework for understanding people's requirements for an information service, PhD thesis, Sheffield University.

Hepworth, M. (2004a) A framework for understanding user requirements for an information service: defining the needs of informal carers, *Journal of the American Society of Information Science and Technology*, 55 (8), 695–708.

Hepworth, M. (2004b) Information literacy from the learner's perspective. In Martin, A. and Rader, H. (eds) *Information and IT literacy: enabling learning in the 21st century*. London: Facet, 217–233.

Hepworth, M. and Brittain, J. (in press) A method for the design, delivery and evaluation of an information literacy intervention for development workers studying participation, power and social change, World Library and Information Congress, 75th IFLA General Congress and Assembly, 'Libraries Create Futures: Building On Cultural Heritage', 23–27 August 2009, Milan, Italy.

Hepworth, M. and Smith, M. (2008) Workplace information literacy for administrative staff in HE, *Australian Library Journal*, 57 (3), 212–236.

Hepworth, M. and Wema, E. (2006) The design and implementation of an information literacy training course that integrated information and library science conceptions of information literacy, educational theory and information behaviour research: a Tanzanian pilot study, *ITALICS*, 5 (1), *http://www.ics.heacademy.ac.uk/italics/vol5iss1.htm*, accessed 19 March 2009.

Hinett, K. (2002) *Improving learning through reflection – part one*, Higher Education Academy, *http://www.heacademy.ac.uk/resources/detail/id485_improving_learning_part_one*, accessed 6 March 2009.

Hollingham, R. (2004) In the realm of your senses, *New Scientist*, 181 (2432), 40–43.

Honey, P. and Mumford, A. (1982) *The manual of learning styles*. Maidenhead: Peter Honey. Cited in: Fry, H., Ketteridge, S. and Marshall, S. (eds) (1999) *A handbook for teaching and learning in higher education: enhancing academic practice*. London: Kogan Page, 25.

Horton, F. W. (2007) *Understanding information literacy: a primer*. Paris: UNESCO, *http://portal.unesco.org/ci/en/ev.php-URL_ID=25956&URL_DO=DO_TOPIC&URL_SECTION=201.html*, accessed 17 April 2009.

Hounsell, D. (1999) The evaluation of teaching. In: Fry, H. et al., *A handbook for teaching and learning in higher education: enhancing academic practice*. London: Kogan Page, 161–174.

Howe, N. and Strauss, W. (2000) *Millennials rising: the next generations*. New York: Vintage Books.

Hughes, H., Bruce, C. and Edwards, S. (2007) Models for reflection and learning: a culturally inclusive response to the infomation literacy imbalance. In: Andretta, S. (ed.), *Change and challenge: information literacy for the 21st century*. Blackwood: Auslib Press.

Hung, D. W. L. and Chen, D. (2001) Situated cognition, Vygotskian thought and learning from the communities of practice perspective:

implications for the design of web-based e-learning, *Education Media International*, 38 (1), 3–12.

Hutchings, W. (2007) *Enquiry-based learning: definitions and rationale.* Manchester: Centre for Excellence in Enquiry-Based Learning.

Ingwersen, P. and Jarvelin, K. (2005) *The turn: integration of information seeking and retrieval in context.* Dordrecht: Springer.

JISC infoNet (2004) *InfoKit: effective use of VLEs: introduction to VLEs*, *http://www.jiscinfonet.ac.uk/InfoKits/effective-use-of-VLEs/intro-to-VLEs/index_html*, accessed 19 March 2009.

Jonassen, D., Davidson, M., Collins, M., Campbell, J. and Haag, B. B. (1995) Constructivism and computer-mediated communication in distance education, *American Journal of Distance Education*, 9 (2), 7–26.

Keller, J. M. (1987) Development and use of the ARCS model of motivational design, *Journal of Instructional Development*, 10 (3), 2–10.

Kelly, G. A. (1955) *The psychology of personal constructs.* New York: W. W. Norton.

Kolb, D. A., Rubin, I. M. and Osland, J. (1991) *Organizational behavior: an experiential approach*, 5th edn. Englewood Cliffs, New Jersey: Prentice-Hall.

Kuhlthau, C. (1991) Inside the search process: information seeking from the user's perspective, *Journal of the American Society of Information Science*, 42 (5), 361–371.

Kuhn, T. S. (1970) *The structure of scientific revolutions*, 2nd edn. Chicago: University of Chicago Press.

Lakoff, G. (1999) *Philosophy in the flesh: the embodied mind and its challenge to western thought.* New York: Basic Books.

Laurillard, D. (2002) *Rethinking university teaching.* London: Routledge.

Lave, J. and Wenger, E. (1991) *Situated learning: legitimate peripheral participation.* Cambridge: Cambridge University Press.

Leckie, G., Pettigrew, K., Sylvain, C. (1996) Modeling the information seeking of professionals: a general model derived from research on engineers, health care professionals and lawyers, *Library Quarterly*, 66 (2), 161–193.

Ledochowski, C. (2008) Personal communication between Chris Ledochowski and Mark Hepworth in 2008.

Levy, P. and Petrulis, R. (2007) Towards transformation? First year students, inquiry-based learning and the research/teaching nexus. In: *Proceedings of the Annual Conference of the Society for Research into Higher Education* (SRHE), 11–13 December 2007, Brighton.

Littlejohn, A. and Higgison, C. A. (2003) *A guide for teachers*, e-Learning Series 3. York: LTSN Generic Centre, *http://www.dur.ac.uk/ resources/its/lt/elearning/ELN063.pdf*, accessed 19 March 2009.

Lloyd, A. (2007) Recasting information literacy as sociocultural practice: implications for library and information science researchers, *Information Research*, 12 (4), *http://InformationR.net/ir/12-4/ colis34.html*, accessed 17 April 2009.

MacKeracher, D. (2004) *Making sense of adult learning*, 2nd edn. Toronto: University of Toronto Press.

Marchand, D., Kettinger, W. and Rollins, J. (2001) *Information orientation: the link to business performance.* New York: Oxford University Press.

Marchionini, G. (1995) *Information seeking in electronic environments.* Cambridge: Cambridge University Press.

Markless, S. and Streatfield, D. (2007) Three decades of information literacy: redefining parameters. In: Andretta, S. (ed.) *Change and challenge: information literacy for the 21st century.* Adelaide: Auslib Press, 15–36.

Marton, F. and Saljo, R. (1997) Approaches to learning. In: Marton, F., Hounsel, D. and Entwhistle, N. (eds) *The experience of learning*, 2nd edn. Edinburgh: Scottish University Press, 39–58.

Mayes, T. and de Freitas, S. (2004) *JISC e-learning models desk study: stage 2: review of e-learning theories, frameworks and models (issue 1)*, *http://www.jisc.ac.uk/uploaded_documents/Stage%202%20Learning %20Models%20(Version%201)pdf*, accessed 19 March 2009.

McFarlane, A. E. (2000) Communicating meaning – reading and writing in a multimedia world. In Easingwood, N. and Gamble, N. (eds) *ICT and literacy.* London: Continuum.

McKillop, C. (2005) *Storytelling grows up: using storytelling as a reflective tool in higher education*, paper presented at the Scottish Educational Research Association (SERA) conference, 24–26 November, Perth, Scotland, *http://www.storiesabout.com/files/ McKillop%202005%20SERA.pdf*, accessed 17 April 2009.

Metcalfe, J. (1994) *Metacognition: knowing about knowing.* Cambridge, MA: MIT Press.

Moseley, D., Baumfield, V., Higgins, S., Lin, M., Newton, D., Robson, S., Elliot, J. and Gregson, M. (2004) *Thinking skills frameworks for post-16 learners: an evaluation*, a research report for the Learning and Skills Research Centre. Trowbridge: Cromwell Press.

Narayanan, S. (1997) Knowledge-based action representations for metaphor and aspect (KARMA), PhD thesis, University of California at Berkeley.

Newstead, S. E. and Hoskins, S. (1999) *Encouraging student motivation.* In: Fry, H., Ketteridge, S. and Marshall, S. (eds) *A handbook for teaching and learning in higher education: enhancing academic practice.* London: Kogan Page, 70–82.

Northedge, A. and Lane, A. (1997) *What is learning?* In: Northedge, A., Lane, A., Peasgood, A. and Thomas, J., *The sciences good study guide.* Milton Keynes: Open University Press.

OED (1998) *Oxford English Dictionary*, 2nd edn. Oxford: Oxford University Press.

Online Computer Library Center (2006) *College students' perceptions of library and information resources, http://www.oclc.org/reports/ perceptionscollege.htm*, accessed 19 March 2009.

Orna, E. and Stevens, G. (2000) *Managing information for research.* Buckingham: Open University Press.

Pask, G. (1976) Learning styles and strategies, *British Journal of Educational Psychology*, 46, 4–11. Cited in: Fry, H., Ketteridge, S. and Marshall, S. (eds) (1999) *A handbook for teaching and learning in higher education: enhancing academic practice.* London: Kogan Page, 31.

Pope, A. and Walton, G. (2009) *Information and media literacies: sharpening our vision in the twenty first century.* In: Leaning, M. (ed.), *Issues in information and media literacy: education, practice and pedagogy.* Santa Rosa, CA: Informing Science Press, 1–29.

Prensky, M. (2001) Digital natives, digital immigrants, part 11: do they really think differently? *On the Horizon*, 9 (6), *http://www.marcprensky .com/writing/Prensky%20-%20Digital%20Natives,%20Digital% 20Immigrants%20-%20Part2.pdf*, accessed 19 March 2009.

Quality Assurance Agency for Higher Education (2006) *Code of practice for the assurance of quality and standards in higher education, section 6: assessment of students*, 2nd edn, *http://www.qaa.ac.uk/academic infrastructure/codeOfPractice/section6/default.asp*, accessed 19 March 2009.

Race, P. (2001a) *The lecturer's tool kit: a resource for developing learning, teaching and assessment*, 2nd edn. London: Kogan Page.

Race, P. (2001b) *Using feedback to help students learn, http://www .heacademy.ac.uk/resources/detail/id432_using_feedback*, accessed 19 March 2009.

Race, P. (2002) *Evidencing reflection: putting the 'w' into reflection, ESCALATE Learning Exchange.* Cited in: Hinett, K. (2002) *Improving learning through reflection – part one*, Higher Education Academy, *http://www.heacademy.ac.uk/resources/detail/id485_improving_ learning_part_one*, accessed 19 March 2009.

Race, P. and Brown, S. (2001) *The ILTA guide: inspiring learning about teaching and assessment*. York: Institute for Learning and Teaching in Higher Education.

Ramsden, P. (1992) *Learning to teach in higher education*. London: Routledge.

Reason, P. (1994) Three approaches to participative inquiry. In Denzin, N. K. and Lincoln, Y. S. (eds), *Handbook of qualitative research*. Thousand Oaks: Sage, 324–339, *http://www.bath.ac.uk/~mnspwr/Papers/YVONNA.htm*, accessed 19 April 2009.

Reason, P. and Bradbury, H. (2001) *Handbook of action research: participative inquiry and practice*. London: Sage, 1–14, *http://www.bath.ac.uk/~mnspwr/Papers/HandbookIntroduction.htm*, accessed 19 April 2009.

Reeler, D. (2005) *Experiencing freedom's possibilities: horizontal learning in CDRA's home weeks*, CDRA Annual Report 2004/2005, Community Development Resource Association, *http://www.cdra.org.za/LibraryandResources/Articles%20by%20CDRA.htm*, accessed 7 April 2009.

Reigeluth, C. (1987) Lesson blueprints based on the elaboration theory of instruction. In: Reigeluth, C. (ed.), *Instructional theories in action: lessons illustrating selected theories and models*. Hillsdale, NJ: Erlbaum, 245–288.

Rogerson, S. and McPherson, M. (2005) *Inclusive online learning*. Leicester: Centre for Computing and Social Responsibility, De Montfort University, *http://www.ccsr.cse.dmu.ac.uk/resources/general/ethicol/Ecv15no4.html*, accessed 26 May 2009.

Rowlands, I. and Fieldhouse, M. (2007) *Trends in scholarly information behaviour*. London: British Library and Joint Information Systems Committee.

Savin-Baden, M. (2007) *A practical guide to problem-based learning online*. Oxford: Routledge.

Savolainen, R. (2005) Everyday life information seeking. In: Fisher, K., Erdelez, S. and McKechnie, L. (eds), *Theories of information behavior*. Medford, NJ: Information Today, Inc., 143–148.

Schon, D. (1987) *Educating the reflective practitioner*. San-Francisco: Jossey-Bass. Cited in: Bell, M. (2001) Supported reflective practice: a programme of peer observation and feedback for academic teaching development, *International Journal for Academic Development*, 6 (1), 29–39.

SCONUL (1999) *Information skills in higher education: a SCONUL position paper*, Society of College, National and University Libraries, *http://www.sconul.ac.uk/groups/information_literacy/papers/Seven_ pillars.html*, accessed 7 April 2009.

Simister, C. (2007) *How to teach thinking and learning skills: a practical programme for the whole school.* London: Sage.

Shevlin, M., Banyard, P., Davies, M. and Griffiths, M. (2000) The validation of student evaluation of teaching in higher education: love me, love my lectures? *Assessment and Evaluation in Higher Education*, 25 (4), 397–405.

Smith, M. (2009) personal communication between Marian Smith and Mark Hepworth concerning her PhD research topic on children's perception of information.

Smith, M. and Hepworth, M. (2007) An investigation of factors that may demotivate secondary school students undertaking project work: implications for learning information literacy, *Journal of Librarianship and Information Science*, 39 (1), 3–15.

Snowball, R. (1997) Using the clinical question to teach search strategy: fostering user education by active learning, *Health Libraries Review*, 14, 167–172.

Snowden, D. (1999) Storytelling: an old skill in a new context, *Business Information Review*, 16 (1), 30–37.

Snowden, D. (2001) *Archetypes as an instrument of narrative patterning*, *http://www.gurteen.com/gurteen/gurteen.nsf/id/snowden-downloads/ $file/2001%2011%20Archetypes%20as%20an%20instrument%20of %20narrative%20patterning.doc*, accessed 6 April 2009.

Spink, A., Wilson, T. D., Ford, N. and Ellis, D. (2002) Information seeking and mediated searching, part 2: uncertainty and its correlates, *Journal of the American Society for Information Science and Technology*, 5 (9), 704–715.

Squires, G. (1994) *A new model of teaching and training.* Hull: University of Hull.

Taylor, P. and Clarke, P. (2008) *Capacity for a change.* Brighton: Institute of Development Studies.

Teles, L. (1993) *Cognitive apprenticeships on global networks.* In: Harisam, L. M., *Global networks: computers and international communication.* Cambridge, MA: MIT Press, 271–281.

Thomas, S. (2008) *Transliteracy and new media.* Berlin: Springer.

Trigwell, K. (2001) Judging university teaching, *International Journal for Academic Development*, 6 (1), 65–73.

Turow, J. and Tsui, L. (eds) (2008) *The hyperlinked society.* Michigan: University of Michigan Press.

UCL (2008) *Information behaviour of the researcher of the future,* CIBER briefing paper, executive summary, University College London, *http://www.ucl.ac.uk/slais/research/ciber/downloads/ggexecutive.pdf,* accessed 19 March 2008.

Underwood, P. (2002) South Africa: a case study in development through information literacy, July 2002, White Paper prepared for UNESCO, the US National Commission on Libraries and Information Science, and the National Forum on Information Literacy, for use at the Information Literacy Meeting of Experts, Prague, Czech Republic.

Walker, M. (2003) *Lessons in e-learning,* Higher Education Academy, *http://www.heacademy.ac.uk/resources/detail/id456_lessons_in_ e-learning,* accessed 19 March 2009.

Walton, G. (2009) *Developing a new blended approach to fostering information literacy,* PhD thesis, Loughborough University.

Walton, G. (in press) From online discourse to online social networking, the e-learning Holy Grail? In Parkes, D. and Hart, E. (eds) *Web 2.0 and libraries: impacts, technologies and trends.* Oxford: Chandos.

Walton, G., Barker, J., Hepworth, M. and Stephens, D. (2007a) Using online collaborative learning to enhance information literacy delivery in a Level 1 module: an evaluation, *Journal of Information Literacy,* 1 (1), 13–30, *http://jil.lboro.ac.uk/ojs/index.php/JIL/article/view/RA -V1-I1-2007-2/3* (accessed 12 July 2008).

Walton, G., Barker, J., Hepworth, M. and Stephens, D. (2007b) Facilitating information literacy teaching and learning in a Level 1 sport and exercise module by means of collaborative online and reflective learning. In Andretta, S. (ed.) *Change and challenge: information literacy for the 21st century.* Adelaide: Auslib Press.

Webb, J. and Powis, C. (2005) Start with the learner, *Library and Information Update,* 4 (1–2), 36–37.

Wenger, E. (1999) *Communities of practice: learning meaning and identity.* Cambridge: Cambridge University Press.

Whitworth, A. (2006) Communicative competence in the information age: towards a critical theory of information literacy education, *ITALICS,* 5 (1).

Widen-Wulff, G. and Davenport, E. (2007) Information sharing and organizational knowledge production in two Finnish firms: an exploration using activity theory, *Information Research,* 12 (3), *http://informationr.net/ir/12-3/paper310.html,* accessed 19 March 2009.

Wilson, T. (1999) Models in information behaviour research, *Journal of Documentation,* 55 (3), 249–270.

Wilson, T. (2006) A re-examination of information seeking behaviour in the context of activity theory, *Information Research*, 11 (4), *http:// informationr.net/ir/*, accessed 1 March 2009.

Windham, C. (2005) The student's perspective. In Oblinger, D. and Oblinger, J. (eds) *EDUCAUSE: educating the net generation*, Chapter 5, *http://net.educause.edu/ir/library/pdf/pub7101.pdf*, accessed 19 March 2009.

Worthington, A. C. (2002) The impact of student perceptions and characteristics on teaching evaluations: a case study in finance education, *Assessment and Evaluation in Higher Education*, 27 (1), 49–64.

Zipf., G. (1949) *Human Behavior and the Principle of Least-Effort.* Cambridge, MA: Addison-Wesley.

Useful web resources

These sites provide a starting point for exploring web resources concerning information literacy. Many of them provide comprehensive lists of additional resources.

Journals and conferences

Communications in Information Literacy
http://www.comminfolit.org/index.php/cil/index

Information Research: an international electronic journal
http://informationr.net/ir/

ITALICS
http://www.ics.heacademy.ac.uk/italics/vol5iss1.htm

Journal of Information Literacy
http://jil.lboro.ac.uk/ojs/index.php/JIL

Librarians' Information Literacy Annual Conference (LILAC)
http://www.lilacconference.com/dw/2009/award_CILASS.htm

Nordic Journal of Information Literacy in Higher Education
https://noril.uib.no/index.php/noril

Information literacy articles also tend to be indexed in databases such as Library and Information Science Abstracts (LISA) and Emerald.

Information literacy portals (includes models, definitions and pointers to other resources)

Association of College and Research Libraries website
http://www.ala.org/ala/mgrps/divs/acrl/issues/infolit/index.cfm

Australian and New Zealand Institute for Information Literacy website
http://www.anziil.org/

Final report from the Presidential Committee on Information Literacy (American Library Association)
http://www.ala.org/ala/professionalresources/infolit/index.cfm

IFLA website: About the Information Literacy Section
http://www.ifla.org/en/about-information-literacy

Information Literacy (American Association of School Librarians)
http://www.ala.org/ala/mgrps/divs/aasl/aaslissues/aaslinfolit/information literacy1.cfm

Information Literacy (Community Services Group of CILIP)
http://www.informationliteracy.org.uk/

Information Literacy (Staffordshire University)
http://www.staffs.ac.uk/infoliteracy/

Information Literacy: Definitions and Models (Sheffield University)
http://dis.shef.ac.uk/literacy/definitions.htm

Information Literacy on the WWW (Florida International University Libraries)
http://www.fiu.edu/~library/ili/iliweb.html

I-Skills Publications (JISC)
http://www.jisc.ac.uk/publications/documents/pub_sissdocs.aspx

Literacy: Definition (CILIP)
http://www.cilip.org.uk/policyadvocacy/learning/informationliteracy/ definition/default.htm

The Scottish Information Literacy Project (Glasgow Caledonian University)
http://www.gcal.ac.uk/ils/

The Seven Pillars Of Information Literacy (SCONUL)
http://www.sconul.ac.uk/groups/information_literacy/seven_pillars.html

UNESCO and Information Literacy
http://portal.unesco.org/ci/en/ev.php-URL_ID=19812&URL_DO=DO_ TOPIC&URL_SECTION=201.html

Teaching material

Assignment Survival Kit (Staffordshire University)
http://www.staffs.ac.uk/ask/

Handbook for Information Literacy Teaching (Cardiff University)
http://www.cardiff.ac.uk/insrv/educationandtraining/infolit/hilt/

Information Fluency and IT skills (University of Cumbria)
http://www.cumbria.ac.uk/Services/lis/skills/tutorials.aspx

Information Literacy Resource Bank (Cardiff University)
https://ilrb.cf.ac.uk/

Intute Internet Detective
http://www.vts.intute.ac.uk/detective/

LessonPlans 4 Teachers (Nova South Eastern University)
http://www.lessonplans4teachers.com/informationliteracy.php

RefZone (Staffordshire University)
http://www.staffs.ac.uk/uniservices/infoservices/library/find/references/

Study Guides and Strategies
http://www.studygs.net/index.htm

People

Susie Andretta
http://www.londonmet.ac.uk/depts/dass/staff/susieandretta/

Christine Bruce's perceptual worlds research
http://www.perceptualworlds.fit.qut.edu.au/

Sylvia Edwards' web page (Australia)
http://sky.fit.qut.edu.au/~edwardss/

Mark Hepworth's blog
http://markhepworthsblog.blogspot.com/

Sheila Webber's information literacy weblog
http://information-literacy.blogspot.com/

Index